Bob Bontrager
Doris Ingersoll
Ronald Ingersoll

Strategic Enrollment Management:
Transforming
Higher Education

SPONSORED BY

EMAS™ PRO

AMERICAN ASSOCIATION OF COLLEGIATE REGISTRARS AND ADMISSIONS OFFICERS

AACRAO®

American Association of Collegiate
Registrars and Admissions Officers
One Dupont Circle, NW, Suite 520
Washington, DC 20036-1135

Tel: (202) 293-9161   Fax: (202) 872-8857   www.aacrao.org

For a complete listing of AACRAO publications, visit www.aacrao.org/publications.

The American Association of Collegiate Registrars and Admissions Officers, founded in 1910, is a nonprofit, voluntary, professional association of more than 11,000 higher education administrators who represent more than 2,600 institutions and agencies in the United States and in forty countries around the world. The mission of the Association is to provide leadership in policy initiation, interpretation, and implementation in the global educational community. This is accomplished through the identification and promotion of standards and best practices in enrollment management, information technology, instructional management, and student services.

AACRAO adheres to the principles of non-discrimination without regard to age, color, handicap or disability, ethnic or national origin, race, religion, gender (including discrimination taking the form of sexual harassment), marital, parental or veteran status, or sexual orientation.

LIBRARY OF CONGRESS
CATALOGING-IN-PUBLICATION DATA

Strategic enrollment management : transforming higher education / edited by Bob Bontrager, Doris Ingersoll &
Ronald Ingersoll.
    p. cm.
 Includes bibliographical references and index.
  ISBN 978-1-57858-100-9
  1. Universities and colleges--United States--Business management. 2. Universities and colleges--United States-
-Finance. 3. College attendance--United States--Planning. I. Bontrager, Bob. II. Ingersoll, Doris. III. Ingersoll,
Ronald J.
  LB2341.93.U6S87 2012
  378.1'06--dc23
                        20120269

TABLE OF CONTENTS

PREFACE

This book came about from collaboration between Bob Bontrager and Ron and Dori Ingersoll to explore emerging and future dynamics in the practice of strategic enrollment management (SEM). To this endeavor we bring more than 100 years of collective involvement in the evolution of SEM theory and practice. To say the least, we have seen many changes in how students are recruited and retained. Today there are opportunities to do things we had only dreamed of in the past, driven by external forces that are demanding change in the delivery of postsecondary education, even as we continue to learn from our own missteps and seek to take advantage of new opportunities. The potential for achieving higher levels of student and institutional success is vast. New technologies, communication tools, data use, and organizational constructs will be key factors in improving the delivery of higher education.

Within this context, describing emerging and future SEM practice is a daunting task, illuminated by two allegories. One is the proverbial group of blind persons seeking to describe an elephant, with each person describing it differently depending on the part they happen to touch. With SEM, the "elephant" is the comprehensive, campus-wide nature of the SEM enterprise. Even those with clear and accurate vision will find it a challenge to effectively coordinate the many aspects of SEM. Blindness in this case is not intended as a pejorative reference to the many authors who contributed to this work nor any other SEM practitioners. Rather, it recognizes that our understanding of SEM is shaped by the institutional circumstances with which we have had direct experience. It also reflects that fact that the creation of SEM organizations is subject to continuous refinement as the internal and external factors that affect enrollment are in a constant state of flux, which leads to our second allegory.

The second allegorical description of SE M is that of taking aim at a moving target. In this instance, the "movement" is evolutionary. That is, our overall understanding of SEM, as well as the components we emphasize, continues to change over time. The earliest "enrollment management" literature focused on college choice, admissions, marketing, and structural issues. The movement to a more "strategic" approach produced added emphasis on retention, connections with academics, financial aid and net revenue strategies, and promoting institutional change. The chapters of this book bring us up to the present and into new territory by addressing many, if not all, of the latest SEM emphases.

The book begins with establishing a historical baseline for SEM practice. Following that the section on "Shifting Context of SEM Practice" presents an in-depth treatment of student success as a higher-order retention construct, including the introduction of a student success program at a major university. As seen previously in SEM literature, change management is addressed here as well, but in newly-imagined contexts of "constructive conflict cultures" and the development of institutional "SEM communities."

The second section focuses on the "Emerging Tools of SEM." Here, understandings of cost and financial aid receive updated treatment. Current understandings of the intensely data-driven nature of effective SEM practice are evidenced by two chapters devoted to that topic, followed by two topics that have received significant attention in recent years: SEM in graduate and professional schools and the enrollment dynamics of international students.

The final section of the book focuses on the "Future of SEM," addressing issues of leadership, staff development, and newly-refined models for implementation. This culminating section highlights an underlying theme throughout the book: the institutional transformation that SEM implies. That is, in the face of the significant, ongoing change inherent to higher education, tinkering at the margins of an institution's enrollment programs will not be sufficient.

Successful enrollment outcomes, across a broad spectrum of indicators, will require institutions to develop new paradigms for enrollment and student success. The overarching purpose of this book is to provide a roadmap for the required paradigm shift, building on the solid foundation of prior SEM practice and offering insights to new approaches that will lead to sustainable SEM efforts into the future.

Bob Bontrager
Senior Director, AACRAO Consulting and SEM Initiatives

Doris M. Ingersoll
Sr. Consultant Advisor, EMAS Pro.

Ronald J. Ingersoll
Sr. Consultant Advisor, EMAS Pro.

ABOUT THE AUTHORS

Dr. Bob Bontrager

Bob Bontrager is Senior Director of AACRAO Consulting and SEM Initiatives. He has 25 years of experience in enrollment management at all types of institutions. In his most recent institutional role as Assistant Provost for Enrollment Management at Oregon State University, Bontrager's leadership resulted in a 40 percent increase in enrollment, including increases in the academic and diversity profile of the student body. He previously served as Vice President for Enrollment Management at Eastern Mennonite University in Virginia and was Assistant Registrar at Arizona State University.

Dr. Bontrager has contributed to the ongoing evolution of the strategic enrollment management profession in the U.S. and abroad as a frequent conference speaker, workshop presenter, consultant, and contributor to the SEM literature. He recently edited two books, *SEM and Institutional Success: Integrating Enrollment, Finance and Student Access* and *Applying SEM at the Community College*. His work has extended internationally to Australia, Canada, India, Ireland, Kazakhstan, Mongolia, New Zealand, Syria, and the United Arab Emirates. This has included featured speaking roles at the European Association of International Educators conference in Dublin, Ireland and the Association of Tertiary Education Management Conference in Adelaide, Australia.

Dr. Bontrager earned his Master of Counseling degree and Ed.D. in Educational Leadership & Policy Studies at Arizona State University, and his bachelor's degree at Goshen College in Goshen, Indiana. He is married with three grown children and works from his home in Corvallis, Oregon.

Guilbert Brown

Guilbert Brown is Assistant Vice President for Planning & Budgeting and Chief Budget Officer at George Mason University, and has previously served as the chief budget officer for Rice University, Georgetown University and Oregon State University. He is co-author of the book *SEM and Institutional Success: Integrating Enrollment, Finance and Student Access*. During a higher education administration career spanning nearly three decades Mr. Brown has made presentations to AACRAO, the National Association of College & University Business Officers (NACUBO), the Society for College & University Planning (SCUP), the Association of Governing Boards of Universities and Colleges (AGB), the Association for Institutional Research (AIR) and other organizations. He is a Phi Beta Kappa graduate of the University of Denver with a Bachelor of Arts degree in political science and philosophy and in 2012 received a Master of Arts degree in Interdisciplinary Studies from George Mason University.

Jonathan Compton

Jonathan Compton is Senior Research Analyst in the Office of the Registrar at Iowa State University. He conducts research on student success and retention issues and oversees enrollment reporting and enrollment projections. Jonathan holds a Ph.D. in Educational Leadership and Policy Studies from Iowa State University, a master's degree in English from Iowa State and a bachelor's degree in English from Bryan College.

Zebulun R. Davenport

Zebulun Davenport is the Vice Chancellor for Student Life at Indiana University-Purdue University Indianapolis. He has over 20 years' experience in higher education. Until his recent appointment, he served as the Vice President for Student Affairs at Northern Kentucky University, where he left a strong legacy on student success, working to connect all dimensions of student affairs to the university's efforts to improve retention and graduation rates. Under his leadership, the student affairs division worked hand-in-hand with other campus divisions to form collaborative partnerships in the interest of student achievement and success. Davenport was instrumental in the opening of four new buildings on the Kentucky campus, including the student union building, state-of-the-art sports and entertainment facility, a 462-bed residence hall, and a soccer stadium.

Davenport's most recent accomplishments include being recognized by the National Association for Student Personnel Administrators (NASPA) for his work on co-founding a student retention model, being elected to the Governing Board for the Association for College Personnel Administrators (ACPA), being selected as a faculty for the New Professional's Institute within the National Association of Student Personnel Administrators (NASPA), and co-authoring a book, *First-Generation College Students: Understanding and Improving the Experience from Recruitment to Commencement*, for release in 2012.

Davenport earned a doctorate in higher education and leadership from Nova Southeastern University. He holds both a bachelor's degree and a master's degree from James Madison University.

Paul J. Dosal

Paul Dosal is the Vice Provost for Student Success at the University of South Florida. He is responsible for coordinating and promoting the university-wide student success initiative, launched by a 100-member task force in November 2009. He supervises Undergraduate Admissions, Financial Aid, the University Registrar, Enrollment Planning and Management, the Academy for Teaching and Learning Excellence, and the Office of Community Engagement and Partnerships. He also coordinates a wide range of initiatives that include the promotion of on-campus student employment; the development of a computer lab to support course redesigns in gatekeeper courses; the expansion of Tutoring and Learning Services; peer tutoring in the career center; centralization and professionalization of academic advising; a new degree audit system that includes an academic tracking module; and the implementation of a financial aid leveraging model.

Prior to his appointment as Vice Provost, Dr. Dosal served as the Executive Director of EN-LACE Florida (now the Florida College Access Network), a statewide network formed to promote college and career readiness, access, and college completion. Dr. Dosal is a professor of history, specializing in the history of Cuba and Central America. He has published four books and dozens of articles and book reviews, most recently a military biography of Ernesto "Che" Guevara. He earned a Ph.D. in History and a M.A. in Latin American Studies from Tulane University in New Orleans.

Chris J. Foley

Chris Foley is the Director of Undergraduate Admissions at Indiana University-Purdue University Indianapolis. He has presented nationally and internationally on domestic and international admissions, recruitment, enrollment management, transfer credit, urban higher education, and technology issues. An active member of both NAFSA and AACRAO, he is the author of several articles and book chapters on these topics as well as the author/editor of AACRAO's books on the educational systems of the Russian Federation and the Kyrgyz Republic. Most recently, he was an author of the *The AACRAO International Guide*. He was a Sturgis Fellow at the University of Arkansas where he completed his undergraduate studies, and he holds master's degrees from Indiana University in English and Creative Writing.

Ann Gansemer-Topf

Ann Gansemer-Topf is Assistant Professor in Educational Leadership and Policy Studies in the School of Education at Iowa State University. She teaches courses in program evaluation and assessment and higher education organization and administration. Prior to joining faculty, she was the Associate Director of Research for the Office of Admissions at Iowa State University. She worked in Institutional Research at Grinnell College and also has experience working in the areas of residence life, academic advising, new student orientation, and student financial aid. Her research areas of interest include assessment of student learning, institutional and personal factors related to student success, strategic enrollment management, and effective teaching/learning pedagogies. She holds a Ph.D. in Educational Leadership and Policy Studies and an M.S. degree in Higher Education, both from Iowa State University, and a B.A. in Psychology from Loras College in Dubuque, Iowa.

Tom Green

Dr. Tom Green is a Senior Consultant with AACRAO Consulting. In his career, he served as dean or vice president of enrollment management at a number of private and public institutions. Dr. Green led admissions, financial aid, registrar, student accounts, academic advising, student support, adult re-entry services and one-stop shop areas, twice serving as director of financial aid. His expertise in SEM planning, recruitment techniques, enrollment marketing and communications, financial aid analysis and resource utilization and student success techniques resulted in enrollment increases, improvements in student profile and retention rates, as well as net revenue.

In 2006, Dr. Green joined AACRAO Consulting and since 2008 has devoted his career full-time to helping institutions reach their enrollment goals. His work has included both private and public institutions, from small private colleges to public flagships, from rural to highly urban, and specializations such as online programs, law schools, Hispanic Serving Institutions and Historically Black Colleges and Universities. His consultations have been performed in every region of the United States, in Canada and in the United Kingdom.

Tom Green holds a bachelor's degree from the University of Iowa, a master's degree from the American Conservatory of Music, where he later began his academic career as a faculty member in music performance, and a Ph.D. in higher education leadership, management and policy from Seton Hall University. He is a frequent speaker and workshop leader at national conferences and has published articles and book chapters on a wide variety of SEM issues.

Stanley E. Henderson

Stanley Henderson is Vice Chancellor for Enrollment Management and Student Life at the University of Michigan-Dearborn. He has long been a national leader in developing new models for universities to better recruit and retain students. Before joining the University of Illinois in 2003 as associate provost for enrollment management, he was associate vice president for enrollment management at the University of Cincinnati from 1995 to 2003. Previously, he was director of enrollment management and admissions at Western Michigan University and director of admissions at Wichita State University.

He also has been deeply involved at the national level in AACRAO, where he served as the association's first vice president of enrollment management in 1991-93 and as president in 1995-1996. He was a founder of the SEM Conference, now in its 22nd year. He is a frequent contributor to AACRAO publications, including the first history of enrollment management. He is also a recipient of the Distinguished Service Award and the Founders Award for Leadership.

Henderson earned his bachelor's degree in political science from Michigan State University in 1969, and a master's degree in government from Cornell University in 1971. He also completed course work in the doctoral program at the University of Illinois.

Doris M. Ingersoll

Dr. Doris M. Ingersoll has been active in a variety of higher education roles beginning with Dean of Women in a private liberal arts college to chairing the faculty of the Department of Communication in a private university. She has primarily worked with her husband Ronald J. Ingersoll as co-owner of The Enrollment Management Center, Inc., working to help over 500 colleges and universities create and develop their enrollment management programs to more effectively meet the goals of the institution.

Her Doctorate in Organizational Communication from the University of Denver covers many facets of communication found in the organization such as interpersonal, small group, culture, conflict management, networking, methods of communication and change within the organization, and the processes set up to work most effectively. She has conducted quantitative research in institutions to describe organizational culture, has provided workshops for senior staff regarding group process, and has provided professional development workshops for admissions representatives over many years.

Over the past 20 years, she has taught in various universities as an adjunct instructor while consulting with colleges. Her teaching has given her inside experience with organizational issues and provided a connection with students that helped her stay focused on student success in her work with enrollment management. She has presented several seminars for the Council for the Advancement and Support of Education (CASE) and the American Marketing Association (AMA) and has co-written papers and articles for College Student Journal and AMA.

Dori and Ron live in Florida where their two daughters and one granddaughter all live relatively close by.

Ronald J. Ingersoll

Dr. Ronald J. Ingersoll has been involved in a number of positions in higher education including faculty, researcher, Dean and Vice President of Enrollment Management, and has been a consultant in the area of enrollment management since 1974. He has been the President of the Enrollment Management Center and worked with the first schools starting enrollment management efforts. He was one of the first to take a systematic and data oriented approach to enrollment management issues.

His doctorate is in Physical Biology from Cornell University. He was involved in research and the metabolism of vitamin D before moving into undergraduate and graduate teaching and administration. His skills and knowledge in organizations, institutional research, strategic planning, marketing, communication, and quantitative/ qualitative studies have been extensive and formed from experience and courses taken over several years. His book, *The Enrollment Problem: Proven Management Techniques*, published in 1988, was one of the first books on this subject that included the whole school in enrollment efforts.

He has done workshops for Council for the Advancement and Support of Education (CASE), The Association of Governing Boards (AGB), The American Council on Education (ACE), and the American Marketing Association (AMA) and has written papers for each of these organizations. Ron's current interest is in the future of enrollment management and its role in higher education and in mentoring potential leaders in enrollment management. He is currently doing writing and research in this area. Ron is also doing research and writing about Parkinson's disease and its impact on individuals and families.

Tricia S. Jones

Tricia S. Jones is a Professor of Adult and Organizational Development in the Department of Psychological Studies in Education at Temple University. She teaches courses at the graduate and undergraduate levels in conflict processes, conflict resolution education, negotiation and mediation, interpersonal communication, organizational communication, and qualitative and quantitative research methodology. Her conflict coaching work has focused on training programs for government agencies, higher education, health care and state offices of dispute resolution. In 2009-2011, she designed and implemented the Department of Veterans Affairs' conflict coaching program as a component of the VA ADR systems nationwide under the auspices of the Office of Resolution Management. She has authored 6 books and over 50 articles and book chapters on conflict management and has given more than 200 presentations at national and international conferences. From 2001-2007 she served as the Editor-in-Chief of Conflict Resolution Quarterly, the scholarly journal of the Association for Conflict Resolution, the nation's largest professional association for conflict management and dispute resolution.

Christine Kerlin

Dr. Christine Kerlin recently retired as the Vice President for the University Center and Strategic Planning at Everett Community College, Washington, and continues her service as Senior Consultant with AACRAO Consulting. Dr. Kerlin is a nationally-known expert on enrollment management in community colleges with previous experience as Director of Admissions and Records at Central Oregon Community College and as Director of Admissions at The Evergreen State College, Washington.

Her areas of experience include admissions, registration, records, international programs, credential evaluation, high school dual enrollment, placement testing, advising, articulation, and strategic planning.

Dr. Kerlin has authored chapters in a variety of AACRAO publications, including *Applying SEM at the Community College*, and she presents regularly at national and regional conferences.

Scot Lingrell

Dr. Scot Lingrell has been the Vice President for Student Affairs and Enrollment Management at the University of West Georgia since 2011. Formerly the Associate Vice President for Enrollment Management, he has direct responsibility for the offices of Undergraduate Admission, Financial Aid, Excel Center for Academic Success (Advising), Student Affairs Web and Technology, Registrar, Housing and Residence Life, Multicultural Affairs, Health Center, Career Services, Counseling and Career Development, Center for Student involvement, and University Recreation.

After receiving his Masters of Arts in College Student Personnel and Guidance and Counseling in 1992, Dr. Lingrell began his professional career as an Academic Advisor and then an Assistant Director of Admission at Wayne State University in Detroit, Michigan. In 1996 he became the Associate Director of Admissions at the University of Toledo and directed all recruitment and outreach efforts as well as supervised Scholarships and Recruitment Publications. In 2000 Dr. Lingrell moved to Rhodes State College, in Lima, Ohio, to become the Director of Student Advising and Development. While there, he assumed two additional roles, first becoming the Director of Admissions and Advising and later becoming the Associate Dean of Enrollment Management. At this same time, he finished his Ph. D. in Higher Education Administration at Ohio University.

Dr. Lingrell was the 2009 recipient of the AACRAO SEM Award of Excellence. He lives in Carrollton, Georgia with his wife Karen and their two children Hannah and Drew.

Miguel Martinez-Saenz

Miguel Martinez-Saenz is the Associate Provost for Undergraduate Education and Student Support Services at St. Cloud State University. Prior to St. Cloud State he was Associate Provost and Associate Professor of Philosophy at Wittenberg University. As an educator he strives to make philosophy relevant to those he engages. He has written and presented on issues including but not limited to international development, Jorge Luis Borges, student development, diversity in higher education, liberal education and the birth of his son.

Outside the University setting, he has worked with his wife, a former 8th grade public school Social Studies teacher, tutoring teens at or below the poverty-line, has accompanied student groups to build houses in rural communities in Nicaragua as part of trips organized by Bridges to Community and, while in Ohio, had been heavily involved in non-profit work in Clark County, Montgomery County and Green County.

Kevin A. Pollock

Dr. Kevin A. Pollock is the President of St. Clair County Community College. He previously served as vice president of student services at West Shore Community College.

Nationally recognized as a public speaker, Dr. Pollock has presented more than 75 sessions at conferences and colleges on topics including community college issues, the executive role in SEM, at-risk students, continuous quality improvement, mentoring, student retention, strategic planning and student success.

Dr. Pollock has written more than a dozen articles and book chapters, including a chapter in *Applying SEM at the Community College.*

Dr. Pollock earned his Bachelor of Science in Education and his Master of Arts in Education degrees from Central Michigan University. He earned his doctorate degree in Higher, Adult and Lifelong Education from Michigan State University.

Lisa B. Rhine

Lisa Rhine has over 23 years of experience in retention, academic support services, student success and co-curricular programming in both academic and student affairs at four colleges and universities in Ohio and Kentucky. She holds a bachelor's degree in Rehabilitation Counseling from Wright State University, a master's degree in Special Education from the University of Dayton and a Ph.D. in Educational Administration from Capella University. Her career focus is on developing systemic approaches of institutional action aimed at improving student success, persistence and graduation. Dr. Rhine is co-creator of the Changing Institutional Retention through Co-Curricular Learning Experiences (CIRCLE) Model which engages and links co-curricular service providers in academic and student affairs in a systemic collegial process of institution-wide service delivery.

Dr. Rhine currently serves as the Vice President for Student Affairs at Northern Kentucky University (NKU). Previous positions include Assistant Vice President for Student Affairs at NKU, Associate Provost for Student Success and Retention at Wittenberg University, OH, Director of Learning Enhancement and Academic Development at the University of Dayton, OH, and Manager of Educational Support Services at Sinclair Community College, OH.

Monique L. Snowden

Dr. Monique L. Snowden is the Associate Provost for Academic and Enrollment Services at Fielding Graduate University in Santa Barbara, CA. She has approximately 20 years of higher education administration experience. In her current position, at a free-standing graduate university, Dr. Snowden specializes in employing and advancing strategic enrollment management for graduate and adult education.

Dr. Snowden is the former assistant dean of enrollment management at Northwestern University School of Continuing Studies and the founding director of enrollment research and technology for the Office of Admissions and Records at Texas A&M University. She held several positions during her 12-year tenure at Texas A&M, including interim director of admissions, managing director of admissions processing, and senior analyst for the university's Student Information System.

Dr. Snowden holds an adjunct faculty appointment in Fielding's School of Human and Organizational Development. Her current research interests include examining the communicative role and impact of professional associations on profession identity, knowledge and practice. She is an engaged scholar-practitioner leader in AACRAO, currently chairing the AACRAO Graduate and Professionals Schools Committee and serving on the Public Policy Advisory Committee.

Dr. Snowden earned three degrees from Texas A&M University: a bachelor's degree in Business Analysis, a master's degree in Management Information Systems and a doctorate degree in Communication, with an emphasis in organizational communication. Dr. Snowden is a certified Project Management Professional (PMP) and Certified Information Systems Auditor (CISA).

Darin Wohlgemuth

Darin Wohlgemuth is the Director of Research for Enrollment and Director of Budget Research & Analysis at Iowa State University. In this split appointment he reports to the Associate Vice President for Student Affairs and the Associate Vice President for Budget and Planning. His responsibilities include developing empirical models of enrollment decisions, forecasting enrollment, developing strategic recruitment initiatives, as well as conducting research and policy analysis for the implementation and operation of the Resource Management Model (Iowa State's responsibility centered management budget) which provides tuition revenue to colleges based on enrollment and credit hours taught. He leads the Enrollment Research Team, comprised of researcher staff in the Offices of Admissions, Student Financial Aid, and Registrar, in research efforts in numerous areas including enrollment planning, strategic recruitment, strategic financial aid and retention. He also teaches in the MBA program at Iowa State University.

Darin's graduate research focused on the demand for higher education. He earned a master's degree (1993) and doctoral degree (1997) in Economics at Iowa State University. He earned a bachelor's degree in Secondary Math Education from the University of Kansas (1991), and an associate's degree from Hesston College (1988).

1

INTEGRATING EVOLVING PERSPECTIVES: THE ROOTS AND WINGS OF ENROLLMENT MANAGEMENT

Stanley E. Henderson
Vice Chancellor for Enrollment Management and Student Life
University of Michigan-Dearborn

CHAPTER 1

If, in 2001, strategic enrollment management was "on the brink of a profession" (Henderson), in the intervening years it has been consolidating itself as a strategic partner in the administration of higher education. SEM has seen explosive growth as an administrative construct, reaching into every level of higher education. Virtually every two- or four-year school today engages in some kind of enrollment management. In some places it is upper case Strategic Enrollment Management; in others, it is lower case managing enrollments. "Strategic Enrollment Management" is the purview of institutions working to determine and reach their optimum enrollments and "managing enrollments" is generally found at institutions concerned with maintaining their position and profile. The threads of SEM that emerged in the first thirty years of the field are still around after almost forty years, but the perspective is different, and the tapestry richer and more complex in design. The simplistic functional SEM designs of the mid-70s now include a web of offices, services, strategies, and technologies that reach into every facet of the academy.

Strategic enrollment management is still demonstrating the resiliency that has characterized American higher education from colonial times. As society expresses needs, new types of higher education emerge. Whether giving rise to institutions to educate the clergy and political leaders in the 17th century, or Land Grant colleges to provide upward mobility for the children of farmers and merchants in the 19th or community colleges for the masses in the 20th, the face of higher education has changed to meet the demands of the citizenry (Henderson 1998). Likewise, the processes of higher education have changed to meet the needs of students, from the elective curriculum with science and math, to graduate education, to the student services offices, to the use of technology to streamline and collapse services. Enrollment management (EM) is a quintessential outgrowth of that need-based development cycle of American higher education to ensure that enough students of the right quality are pursuing higher education.

IN THE BEGINNING: A SYNERGY OF FUNCTIONS

When the Baby Boom went bust in the early 1970s, traditional residential colleges scrambled to meet the crisis. In some cases, such as Boston College, private schools considered seeking state affiliation. Two administrators at BC rejected that approach, however, and instead launched one of the most significant new administrative constructs in higher education—enrollment management.

Jack Maguire, a junior physics professor at BC, had just been named Dean of Admissions. Along with his boss, Executive Vice President, Harvard-educated **Frank Campanella**, he struggled to apply academic planning and reengineered processes and policies in Admissions to meet the enrollment crisis. Campanella soon came to the conclusion that admissions alone could not meet the challenges facing the campus. He believed that enrollment needed a broader perspective than Maguire and his admissions staff could provide. Administrative oversight, attention to faculty matters such as teaching loads and schedules, and strategies for tuition generation and pricing all needed to be integrated into a new approach to enrollment planning. Campanella could see relationships between market demands and academic planning that people in traditional office silos missed. His comprehensive view took him to a new level. In his own words, "managing enrollments was a way of managing the business of higher education" (Maguire 1999; Scannell 1999).

In 1974, Campanella told Maguire that he wanted to restructure the way in which BC handled enrollment planning and call it "enrollment management." On November 11 of that year, he wrote a memo "to introduce the idea of 'enrollment management'" (Campanella 1974). He envisioned enrollment management as directing admissions resources, minimizing student attrition, predicting market demands, and developing financial aid strategies. "I am convinced," he wrote, "that enrollment management will shortly be the 'name of the game.' I am equally convinced that it will require a coordinated and integrated effort of the highest order." The rest, as they say, is history (Henderson 1998).

Maguire became the chief implementer of this new paradigm at BC. In breathing life into enrollment management, he fundamentally changed admissions in higher education. "Simply stated," he wrote, "enrollment management is a process that brings together often disparate functions having to do with recruiting, funding, tracking, retaining, and replacing students as they move toward, within, and away from the university." It was, he said, a "grand design" (1976). Years later he would say that "enrollment management was developed to bring about a synergy among functions such as admissions, financial aid, and retention, which too often were viewed as independent and working at cross purposes" (Britz 1998).

Maguire put together a team of specialists in these disparate functional areas to look at their work with a new lens. The names of **Jim Scannell**, **Bob Lay**, and **Louise Lonabocker** still resonate as early pioneers in enrollment management (EM). Their collective experience and perspectives allowed a deeper and broader approach to tracking prospective students and influencing their choices in order to solve BC's enrollment problems. The enrollment management team "spent a lot of time trying to figure out how these functions interacted. And instead of viewing them as four separate functions [admissions, financial aid, retention and marketing], we realized we were also managing six different interactions for a total of ten. This realization led to a very careful management of these important interactions, such as admissions/financial aid and marketing/retention, and ultimately to the success of enrollment management at Boston College." Maguire took Campanella's concept and created the components of an enrollment management system: outstanding people using the right information in the right organizational structure (Henderson 2001). The synergy of that blending is still very much a part of EM today.

To understand the roots of enrollment management, it is important to emphasize that a significant part of Maguire's enrollment management concept was its relationship to marketing. While Maguire saw the goals of enrollment management as "fluid and overlapping," he also saw them as all being related to marketing. "Indeed," he wrote, "in a restricted sense some would consider enrollment management to be a euphemism for marketing" (Maguire 1976).

MARKETING ROOTS

The heritage of marketing is unmistakable in the work of another early pioneer in the field of enrollment management. If John Maguire and Frank Campanella are the fathers of enrollment management, then **Tom Huddleston** is its godfather. At about the time enrollment management was emerging in Boston, Huddleston, then Dean of Admissions and Financial Aid at Bradley University, was applying formal market research with considerable success in Peoria (1976, 1977, 1978). Because Huddleston saw marketing as a "comprehensive rather than singular approach to conception and implementation" (1980), he saw efforts to bring marketing to an institution through the admissions office as shortsighted. The admissions office could not undertake the full institutional approach that marketing required. By 1980, he was suggesting that marketing should drive new organizational structures: "Simply stated, there needs to exist an administrative component that formally examines the needs of internal and external student publics and considers the most appropriate organizational structures to further define and support their needs. This group of units should become the foundation for institutional marketing efforts" (1980).

Following a College Board meeting in New Orleans, Huddleston spent three days at the library of Spring Hill College writing about the comprehensive nature of marketing in a higher education institution and sketching out the components of a new organization to reflect that comprehensiveness (1999). Included in his ideal marketing structure were the areas of admissions, financial aid, orientation, academic advisement, retention, cooperative education, and career development. These offices "should enhance a student's use of the varied educational opportunities and provide the nucleus for an initial entry into institutional marketing" (1980).

Huddleston saw the benefits of marketing institution-wide such that "in essence, colleges should reconsider the traditional organizational structure being used to respond to the interests and needs of their prospective and current clients. The integration of efforts of certain relevant areas will be greater than the sum of the individualized activities" (1980). In identifying the ideal combination of areas, Huddleston also defined what many would call the "classic combination" of enrollment management units for the most effective impact.

Huddleston also saw partnerships with the academic areas of the institution as essential. Successful marketing had to address academic quality and reputation. Enhancing and communicating that portion of the institutional image would be more effective if it happened in collaboration with faculty and academic administrators. This vision had led to the establishment of the first office of retention at Bradley (1999). For the first time, specific staff members were made accountable for retention. Previously, no one had responsibility, so no one took charge. With this model, EM had hitched its wagon to the academic stars.

The Structural Strategists

While Huddleston focused on marketing as the defining link between the structure and practice of enrollment management, the first book devoted to the new enrollment management field emphasized multiple strategies. Writing in 1982 for the American Association of State Colleges and Universities (AASCU), **Frank Kemerer, Victor Baldridge,** and **Kenneth Green** asserted that the institutions that would succeed in the 1980s would need to "develop a set of concrete, practical steps specifically designed to enhance enrollment management" and, in doing so, "adopt a strategic planning approach."

These academics saw enrollment management as both a concept and a procedure. Conceptually, it provided institutions with the steady supply of students necessary to maintain institutional vitality. Procedurally, it was "a set of activities to help institutions interact more

UNIVERSITY *of* WASHINGTON | TACOMA

STUDENT & ENROLLMENT SERVICES

Ted Olsen
Associate Director Admissions Operations

ADMISSIONS

Box 358400
1900 Commerce Street   Tacoma, WA 98402
253.692.4757   fax 253.692.4414   TTY 253.692.4413
olsent2@uw.edu   http://www.tacoma.uw.edu/admissions

W

itial students." Enrollment management was perceived as including
vities: "clarification of institutional mission, program development,
issions, financial aid, orientation, and retention." The list implied
proach" with "clearly linked" components. Enrollment management
rollment management is the antithesis of the quick fix and involves
attention and resources for recruitment activities" (1982).

d Green laid out enrollment management in practical ways. If the
onal vitality, then this view of enrollment management represented a
s. "Effective enrollment management," they wrote, "begins at home
edgeable administrators and faculty who realize that they possess the
vely to environmental pressures in the interest of long-term institu-
e increasingly specialized nature of offices dealing with enrollments
culture" in which decisions in one area were made without any assess-
en in another area. Senior administrators would need to concentrate
s and on communication to break down the silos and pave the way for
ple strategies of "the day-to-day, middle-range type." They shunned
ign because the world of higher education management doesn't oper-
e lure of quick-fix solutions like those so often portrayed in marketing
literature" (1982).

Kemerer, Baldridge, and Green's greatest contribution to the development of enrollment management may have been their presentation of a continuum of structures, each expressing a progressively more complex system of enrollment management. Drawing on the work of Campbell (1980), Fram (1975), Kreutner and Godfrey (1981, the only bibliographic entry in Kemerer, Baldridge, and Green to use the words "enrollment management"), and Caren and Kemerer (1973), they outlined what became the quintessential enrollment management structural forms. Every major researcher and practitioner to follow would refer to and refine the Kemerer, Baldridge, and Green architecture of the "marching millions" enrollment committee, the "somebody has enough time" to be the enrollment coordinator, the "shared turf" matrix with multiple senior officers cooperating to reach enrollment goals, and the full-blown enrollment division with its own senior officer. Given their emphasis on middle-ware strategies and structural continuums, Kemerer, Baldridge, and Green might be called structural strategists. They responded to the need for solutions to unnerving environmental problems confronting higher education institutions in the early 1980s.

EM MOVES INTO THE FACULTY

While a doctoral student of Howard Bowen, **Don Hossler**, EM's preeminent academic, began to focus his research on college choice. He tells of seeing a *Time* magazine photo of two students in caps and gowns digging ditches. The cover story was about college graduates unable to find jobs. Hossler found himself wondering how the promise of employment after graduation could impact the decision to attend college. Thus was born his life's work to inform practice with research (1999).

Hossler describes his first book as "a modest crusade" (1999) to show how research could improve practice, as well as affirming that practice can shape research. In this work (1984) Hossler expanded the components of enrollment management. Student marketing and recruitment, along with pricing and financial aid, were essential elements of Hossler's enrollment management model. In addition, the enrollment management area would need to exert strong influence on academic and career counseling, academic assistance programs, institutional research, orientation, retention programs, and student services (e.g., athletics, activities, career planning, counseling, residence life). "It is not simply an administrative process. Enrollment management involves the entire campus" (1986).

More important, Hossler was turning the field toward a research base. The competition and the smaller applicant pools intensified the imperative for those in enrollment management to understand higher education demand and college choice, pricing, fit between student and institution, retention, and outcomes. Hossler was challenging enrollment management officers to recognize the "need for a new level of professionalism vis à vis a sound knowledge base and the need for a strong research and planning effort for enrollment managers" (1986). Hossler was describing a new kind of enrollment management professional—more than "just" an admissions officer.

The crucial role of research in enrollment management would be reemphasized in Hossler's second book in 1986. Here he suggested that the groundwork for enrollment management had not come from organizational theory but from "convergence of (1) institutional concerns regarding student enrollments, (2) research on student college choice, (3) student-institution fit studies, (4) retention research, and (5) college impact research." Hossler suggested that the research base goes to the understanding of the entire student experience.

In fact, Hossler saw enrollment management as providing a lens on the total student experience. Each of the parts of enrollment management—admissions, financial aid, retention offices, orientation, etc.—sees students from a particular vantage point. Decisions in these areas are made in different parts of the campus, in different divisions, with different administrators. It is little wonder that the resulting views of students conflict! Applying the enrollment management lens enables the institution to see its students from a wider, more comprehensive angle. It also helps the institution see itself through the eyes of students, thus providing a valuable student-centered view.

Hossler continually emphasized the research nature of enrollment management. Whereas the common characteristics of early efforts in the field included continual analysis of institutional image in the student marketplace; attention to the connections between recruitment and financial aid policies; an early willingness to adopt marketing principles in recruitment activities and recognition of the importance of gathering and utilizing information for institutional practices and policies, his enrollment management paradigm proved richer. A combination of the evolution of admissions and financial aid offices, as well as that of other student services offices; the emergence of marketing in higher education; and research on student college choice and student persistence: these factors, and more, comprise enrollment management. Hossler characterized enrollment management as a complex and holistic approach to analyzing and influencing college enrollments (1986).

By 1990, Hossler and Bean had refined the definition of enrollment management. It is, they said:

> *An organizational concept and a systematic set of activities designed to enable education institutions to exert more influence over their student enrollments. Organized by strategic planning and supported by institutional research, enrollment management activities concern student college choice, transition to college, student attrition and retention, and student outcomes. These processes are studied to guide institutional practices in the areas of new student recruitment and financial aid, student support services, curriculum development and other academic areas that affect enrollments, student persistence, and student outcomes from college.*

Bean suggested a significant connection between strategic planning and enrollment management. Although strategic planning had been mentioned in the literature, Bean's explanation was more explicit, especially in distinguishing between long-range and strategic planning.

Issues versus goals, vision versus objectives, open versus closed, environmental versus internal, do versus talk, process versus blueprint—the very language of strategic versus long-range planning provides enrollment management with the flexibility and process orientation to foster greater and more significant change. Hossler and Bean suggested that the steps of strategic planning provide a new context for enrollment management:

- Initiating and agreeing on a strategic planning process.

- Identifying organizational mandates.
- Clarifying organizational mission and values.
- Assessing the external environment: opportunities and threats.
- Assessing the internal environment: strengths and weaknesses.
- Identifying the strategic issues facing an organization.
- Formulating strategies to manage the issues.
- Establishing an effective organizational vision for the future (1990).

Strategic Enrollment Management: Optimum Defined in the Academic Context

By 1993 **Michael Dolence**, a former strategic planner at California State University-Los Angeles, was defining *strategic* enrollment management (SEM) as "a comprehensive process designed to help an institution achieve and maintain the optimum recruitment, retention, and graduation rates of students, where 'optimum' is defined within the academic context of the institution. As such, SEM is an institution-wide process that embraces virtually every aspect of an institution's function and culture."

Dolence introduced the "linking" of academic programs and SEM:

An institution's academic program is inexorably co-dependent on enrollment management. The quality of the academic program can only be developed and maintained in a stable enrollment environment, and stable enrollments are only possible through sound planning, development, and management of academic programs. The alignment of institutional academic policies with SEM goals and objectives is essential to successfully structuring the SEM process (Dolence 1993).

This focus on academics was the "heart and soul" of SEM (1999). Dolence's view of SEM is not just student-centered, but learner-centered (Henderson 2001).

Dolence's primary contribution to enrollment management may have been developing a framework for implementation and evaluation of EM applicable to all institutions. All those who preceded him agreed that the look and feel of enrollment management systems would vary greatly. Dolence, on the other hand, set forth criteria for every enrollment management system to work toward and be evaluated accordingly, no matter the system's "look" or "feel." The Dolence model provided a template for measuring the success of enrollment management systems while providing sufficient flexibility for institution-specific development. By suggesting a set of primary goals that all enrollment management systems would share, regardless of the unique institutional features that created and drove the systems, Dolence standardized the field while respecting its inherent variability (Henderson 2001).

The SEM Template: A Roadmap for Campus Units

Dolence's strategic enrollment management goals showcased the comprehensive nature of enrollment management and provided a roadmap for how every component of the campus, from admissions to the faculty to the groundskeepers, could participate to:

- Stabilize enrollments (stop declining enrollment, control growth, and smooth out fluctuations);
- Link academic programs and SEM (align the principles of SEM with those of the academic nature of the institution);
- Stabilize finances (eliminate deficits, pay off debts, and reinvest strategically);
- Optimize resources (contain growth in the number of employees and redirect and refocus employees);
- Improve services (shorten response time, increase satisfaction, and reduce paperwork);
- Improve quality (eliminate errors and increase student quality ratings);
- Improve access to information (put information systems online);
- Reduce vulnerability to environmental forces (mitigate the negative impact of local and regional events and expand the pool of qualified prospects);
- Evaluate strategies and tactics (track what works, and change what doesn't) (Dolence 1993).

SEM Critical Success Factors (Dolence)

After laying out the SEM goals as a framework, Dolence went on to develop a set of critical success factors against which institutions could evaluate their SEM plans and practices:

- Leadership: No enrollment management system or organization can be anything more than incremental without support and understanding from the top.
- Strategic Planning: Enrollment management is a form of strategic planning and must be tied to the institution's strategic plan.
- Comprehensiveness: Enrollment management cannot operate as a silo. The enrollment management system must be embedded in the total university system in order to function, which means that everyone must be involved in enrollment management.
- Key Performance Indicators (KPIs): Institutions must identify and track progress against metrics that reflect the institution's goals. KPIs are measures of institutional health.
- Research: Analysis of data and information must inform strategies and decision making.

- Academic Foundation: Strategic enrollment management must function in the academic context of the institution. Academics are at the heart of an institution, so they are at the heart of enrollment management.
- Information Technology: State-of-the-art information systems are essential to provide service, track data, and inform decision making.
- Evaluation: Assessment of strategies' effectiveness is essential to allow feedback for change. (Henderson 2001, adapted from Dolence 1999)

EM MOVES INTO THE PROFESSIONAL DEVELOPMENT REALM

As EM gained more traction both in practice on college campuses and in the academic literature among researchers, specialized topics conferences began to appear. When the demand for EM pre-conference workshops at AACRAO Annual Meetings led to repeat performances, the AACRAO Board began to consider looking at other venues that could expand enrollment management offerings and reach a broader market. In January 1991, AACRAO's first Vice President for Enrollment Management and Admissions, **Stanley Henderson**, convened a meeting in Chicago with Ernest Beals (Enrollment Management Committee Chair), Michael Dolence, Tom Colaner (from ACT), and Doris Johnson (from the AACRAO national office). The purpose of the meeting was:

- To explore the feasibility of an enrollment management conference to be cosponsored by AACRAO and other organizations.
- To brainstorm goals and objectives for such a conference.
- To map out a tentative agenda.
- To discuss logistics of time, place, cost, and marketing.

This planning committee developed a conference with an ambitious set of goals:

- Define/refine concept of enrollment management.
- Increase campus-wide awareness of enrollment management.
- Build a campus coalition to address enrollment management.
- Provide a structure for human resource development, training, and accountability.
- Provide new paradigms.

The targeted audience was not just AACRAO professionals, but also college presidents, vice presidents for academic and student affairs, and information systems personnel. In true enrollment management form, the committee also developed Key Performance Indicators to be used in evaluating the program.

Five tracks were created, and the planners solicited nationally-recognized presenters. Don

Hossler, John Bean, Vincent Tinto, and John Gardner were to be featured speakers on organizational structures, research, the freshman year experience, and retention and recruitment activities. Jan Janzen of Xavier University, Chris Munoz of California Lutheran University, Susan Clouse of Arizona State University, and Tom Abrahamson of DePaul University would present practitioner sessions and/or case studies. Four college presidents were invited to give plenary presentations (Johnson 1991).

The committee felt that a strategy of cosponsorship would help to convince the AACRAO Board to support the conference. Some sharing of the financial risk might be the hook that could convince the Board to take on another national conference, the first AACRAO would do outside the Annual Meeting. However, when Henderson presented the idea of co-sponsorship to the Board, President Jerry Bowker said, "This is too important to AACRAO to co-sponsor. Let's do it ourselves." Thus was born the AACRAO SEM Conference.

The first AACRAO Strategic Enrollment Management conference was held in Atlanta, Georgia, in November 1991. The SEM conference promotional materials assured prospective attendees, "Building on the successful enrollment management sessions at the AACRAO Annual Meeting, this conference is a 'must attend' event...." Nearly 200 participants attended, with 95 percent rating it either "excellent" or "good." One evaluation enthused, "This SEM program absolutely needs to be continued, no exception. It has been the most valuable conference in years." "This was the most outstanding conference sponsored by AACRAO I've attended in my 17 years of experience," said another participant (Johnson 1991). A former AACRAO president who attended wrote, "I know the [Board] had a difficult decision to make...when debating whether to offer [SEM] or not. I think you'll find the participants are most grateful for your decision. ...The area of enrollment management needs more attention from us now, not less, and most institutions need help in this area" (Randall 1991). The conference cleared $13,000—a substantial sum from a professional development activity, and enough to convince the Board of Directors to continue the program the following year.

In the 22 years since the first SEM conference, EM professionals from around the world have found the conference true to its original guiding principles. Cutting edge practice sessions, pre-conference papers, keynote presentations from higher education policy makers, as well as technology leaders have helped to shape and define EM through its own preeminent national conference. From the first SEM attendance of 200, the annual conference grew to 1,000 participants in the early 2000s. Four individuals have directed the conference since its inception: Roger Swanson, Jim Black, Bob Bontrager, and William Serrano.

The success of the SEM conference in developing and refining EM practices may also have helped focus criticism of the emerging field by giving a platform to some who opposed its goals and outcomes. By the early 21st century, enrollment management was in the center of a passionate debate over its role in higher education and its treatment of students through the admissions and financial aid processes. Wildly popular among many campus CEOs and board members, EM was not uniformly embraced by faculty, advocates for underserved students, high school counselors, and even a number of professionals in the field. A significant—and vocal—segment of higher education was beginning to see the new EM paradigm as a blight upon higher education. *The Chronicle of Higher Education* went so far as to include the quote, "Enrollment managers are ruining higher education" (Quirk 2005).

The "Enrollment Arms Race" and the Impact on Access

Kati Haycock, President of The Education Trust, gave voice to widely held perceptions:

> *"… Through a set of practices known as enrollment management, leaders in both public and private four-year colleges increasingly are choosing to use their resources to compete with each other for high-end, high scoring students instead of providing a chance for college-qualified students from low-income families who cannot attend college without adequate financial support. In institution after institution, leaders are choosing to use their resources to boost their 'selectivity' ratings and guidebook rankings rather than to extend college opportunities to a broader swath of American young people"* (Haycock 2006).

SEM's critics charged that a college arms race was underway. Escalating costs of technology, recruitment strategies, and financial aid leveraging burdened institutions that felt they could not afford *not* to join the headlong rush to shape their class. Money for academic programs or for student access was sucked into enrollment management schemes, often with the explicit support, if not the pressure, of the institution's president or Board of Trustees.

With special emphasis on the use of financial aid leveraging, SEM was frequently criticized most severely for the role that it played in transforming institutional financial aid from "a tool to help low-income students into a strategic weapon [used] to entice wealthy and high-scoring students" (Haycock 2006).

In the final analysis, the naysayers in relation to enrollment management saw the academy as held in thrall to the enrollment management agenda: "Any aspect of university life that bears on a school's place in the collegiate pecking order is fair game: academic advising, student services, even the curriculum itself. Borrowing the most sophisticated techniques of business strategy, enrollment managers have installed market-driven competition at the heart of the university" (Quirk 2005).

Haycock also questioned whether SEM measurements of quality were valid for college campuses, and whether the value of institutions was accurately captured by SEM methods:

> *"We must begin to think very differently about what constitutes 'quality' in higher education. At the moment, colleges and universities get a lot of their status from things that have very little to do with the fundamental purposes of higher education. Things like how many applications they get for every one they accept, the average SAT or ACT score of their freshman class, or how well their sports teams do. Indeed, new college presidents are often charged with improving their institution's performance on these rankings, and retiring presidents' accomplishments are often celebrated in much the same way....If higher education is to play the role of widening opportunity that the nation needs it to play, we need very different metrics for assessing quality"* (Haycock 2006).

In Defense of Enrollment Management

The indictment was damning against SEM, but practitioners such as **Bob Bontrager** managed to mount an eloquent and elegant defense. Charging that the critics were too often simplistic in their characterization of SEM as worshipping at the altar of material gain at the expense of academic values and kids' best interests, Bontrager outlined the level of complexity in SEM that critics often missed. When an institution began to lay out its enrollment goals, "a focus on aggregate numbers will evolve into detailed analyses of the 'mix' of students that best fulfills the institution's mission. A single goal for overall enrollment becomes multiple goals for undergraduates, graduates, residents, nonresidents, first-year students, transfer students, students of color, retention and graduation rates, and any number of other student subgroups depending on an institution's unique circumstances" (Bontrager 2006).

Bontrager further argued that institutions could use SEM to achieve clarity on enrollment goals and institutional priorities, redefine academic ability, potential, and success, and realign institutional financial aid programs. If some in this profession abused the trust of students and institutional mission, unscrupulously seducing presidents and boards into the enrollment arms race, the true professionals, far from "checking their morals at the door," would be looking at how to use SEM for "other things, like needy students" (Tally Hart quoted in Quirk 2005). Even some of those quick to criticize acknowledged that "although competition increasingly threatens a university's principles, the most innovative work in the profession comes from enrollment managers who attempt to align market with mission" (Quirk 2005).

It is that innovative spirit of service in enrollment management that will "guarantee enough revenue to support the academic mission, or even to expand low-income access to higher education. Indeed, the sophisticated methods of enrollment management may be the only way for schools to hang on to their principles while surviving in a cutthroat marketplace" (Quirk 2005).

Enrollment Management in the Academic Context

By 2005 Henderson was suggesting that a return to the emphasis on the academic context was one way to help ensure that SEM could avoid the excesses practiced by some in the academy. As strategic enrollment management matured as an administrative construct, it had lost sight of the academic context and became "stuck on structure." The emphasis on determining which offices went into the enrollment management division, whether they reported to Academic Affairs or Student Affairs, and what title the chief enrollment officer carried obfuscated the interaction of SEM with the academic mission of an institution. Institutions were even building structures for structure, moving offices from various buildings into one-stop facilities for a SEM-in-a box approach. Henderson asserted that SEM needed to lose structure and refocus on the academic context.

This view of SEM as embedded in the academic mission and principles of the institution sought to return the SEM concept to its origins as a synergy of functions interwoven into the academic mission and values of institutions. Technology and data-mining exist not as ends in themselves but as expressions of what the institution is all about. The offices of SEM should be using financial aid leveraging and predictive modeling to express the academic mission of the university and ensure fit and enhanced student success. And enrollment management professionals—and senior officers in the institution—should ensure that they view SEM through an academic lens. A re-defined SEM Ethos—the underlying fundamental character and spirit of a higher education institution's culture—could give new import to Dolence's definition of "optimum" as being defined in the academic context of the institution.

Looking at enrollments through the academic lens of the culture and principles of the institution provided the integration that Campanella and all the early SEM theorists and practitioners sought as a way to combat the scourge of the "silo mentality." Isolation from the academic mission into a separate SEM structure—SEM for the sake of SEM—led to practices that would draw such passionate criticism of SEM. By contrast, the institution that held onto a more broadly conceived "SEM Ethos" that combined the academic context with SEM practice would seek students who would graduate rather than merely those who would fill empty seats. Such a SEM Ethos could guide an institution to define its market niche according to its academic strengths. In addition, thinking in terms of the academic context could lead SEM to develop enough net revenue increases to plow back into access for the benefit of the "new" students emerging from high schools today.

Henderson wrote:

The academic Ethos of SEM will set the tone for a comprehensive approach. The academic enterprise will, by definition, by its underlying assumptions and values, encompass all components of the institution....The academic lens not only confirms the comprehensive nature of SEM, it reshapes every fundamental element that gives SEM its identity. To rethink these SEM principles in the academic context ensures that the SEM Ethos on any campus will be consistent with the institution's academic being" (Henderson 2005).

In sum, enrollment structure should follow an institutional commitment to the SEM Ethos, and each of the separate offices of any enrollment management structure should reflect the institution's academic culture.

With a full integration of SEM in the academic context, certain principles would rise to give a new template for developing SEM.

SEM Is Shared Responsibility

If enrollment policy and practice reflects the academic culture of a campus, then responsibility for the success or failure of enrollment efforts must belong to every member of the community. No longer does the fickle finger of blame point solely at the admissions office when enrollments decline. To be sure, admissions will bear the responsibility for the execution of recruitment strategies. But faculty must look to the program mix; business affairs officers must look to tuition policy and staff must look to client relationships. It takes a village to raise a child, and it takes an academic community to ensure enrollment health for an institution.

SEM Is Integrated Institutional Planning

The SEM role in institutional planning is much like the Roman god Janus, whose two faces look in opposite directions. On the one hand, SEM speaks as the voice of the campus, representing the academic strengths and messages to various external constituencies. On the other hand, the SEM staff also functions as the eyes and ears of the institution. SEM has access to data and experience that tell the institution what students and parents want and need. The integration of input from both external and internal constituencies into institutional planning informs and enriches the SEM Ethos of the campus.

SEM Is Focus on Service

In the SEM Ethos, service is more important than structure. Business practices flow from the academic foundation of the institution, and the business of a campus becomes student academic success. The campus community should want to test its students' talents in the classroom rather than their patience in navigating the institutional bureaucracy. In the SEM Ethos, the admissions function becomes the first step in retention. *The SEM-focused Admissions Office recruits graduates, not just freshmen.*

The academically centered SEM moves service offices such as admissions, financial aid, records, orientation, academic support, etc., away from isolated and insulated silos into a part of the whole—a big tent approach to enrollment. The big tent, where students access those services they need and ignore the others, provides an intuitive way to look at student service. Do policies and practices make sense to students? Do they meet student expectations? Offices in a SEM environment will be focused on service from the student perspective. Why is the student drawn to the campus? Why does the student stay? To find a mate? To have a good time? To join a fraternity? To play sports? To save money? To prepare for a job? Or, possibly, to get an education? In any event, the SEM-oriented office will recognize that the only way a student stays in school is if he or she is successful *academically*. Recruitment in the academic context seeks ways to show prospective students how they can be successful on the campus. "They recruit best who serve best."

SEM Is Key Performance Indicators (KPIs)

KPIs are placeholders for the institutional values of the SEM Ethos. If the driving force for the admissions office is "get the bodies, not the fit," the process is out of sync with the academic values of the institution. In too many places we have put the emphasis on how *many* students we recruit rather than *which* students we recruit. The academic culture should define the appropriate characteristics of the enrolled student. Those characteristics, then, become what the admissions office will track in suspects, prospects, applicants, and admits. And retention services can concentrate on providing what those students need in order to be successful.

SEM Is Research and Evaluation

The people who go into most enrollment management units are not always predisposed to research and evaluation. These are "people people." They are more interested in spending time with prospective students and with those students' families than in doing research on student choice or evaluating recruitment programs. Henderson cautions institutions to evaluate SEM based on academic outcomes, not on perceptions:

> *However, the industry standard is more and more based on data, surveys, research—all the tools of the academic enterprise. Without a data-driven approach to practice and process, the logical outgrowth of a major dip in enrollment is disappointment, recrimination, and finger-pointing. SEM units cannot continue to do 'feel-good' programs where the evaluations say everybody thought it was a great program, and staff felt so positively about how things went. If it didn't make a difference in reaching the institution's academic goals, then it wasn't successful, no matter how positively everyone felt about it"* (Henderson 2005).

SEM Is for the Long Haul

SEM is never finished. Just as academic disciplines evolve with the discovery of new knowledge, or the infusion of new research interests, or the development of new pedagogy, so SEM will remain fluid and responsive to its external environment and institutional culture. Within this environment, SEM practitioners must follow the deliberate, purposeful path of the long-term academic, not the quick fix of the repairman.

These principles provided a roadmap, if you will, for institutions to apply a SEM Ethos that would express the culture and values of the campus for tailor-made enrollment management.

RETHINKING SEM'S MARKETING ROOTS

David Kalsbeek, arguably SEM's ablest theoretician and consummate practitioner, used a pre-conference paper at the 15th Annual SEM Conference in 2005 to review the evolution of SEM from Maguire's synergy of functions to Hossler's process and "systematic set of activities" to Dolence's academic context and Henderson's call to de-emphasize structure and return to the academic context. Noting SEM's roots in marketing, Kalsbeek put forward a more complex and nuanced view of SEM as a "systematic evaluation of an institution's competitive market position, the development of a research-based definition of [that]…position…, and then marshalling and managing institutional plans, priorities, and resources to…that market position in pursuit of the institution's optimal enrollment, academic, and financial profile" (2003).

Kalsbeek and Hossler in 2009 amplified the market context of SEM by suggesting that "enrollment managers must begin by assessing the dynamics that create the competitive market context which in real and measureable ways prescribes and circumscribes the range of strategic futures an institution in all likelihood has to choose among. Understanding that marketplace is the prerequisite to all strategic enrollment planning."

The very issues that SEM has concentrated on as strategic initiatives—demand for admission and resulting selectivity, tuition price from a willingness to pay perspective, tuition discounting and net tuition revenue, enrollment diversity, student expectations and aspirations, retention and graduation rates—may in fact be a reflection of market indicators. Hossler and Kalsbeek (2009) wrote:

> *These measures are not just indicators of institutional performance but indicators of institutional position, indices of a school's place in the competitive market.*
>
> *What a strategic enrollment management perspective brings to campus planning is this realization that many academic decisions about curricular offerings, and new academic initiatives and many student life initiatives should be and typically are influenced more by an institution's market position than its mission statement.*
>
> *Market position defines the interpretative context within which any enrollment goals for academic profile, pricing or retention can be meaningfully understood. Embracing that fact shifts enrollment management and planning from traditional, internal, tactical, and structural concerns to external, strategic realities and opportunities.*

This echoes Dolence's Strategic Level of the SEM Transition Model in the 1990s that carried the institutional message of "We control our enrollment outcomes." Institutions in this advanced stage of SEM stayed ahead of the changing environment with nimble responses from the alignment of both academic and planning enterprises fused with enrollment management. The resulting embedding of an outward focused SEM in the campus culture assured integrated institutional decision-making processes and provided for consistent planning and assessment to meet any challenge the environment could throw.

However, Hossler and Kalsbeek recognize that the market-driven approach to SEM is not in sync with the academy. They insightfully point out that higher education leaders are convinced that their future is determined by the academic programs and the learning outcomes of their students. Two common misconceptions of the academy are that the institution's academic programs are so strong that if students aren't coming to them, there must be something wrong with the process of recruitment, and that if too many students fail to graduate, the admission standards must be flawed. The hard truth is that decisions are too often based on faculty interest rather than student interest, and the evergreen interest in raising admission standards fails to realize that the bottom quartile of the class will always be disadvantaged because the students who fall there will be outclassed by those in the higher quartiles. Because raising admission standards is easier than building in the hard slog of retention support to get the bottom quartile to graduation, raising admissions standards has been done again and again on campuses.

While the insular view of faculty holds sway in the academy, institutional failure to understand its market position "can lead to errors not only in marketing decisions but also in academic program decisions. In fact, one of the errors many senior campus policy makers and enrollment managers make is to set goals that are simply not realistic given the institution's market position" (Hossler and Kalsbeek 2009). Hence the experience of the enrollment manager whose president in late April decided there weren't enough freshmen in the pipeline for the coming fall, so he made available $500,000 for scholarships. The president disregarded that academically talented students had already decided where they were going and would not be tempted to apply to a new school at such a late date in the cycle.

THE INTEGRATION OF SEM: A MAP FOR THE FUTURE

Kalsbeek (2006) has also given focus to four threads of SEM, each of which has roots in the past 40 years of development of SEM theory and practice. Institutional predisposition for one or the other SEM orientation has driven the wide variations in how SEM is structured and how its strategies play out. Each in its own way has strengths, but each taken in isolation may lead to imperfect application of what we have come to know about the integrated nature of SEM. The future of SEM will surely lie in how well the field can integrate the threads into a tapestry that is greater than the individual perspectives.

The Administrative Orientation is about process and business practices. From the earliest days of SEM the field has been about reengineering how we process students in enrollment areas. The practices of how to use technology, the Web and communications all lead to a process-driven approach. The drawback of this orientation is its slavish devotion to the institution's efficiency and effective use of resources. It is administrative and may detract from the end goals of SEM: student success and the academic mission.

The Student-focused Orientation corrects the ultra-process of the Administrative approach by putting the individual student in the center of SEM. This approach to SEM is often couched in terms of Student Affairs student development theory, leadership training, and experiential learning. It is in conflict with process because it often requires individualized treatment to find the path for student success. Redundancy is the logical outcome. And faculty can become impatient with too much emphasis on student wants rather than academic expectations for students.

The Academic Orientation puts the academic mission of an institution into SEM. The focus is on academic programs, curricula, research and teaching through the eyes of the faculty. Students are important as they interact with the academic core of the school, and SEM will have to deal with program delivery, scheduling, and other processes related exclusively to the well-being of the academic side of the house. Faculty control in this orientation may make SEM—and the institution—insular, isolated from what is happening outside the walls of the institution.

The Market-centered Orientation looks externally at the market perspective (not marketing) and the market position an institution has among its competitors. The market-centered approach to SEM makes an institution nimble and able to respond to changing market conditions by bringing strategies and tactics to bear that will maintain or shift the market position. The drawback of this approach is the inherent opposition on campuses to such external influence.

Kalsbeek has an appreciation that successful SEM efforts will incorporate pieces of each of these perspectives. While clearly in his taxonomy the market-centered approach is the most mature, it may also be the most difficult to bring to successful implementation in a faculty governance structure.

The use of integrated approaches to SEM has also been suggested by Smith and Kilgore (2006), and Henderson and Yale (2008), through the concept of the "three faces of SEM." This approach posits that EM has an Administrative-Structural component, or "face"; a Planning component; and a Leadership component. Each is essential to the successful functioning of the SEM enterprise, and each must be blended with the other two. Getting the right approach for the management of SEM requires planning and leadership. Charismatic leadership without regard to process and structure will bog down SEM. Building a SEM structure that doesn't accommodate the needed strategic processes and the campus's leadership style will, in the final analysis, be empty.

Higher education today can be said to be moving into the age of accountability. A number of recent studies suggest that higher education has fallen on hard times, in part because of the industry's failure to consider the realities of its environment. Endowment assets plummeted in the financial collapse of 2008. Schools are overleveraged; liabilities are increasing; and assets are drying up while costs continue to rise. Public higher education is seeing searing cuts in state appropriations where state universities are going from state-supported to state-assisted to state-located. The result is increasing tuition at a time when more students and their families are unable to afford the cost of education. If a student fails to see the value of an increasingly expensive and out-of-reach education, she will not complete or even attend. Rhodes suggests that "colleges and universities [are] characterized more by their *strategic imitation* rather than *strategic imagination* as their singular pursuit of prestige is shaping to an extreme degree the strategic agendas" (2009).

Bill Gleason (2010) agrees with this assessment when he takes on the University of Minnesota president's "ambitious aspiration" to be one of the top three research universities in the world as "hubristic and clueless." He says that Minnesota's land grant position should lead it to focus on preparing people in the state to be competitive in the job market. Re-establishing priorities that match the market and showing how the university works for the people of the state can make a stronger case for increased state aid. "Ensuring you're in the top 25 favorites of recruiters for big companies is more important than being in the top three in research world-wide."

State legislatures are moving to metrics for allocation of any increases in state funding. Instead of across the board increases, schools will receive funding based on how much growth they realize in total degrees awarded, how many graduates in academic areas needed by the state (e.g., STEM programs), how well the school does in providing access for underserved/underrepresented groups (e.g., number of first generation students enrolled), and how many Pell-eligible students are enrolled.

EM, with its emphasis on data, process, research, and evaluation already in its tool set is ideally situated to meet this push for accountability. However, tools alone will not be enough to ensure that EM continues to evolve. Our attention to process must take into account the needs of a student-centered campus while embedding our actions in the academic mission, all the while acting in concert with the market and our institution's position in it. How well enrollment managers can integrate the perspectives that have evolved through the last 40 years will be the true test of whether we spread our wings to leave the brink of a profession as the future unfolds.

2

THE STUDENT SUCCESS CONUNDRUM

Zebulun Davenport
Vice Chancellor for Student Life
Indiana University – Purdue University Indianapolis

Miguel Martinez-Saenz
Associate Provost for Undergraduate Education
and Student Support Services
St. Cloud State University

Lisa Rhine
Vice President for Student Affairs
Northern Kentucky University

CHAPTER 2

INTRODUCTION

In *Democracy and Education* (1916), John Dewey maintained that "To find out what one is fitted to do and to secure an opportunity to do it is the key to happiness." We need a firm and consistent reminder of the substantial import of Dewey's message so higher education institutions remain effective in fostering these opportunities for students. We should also keep in mind the idea that education, and higher education in our case, serves a public good, and is one of the central experiments in the history of democracy in the United States. Nonetheless, in our present context, the importance of promoting access to higher education appears to have less to do with the common good and an engaged and learned citizenry than with prioritizing competitive advantage, earning potential, and prestige.

Higher education has changed, both in its role in society and its approach to learning. As *America's Perfect Storm: Three Forces Changing our Nation's Future* (Kirsch et al. 2007) conclusively demonstrates, universities and colleges must anticipate and respond to the growing educational inequalities and the substantial disparities in the distribution of skills, the changes in the economy and its effect on college graduates, along with extensive student population demographic changes. As national studies confirm, high school graduates are only marginally prepared to do college-level work, so that higher education institutions must respond to the changing needs of our students (U.S. Department of Education 2006, 8-9). Because of the rapid changes in technology, there has been growth in the demand for college graduates to be able to move into management, professional, technical, health and high-level sales positions, which require a college education that teaches students to think critically and adapt to the changes in their environment (Kirsch 2007, 16-18). Furthermore, due to the expected population growth and the continued increase in international migration, we need to appreciate that there is an urgent need to develop intercultural competencies across campus communities, to develop our students' cognitive abilities, and to foster a diverse campus community.

That said, recently published works such as *Academically Adrift: Limited Learning on College Campuses* (Arum and Roksa 2011) and *Why Does College Cost So Much?* (Archibald and Feldman 2011) elucidate the disparate and contradictory messages about the role higher education ought to play in the life of individuals and, more to our point perhaps, the role of higher education in the public landscape. Amidst all of this, however, one thing appears clear: the student as consumer. The implications are considerable because this view of the student has shaped the way we conceptualize and justify the educational enterprise: both its purpose and its organizational structure. Our hope, then, is to illustrate how the way we talk about education, specifically how we define student success and how we organize our educational institutions, can dramatically affect the transformative potential of higher education.

It is important to note that the language of the market has been pervading higher education through marketing and branding strategies, or the rationale that people should pursue a college degree to increase their earning potential. Higher education, however, is considered by some students as one of the few market arenas where consumers demand less than they pay for. For example, many students have come to believe that the credential, not the education, is the goal. So, when colleges adopt a consumerist approach, we give students more options whether they benefit from these choices or not, and increase amenities even when they reallocate resources from educational initiatives and instructional costs. What is at stake when this narrow market mentality takes hold is that campuses no longer challenge students to engage in a process of self-discovery and knowledge creation that requires commitment, discipline and persistence. So, instead of selling the idea that higher education is about knowledge, growth and development, we sell a sometimes misleading expectation of the student experience for which the "customer" is willing to pay. Put differently, and as Stefan Collini aptly explains, colleges and universities sell a "student experience" that is what students ask us for even if it isn't what they need.

Consider the following:

> *Where all this talk about 'the student experience' starts to betray the purposes of education is in its focus on a narrow form of short-term box-ticking satisfaction. … On graduation ('exiting the student experience', we should say), it's easy to imagine respondents ticking all the boxes to indicate that the goods and services they received corresponded to those promised, and yet being left with the uneasy feeling that they haven't been—as we used to call it—educated. Not that practical things are unimportant or students' views irrelevant or future employment an unworthy consideration. … It is, rather, that the model*

of the student as consumer is inimical to the purposes of education. The paradox of real learning is that you don't get what you 'want'—and you certainly can't buy it. The really vital aspects of the experience of studying something (a condition very different from 'the student experience') are bafflement and effort. Hacking your way through the jungle of unintelligibility to a few small clearings of partial intelligibility is a demanding and not always enjoyable process. It isn't much like wallowing in fluffy towels. And it helps if you trust your guides rather than assuming they will skimp on the job unless they're kept up to the mark by constant monitoring of their performance indicators (Collini 2011).

So, as we continue to develop our understanding of enrollment management, let us remain mindful that the higher education burden is quite unique in the "service industry." Higher education undermines its purpose when it behaves as an enterprise that does everything it can to please the consumer and that adopts the simplistic and misguided refrain that "the customer is always right." In fact, our job as educators is, in large part, one that requires us to create learning experiences that are challenging, rigorous and that require the customer to make a concerted effort if she hopes to reap the "rewards." In short, educational institutions should focus on creating conditions that enable students to pursue an education in which they develop intellectually, emotionally and socially; and we must be honest about the fact that students will have to exert a great deal of effort if they hope to say that they earned a world-class education.

It starts, then, by the way higher education defines what it means to be a successful student.

DEFINING STUDENT SUCCESS

Varying definitions of student success—by multiple entities that aim to improve higher education performance measures—complicate our ability to understand and address student outcomes. The university and state may view and measure student success based on retention or graduation rates. Or perhaps the university may recognize that active involvement in the academic, co-curricular and social life of the university represents student success. Faculty and staff may define student success as learning, growth and development while students may define it as achieving their goals as they personally define them. Even if institutional entities can agree and come to a common definition of student success, they are faced with collaboration barriers that may impede progress toward the desired goal. Let us keep in mind that there is some broad consensus that higher education generally is in a moment of crisis in the United States (and, perhaps, in much of the developed world). Among the factors that have contributed to this predicament are:

- A financial crisis that has significantly lowered the level of support from private and public sources.
- The obsession with rankings based on measures such as peer assessment, graduation rates, alumni giving, class profile and retention.
- An emphasis on accountability that has more to do with financial conditions than the promotion of a public good, or the fulfillment of an institutional mission. (Lalami 2009)

While Kent State University's decision to try a "new and unusual tactic to improve its status, retention rate, and fund raising—paying cash bonuses to faculty members if the university exceeds its goals in those areas," may seem to be a wise strategic choice, we believe there is reason to be concerned (Masterson 2008). The mantra of accountability and the obsession with rankings based on measures like peer assessment, graduation rates, alumni giving, class profile and retention may undermine the vision of higher education. Retention in particular appears to have more to do with the financial conditions impacting a higher education institution than the promotion of student success.

As Robert M. Zemsky (2005) argues, what is being measured by our market taxonomy and *U. S. News* rankings is competitive advantage." If Zemsky is correct, then accountability, as it is being communicated in the national media, also has more to do with financial conditions than with promoting a quality education and fulfilling an institutional mission. And, while some institutions are adapting their missions, it is not clear whether there has been a dramatic shift in the overall focus of higher education. Consider the following commentary by Ben Gose (2005, B6):

> *The conventional wisdom is that the college-admissions process has spiraled out of control in the past decade or so, with the tremendous growth of test-preparation companies; the rise of high-priced independent college counselors; the morphing of the admissions office into a number-crunching "enrollment management" operation; and the fixation by universities on improving statistical measures of quality, like selectivity, even when doing so requires strategies — for example, filling the bulk of the class through early admissions — that many counselors believe are harmful to students. Both admissions deans and guidance counselors get wistful thinking about an earlier time when everyone focused on the right "fit" for prospective students.*

Realizing that the tension between student-centered models of education that purport to promote student success and the many financial constraints that most of the nation's institutions of higher education are facing betrays a fundamental fact: most institutions have to improve retention if they are going to remain viable. We are all aware that the *U.S. News* rankings and other college guides take into account student retention; and there are various retention models and formulas (e.g., Tinto, Noel-Levitz, and Seidman) used to enhance enrollment management strategies, improve retention, and strengthen financial position. Tinto's model makes plain that socially and academically integrated students are likely to complete their courses of study, be retained and incidentally persist. We say "incidentally persist" because it is difficult to determine whether retention is an indicator of persistence. In other words:

> *… [A]greeing with Tinto, [John Bean] acknowledge[s] that students who drop out might have already achieved their goals during their limited time in college. Hence, Bean suggest[s] that neither the student nor the college should be considered a failure. Retention, as he explain[s], needs to be further complicated to consider student educational goals."*
> (Hagedorn 2005, 91)

Yet, retention and graduation rates are frequently and consistently used as indicators of student success in higher education.

Since there is a positive correlation between high retention numbers and level of academic profile, it seems that there is some circularity. Nonetheless, institutions have been convinced that high retention numbers indicate a very good educational experience. For example, John Bean argues that "Student retention is a win-win situation: the student gains an education and increased lifetime earnings and the institution educates a student, fulfilling its mission, and gains tuition income" (Bean 2005, 237). While it is relatively easy to track "lifetime earnings" and "tuition income," it is more difficult to quantify the extent to which a student has gained an education or an institution has fulfilled its mission. As a consequence, the student's education may be considered incidental, while tuition income and earning potential may be viewed as fundamental. So, what does "student success" really have to do with all of this?

Ewell and Wellman (2007) describe student success as a "generic label" for a topic with multiple dimensions:

- *Student flow through the institution and persistence to degree*
- *Quality and content of learning, knowledge and skill attainment, and*
- *Positive engagement experiences.*

Student flow through the institution to degree completion most closely aligns with a description of the retention goal. At degree or certificate completion, students have successfully navigated the pathway from enrollment through degree completion.

Tinto's model, coupled with Alan Seidman's formula, results in the following equation:

Retention = Early identification + Early, Intensive, Continuous Intervention

Thus, "the goal" is to identify at-risk students and achieve better retention numbers. As discussed frequently in the literature, "retention" can be measured in a number of ways, but at best it is an institutional measure to determine the extent to which it retains or fails to retain students. Yet sometimes retention, by a process of equivocation, is championed as a measure of student success.

Student flow describes the student's progress from choosing a college through enrollment to graduation. This process encompasses admission, enrollment, timely and satisfactory completion of general education courses, major declaration and satisfactory major course completion through graduation.

There is an increasing concern that colleges and universities are not producing students with high levels of skill, knowledge and abilities that the college degree is intended to represent (see *Academically Adrift*, Arum and Roksa 2011). A focus on assessment and accountability has resulted in new indicators of student success and effectiveness including learning-based models that emphasize what students know and can actually do (U. S. Department of Education 2006). Focusing on qualitative aspects of education and the content of learning or skill attainment provides the opportunity to emphasize how colleges can, and should be, expected to contribute to the common good. To illustrate this point, the following questions should be considered: Can students understand, articulate, demonstrate and practically apply the knowledge that they've acquired? What do students know that they didn't know before? What can they now do that they couldn't before the learning experience occurred?

Positive engagement experiences may also serve as a definition of a success for students. Consider the National Survey for Student Engagement's (NSSE) report *Experiences That Matter: Enhancing Student Learning and Student Success* (2007). This report sends the message that colleges should focus on high-impact activities—activities that enable students learning—and retention will follow. In other words, retention is a by-product of successful programs. Successful programs, however, are understood in relation to student learning outcomes, not retention numbers. An intentional reorientation toward accountability that places the central importance on student learning outcomes is essential.

The study *Learning Reconsidered: A Campus-Wide Focus on the Student Experience* directed the nation's attention to the challenges and opportunities of adopting new and exciting pedagogical strategies to engage students. The study suggested that classroom strategies through which integrated learning outcomes are paramount were one means to significant learning outcomes. The idea is that student learning is maximized if students are given the opportunity 1) to construct knowledge and meaning from coursework that informs them about its place and their role within the community and 2) to learn across multiple domains, i.e., cognitive, affective and behavioral.

In this discussion we do not intend to oversimplify or be insensitive to the difficult task of assessing student learning, especially as it relates to the education of the whole person. While institutional measures like retention remain a central goal of many institutions, we think it appropriate to highlight the role admissions plays in securing a class that will have a high success rate, with interest in enhancing the well-being of the women and men who choose to enroll at our respective institutions. In other words, if institutions focus on student learning and educating the whole person, they take a risk—a risk of students questioning their long-term goals after arriving at the college and perhaps deciding it is not the place for them.

There is no shortage of commentary on the importance of accountability, transparency and assessment of student learning. In fact, *A Test of Leadership: Charting the Future of U.S. Higher Education* has made plain its recommendation that universities "must become more transparent about cost, price, and student success outcomes, and must willingly share this information with students and families" (U. S. Department of Education, 2006, 4). In fact, the report emphasizes the need to measure student success on a "value-added" basis (24). The Collegiate Learning Assessment (CLA) project is being touted by higher education experts as a useful tool when considering "value-added" assessment. This tool aims to measure learning outcomes in areas including critical thinking, analytic reasoning, problem solving, writing skills, the ability to evaluate and analyze source information, drawing inferences, constructing arguments and using evidence correctly when attempting to establish a position.

There are assessment instruments to "measure" critical thinking, e.g., Collegiate Learning Assessment, instruments to "measure" engagement as self-reported, e.g., National Survey on Student Engagement, and instruments to "measure" institutional effectiveness (Joint Commission on Accountability Reporting, or JCAR); yet, higher education fails to connect the dots between these three so that we end up with organizational structures and behavioral structures and practices derived from the way we have conceptualized the problem or issues before us. Because of our failure to see the whole picture, we fail our most important constituent: the student.

What we label the student success conundrums, then, are a series of problems that result when we take too narrow a view of student learning. We seek to describe here what we see as the perspectives from each respective stakeholder in higher education. Again, what we hope to illustrate, by example and story, is the way stakeholders conceptualize and perceive a problem and the ways these conceptualizations contradict each other.

THE STUDENT SUCCESS CONUNDRUM

The student success conundrum (summarized in Figure 1, page 38) is based on the differing perceptions of student success held by students, faculty and staff, colleges and universities, and state governments which complicate the ability of higher education institutions to understand, assess, and design interventions that enable students to succeed.

The State's Perspective: Only Part of the Picture

A wide variety of productivity and accountability measures that are directly comparable across institutions are not available amongst our colleges and universities. Understandably, state agencies most commonly require retention and graduation rates as performance measures of progress and completion. Policy makers may equate these rates with student success because they answer the questions: How many students return? And how many students graduate? However, these measures are not without their shortcomings. Retention rates and graduation rates reported to state agencies reflect outcomes for only those students that were first-time, full-time degree seeking students at the point of fall entry in any given year to the institution. Many institutions have a significant number of students who attend part-time, began in a term other than the fall semester or transferred into the institution from another college. These students are not included in the reporting on figures of retention and graduation and may represent an important cohort of enrollees.

One four-year public institution in the Midwest had seen a 72 percent increase in degree production in ten years at its university due to the increase in the number of transfer students successfully completing degrees at the institution; however, that number was not celebrated by the state because the institution's graduation rate, based on first time, full time, degree seeking enrollees, had risen only slightly. Similarly, a significant number of students at an institution may plan to complete two years there and move to another university to complete their degree, but those numbers may not be taken into account by state boards requesting only graduation and retention rates as performance measures.

The onus is placed on institutions to develop assessment methods and strategies that demonstrate the impact educational institutions have on students beyond the requisite retention and graduation rates. Some collaborative bodies have begun work in this area. The U.S. Department of Education's Committee on Measures of Student Success aspires to create a more ideal reporting framework. This framework would encompass many more data tracking points than what is currently in the reporting domain. This working group's directive is to prioritize major issues related to progression and completion measures and identify areas for potential recommendation.

The Joint Commission on Accountability Reporting (JCAR) recognizes that current retention and graduation measures fail to take into account variability in the student body and in enrollment patterns at colleges and universities across the nation. JCAR presents a model that is inclusive rather than exclusive called "Student Advancement Rates." This model employs a formula that takes into account not only graduation rates but also transfer rates and continued enrollment rates in its calculation of student success. In 1997, the U.S. Department of Education authorized use of the JCAR method as an acceptable form of reporting student progress.

The Institutional Perspective

Driven by governmental agencies, many institutions align with definitions of success that focus solely on retention and graduation rates. Retention, persistence and graduation are vital to the success of students. In fact, many governing bodies are moving toward a funding formula that is based on persistence and degree attainment in a specified amount of time (i.e., the number of first-time full-time degree seeking students who complete degrees in four years or less). As a result, some institutions have placed major emphasis on faculty involvement and in-class participation; so much so that they have created strategies and, in some cases, policies that enforce course attendance and classroom participation. For instance, faculty may require attendance and assess classroom participation as a component of the grading structure. Other practices include mandatory attendance during the first two years of a student's college career. While attendance and classroom participation are important to student success, there are many factors outside of the classroom that contribute to retention and graduation as well.

Carol Schneider, President of the Association of American Colleges and Universities, contends that retention and graduation are only partial indicators of success. She postulates that there are other core elements that must be considered when defining success, including intellectual powers and capacities, ethical and civic preparation, and personal growth and self-direction (Schneider 2010). As a result, defining and impacting student success must consider the student's involvement in the academic, co-curricular and social life of the institution. Tracking attendance and focusing on participation in the classroom are not sufficient measures of student success. The institutions that recognize retention and graduation rates are influenced by factors both in and out of the classroom have higher retention rates than peer institutions that do not.

Engaging students in meaningful ways outside the classroom is essential to student success.

While Kuh (2008) suggests that "high impact practices" are limited to first-year seminars, common intellectual experiences, learning communities, writing intensive courses, collaborative assignment/projects, undergraduate research opportunities, service learning, internships, and capstone experiences, we contend that such programs and services must also contain the following elements to maximize student success: clear and specific learning outcomes, meaningful connections, expectations that students devote considerable time and effort to purposeful tasks, and interact with faculty/staff and peers about substantive matters over an extended period of time.

What we put forth in this chapter is that the structured and desired learning objective coupled with experiential components result in the greatest positive impact. What impacts retention and graduation rates remains inconclusive. But we can attest that a complex combination of interwoven factors influence student success.

Faculty and Staff Perspective

Faculty and staff may define success as learning, growth and development, measurable outcomes of a particular course, degree program or engagement in co-curricular activities. The call for assessment outcomes from colleges and universities is widespread across the nation. Universities, especially enrollment management and student affairs staff, must answer to issues raised about the competency and value of higher education and the extent to which campus experiences outside of the classroom impact success.

Institutions are working diligently to find reliable ways to identify and measure intended learning outcomes. Enrollment Management and Student Affairs are particularly challenged to align programmatic interventions and services with a set of learning outcomes resulting in student success. Outside the academic realm, service providers are employing learning outcome identification activities and co-curricular alignment processes that tie programmatic activity and service to specific, measurable learning outcomes known to impact retention. One Midwestern four-year university has adopted a sophisticated co-curricular alignment process. By identifying outcomes that the literature defines as impacting success, tying programmatic efforts to those focused outcomes, and developing reliable measures of those outcomes, institutions can begin to demonstrate impact on student learning and utilize the data for continuous improvement of interventions that become best practice in the field.

That data should drive decision-making is not a new concept in higher education. More sophisticated strategies such as the use of predictive analytics for determining which students, based on historical data, are most likely to persist, is a step toward a more comprehensive set of retention data. While learning outcome assessment gets to the heart of what we intend for students to gain from the higher education experience, it is often not used beyond the institution itself to demonstrate student success and educational attainment; therefore, learning outcomes need to be brought into the national discussion and incorporated as measures worthy of consideration alongside measures of retention and graduation rates. And institutions must consider all of these perspectives when designing assessment plans to determine our ability to promote student persistence and graduation. The personal goals of students should also be considered to create a comprehensive assessment picture that can guide institutions.

The Student Perspective

Students attend institutions for many reasons with varying goals in mind. These students may be classified as first-time, full-time, degree-seeking, transfer, returning, and/or adult. Their goals can range from completing a four- or two-year degree, fulfilling general education requirements or prerequisites for a desired major, taking individual courses to improve a skill necessary for employment or taking a class for the purpose of personal fulfillment.

As student goals vary, so do the types of institutions. Thus, institutions play different roles in assisting students in reaching their desired goals. Often this assistance depends upon the institution type, focus, or mission. Some students attend community or technical colleges to obtain a certificate of completion in order to meet identified workforce needs of a specific region. The education obtained from this pursuit is usually tied to the economic advancement for that student and of that region. Other students may attend a community college for the first year as a "primer" with no intentions of completing a two-year degree there. Meanwhile, others may attend community college with a long-term goal of completing a Bachelor's degree. These students seek to fulfill general education requirements at a lower cost and then transfer into a four-year degree granting institution. Finally, some students just want to take courses as a "lifelong learner" with no intentions of ever obtaining a degree.

These various pursuits are all noble, as higher education is vital in advancing the progress of a region, state, and the nation. Institutions serve as valuable vehicles through which students achieve their desired goals. However, incongruence of desired outcomes by the student and the institution can result in negative consequences for both. If an institution falls short of serving students as they pursue their goals, the student may fail to progress academically, lose financial assistance, and even be unable to return in good standing if she drops out. By the same token, when a student's goals misalign with the institution's goals, including local, state, or federal reporting requirements, it can have major adverse implications for the institution. Misalignment between a student and an institution may result in an institution's inability to achieve effectiveness as defined by governing bodies. As a result, it may be very difficult for that institution to add new and necessary programs of study, possibly leading to its inability to secure local, state, and national resources.

For these and other reasons it is vitally important that we, as professionals in higher education, exercise due diligence in identifying students' needs, understanding the type, focus, and mission of institutions, and intentionally matching the two.

Figure 1: The Student Success Conundrum: Varying Definitions of Success

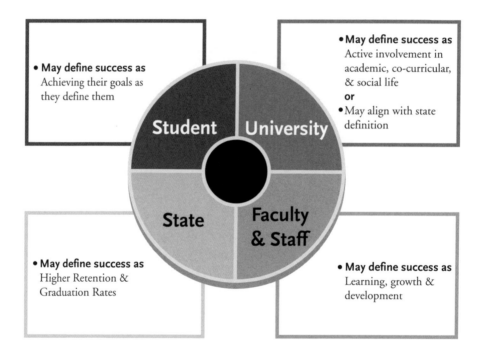

COLLABORATION BARRIERS

Institutions and institutional staff that comprise them often exhibit counterproductive behaviors that complicate our ability to address student success comprehensively. Simply put, individuals that work in higher education institutions often fail to collaborate (see Hersch 2007; Shavelson 2007). Staff and faculty behaviors produce additional obstacles and are rooted in an institution's inability to put all personal, divisional agendas and fears aside in order to collaborate for the good of students. Often, policies and procedures that become obstacles for students are created with the best of intentions and exist to protect an individual's or group's ability to meet a goal or objective. However, when faculty or staff needs conflict with organization or student needs, barriers are constructed that are detrimental to student success.

Gallup has studied organizational management across multiple industries and found that organizational barriers result from five causes: fear, information flow, short-term thinking, misalignment and money (Reiger 2011). While these causes apply to higher education, other barriers include potential loss of credit or recognition, organizational heterogeneity and organizational hierarchy. Units on campus practicing autonomously can also result in organizational barriers that undermine an institution's ability to collaborate.

Structures, policies and strategies used by mature organizations often unwittingly reinforce these barriers. Mature institutions must create collaborative structures and processes to solve problems creatively. An institution's infrastructure can work to undermine or facilitate approaches to improving student success. Though students do not perceive the college experience as a series of discrete experiences or activities, institutions of higher education tend to organize themselves in ways that create separation and perpetuate a "silo mentality" (Schoem 2002). Artificially-constructed divisions keep scholars apart and leave students to make sense of their college experience on their own. These barriers do a major disservice to the innovative, comprehensive efforts imagined to improve or even transform a campus.

If we take a moment to view the college experience through the eyes of students and design our initiatives from their perspective, we would likely take a totally different approach. The view that we would see would be an integrated, holistic, seamless experience that crosses divisional and departmental lines. Keeling, in *Learning Reconsidered 2* (2008), discusses the value of true collaboration. Keeling claims that collaboration matters as it re-orients and links resources and service providers in new ways that make the total value of them greater than the sum of their parts. If institutions continue to adopt fractured, segregated approaches to student retention efforts and learning outcomes assessed without taking into account the whole person, the true potential of the emerging systemic models that can transform our institutions and graduate more students will never be realized. When institutions attempt to address student success from one area, void of cross-divisional collaboration, the result sub-optimizes the student experience.

The inertia of current practice and policy can overwhelm concerted efforts to collaborate and implement change (Hannan and Freeman 1984). Administrative structures and processes, and access to decision making across the organization are necessary to overcome obstacles that impede student success. Flourishing organizations have structures and processes in place to make ongoing decisions, follow through on problems and bring new issues to the table for consideration (Jelinek and Schoonhoven 1990). Collaborative structures should connect both vertically within divisions and laterally across organizational units to ensure that varied expertise, knowledge of widespread impact of decisions and varying perspectives are considered.

Since employee performance in higher education is centered on reward and evaluation, with programmatic or group outcomes tied to resources; individuals and groups take actions and exhibit behaviors that ensure the likelihood of receiving those rewards. Common problematic behaviors are fear of not meeting set goals, short-term thinking and fear of losing credit or recognition to someone else. Such behaviors negatively impact the student experience, and ultimately their success, regardless of how it is defined by the student, the faculty/staff, the institution and/or the state. The impact of these behaviors is manifested in several ways. For example, students may not receive appropriate or timely services, institutions may fall short of addressing the comprehensive needs of students or students may be inadvertently forced to choose sides/ service providers. This can often cause students to segregate themselves by seeking support from single individual departments or service units, resulting in a narrow view of the resources and services available to successfully matriculate into, through and out of the institution.

Fear of not meeting personal or unit goals can result in faculty, staff, and administrators being unwilling to work cross-collaboratively and take risks that could benefit students. When the aforementioned behaviors are prevalent, individuals focus their time and attention on their specified area of influence, failing to consider the good of the whole institution. Another behavioral consequence of fear is an unwillingness to engage in cooperative and collaborative efforts that might threaten individual or departmental outcomes. The result of these actions can create isolated effort and initiatives, often referred to as silos, and unnecessary bureaucratic processes. When staff engages in short-term thinking, they tend to move forward with single initiatives or projects rather than integrating their efforts with others with similar goals or agendas. The consequence of operating in the short-term is not fully vetting potential solutions to problems, thus creating short-term results or "Band-Aid" solutions, inadequate support across the institution and a limited consideration of constituents' needs. The systemic impact of short term thinking is contradictory, disconnected or redundant services which inefficiently use resources and waste the time and effort of multiple units.

Another barrier to collaboration is the unspoken fear of losing credit or sharing recognition for an initiative or innovative idea. Individuals may pass up collaborative opportunities and systemic solutions because someone else might receive or share in the lime light. When this behavior is exhibited institutions fail to leverage the value of a broader perspective. While the success of an immediate area or unit might be optimized, the larger institution can be compromised.

Collaboration barriers in institutions result when there is misalignment among various departments, resources are scarce and/or the organization seeks to preserve the status quo. In the latter case, staff may believe that the way things are being done is best; unfortunately, this thinking can lead to outmoded programs and services that fall short of meeting student needs because the issues they face are left unidentified and unaddressed.

When departments or divisions fail to align their work, goals of one area may be set in opposition to another. Fiercely protecting resources, budgets or headcount can result in improper budgetary planning. Those things that are most important to student success may go underfunded. Resource allocations may be made that are not in the best interest of the institution, inhibiting the university's ability to build a healthy organization focused on continuous improvement. When organizational units fail to align and identify how cross-departmental or cross-divisional functions relate and connect it can undermine institutional goals aimed at the collective success of students. Poor management relations can also result when each manager is fiercely protecting their turf at all costs, and there is a sense that the way things have always been done is the only way to accomplish them. Institutions stuck in this state might resist original ideas from new employees in order to maintain the status quo. The impact of this behavior may lead to stale processes and programs that once met the needs of a bygone era of students. Alternatives for improvement may also be overlooked.

Lack of information flow, a leader's practice of autonomy and an established organizational hierarchy all can block an institution's ability to collaborate effectively. Transmission barriers happen when cascading information from the top fails to flow down. Professionals in one division within an institution may communicate with one another but fail to communicate broadly across the institution. Information flow may also be controlled by one group to block information that another group needs. Conversely, too much information or information overload from units may make it difficult for other areas to assimilate the information.

Also, promoting open dialogue amongst all stakeholders and ensuring clear and consistent communication amongst groups can ensure that information is shared with those who need it to serve students. Stakeholders must be able to reconcile conflicting, or differing interpretations of, information. If they cannot, students may receive inaccurate information, incomplete information or no information at all.

Some leaders promote a culture or practice of autonomy. The leader may fear loss of control or authority and behave in ways that isolate colleagues and direct reports. In this instance, leaders may believe he/she can go it alone. It may be that the leader feels that they do it best or can accomplish tasks faster on their own and not solicit support, cooperation or collaboration from direct reports and colleagues. What manifests is a micro-manager that fails to delegate tasks. Consequently, employee morale plummets and poor performance may ensue. The leader has missed an enormous opportunity to engage his or her staff and model the type of collaboration that ultimately would best serve the organization and students.

Most institutions have some form of organizational hierarchy. However, when vertical chains of command are heavily guarded and enforced, competitive rather than collaborative interactions can result. Mistrust of horizontal, cross-divisional connections can create a mentality of "I lose if you gain" undermining the collective whole. Inefficient, ineffective programs, services and processes that don't meet the comprehensive needs of students are often the by-product of highly structured, formal organizational structures that practice a silo mentality.

Complicating matters further, a number of higher education stakeholders, namely, state governments, institutions, faculty, staff, and students subscribe to different definitions of student success. Subsidy for educational and capital expenditures is allocated to institutions by state governments that expect certain performance measures to be met in order to receive funds. However, faculty, staff, students and sometimes even universities define success differently than state governments. This creates a quandary that is difficult if not impossible to reconcile, complicating our ability to determine institutional actions, and develop appropriate interventions and services that can improve student outcomes, regardless of how they are defined.

IN CONCLUSION: A STUDENT SUCCESS FRAMEWORK FOR CAMPUSES

In summary, it is vitally important for administrators, staff, and faculty to understand that there are many factors that can impact student success; however, we believe that as professionals in higher education, it is incumbent upon the entire institution to understand our collective role in student success. This understanding is particularly important as it relates to messaging/marketing, defining student success, and collaborative approaches, all of which determine an institution's overall impact on a student's ability to succeed.

Rapid changes in technology, the demographic make-up of our country, the globalization of our society, and the ever-changing demands of employers result in the need for college graduates to be critical thinkers who are socially adept and culturally competent. However, more and more high school graduates are coming to college less prepared to handle the rigor of college level coursework. As a result, colleges are spending more time and resources simply getting students ready to be successful in the classroom, much less for the work world. Yet, institutions send messages through marketing strategies that are incongruent with the realities of college life for many students. Many students and parents are being sold an idea that disregards the rigors of college life. We should however, be telling the constituents about the realities of college life that include: a constant state of challenge, frequent dissonance, self-discovery, and the expectation that the student will have to exert a great deal of effort in order to earn a degree.

"Success" can vary based upon the entity defining it; we have discussed the quandary that is created when there are different understandings of student success held by students, faculty and staff, colleges and universities and state governments; hence, the chapter's title: the Student Success Conundrum. These varying definitions/foci make it difficult to understand, assess, and design interventions that impact the success of the student. Students may have a measure of success related to a personal achievement or an accomplishment that may or may not include graduation. Faculty may also have a definition of success that omits graduation but centers on learning, growth and personal development. On the other hand, the State's definition and the University's definition of student success may be similar if it is closely tied to resources. In this case, student success can be equated to retention and graduation rates. Sometimes, however, universities can have definitions that focus on academic, social, and co-curricular involvement in addition to retention and graduation. We addressed in this chapter that the inability to come to a common understanding of student success can create challenges for all involved.

Finally, we addressed the important issue of collaboration and barriers that prohibit collaboration in higher education. The barriers may be intentional, unintentional, conscious, or unconscious and relate to misalignment of unit activities, scarce resources and maintaining the status quo. These barriers are manifested in both organizational and individual behaviors. Figure 2, on page 48, relates how the barriers to collaboration and student success are related. Regardless of why the barriers are present or how they manifest, they all negatively impact student's ability to succeed. We contend that institutions wishing to address these challenges might consider the following key actions and questions to assist them as they work to positively impact the student experience:

- Reframe the conversation with university leaders to discuss the consumerist trap into which some higher education institutions have fallen, and its impact on the institution's ability to create conditions that allow students to develop intellectually, emotionally and socially. Ask:
    * Does the University Mission Statement, Vision Statement and Values incorporate a conception of student learning that is not exclusively driven by market ideals?
    * Are curricular and co-curricular offerings in line with the espoused mission of the institution? Put differently, has your institution enacted your mission?

- Reframe the conversation with students in the pre-enrollment process to clarify expectations, challenges and rigor of the college experience. Ask:
  * Does your initial contact with students outline the educational and behavioral expectations for students?
  * Do your campus visits include experiences that will allow prospective students to see the values, including the importance of challenging students, of the institution in practice?

- Discuss with students during academic advising their reasons for attending college, rather than assuming a degree is the goal and proceeding from that assumption. Ask:
  * Does academic advising challenge students to take responsibility for their education by enabling them to articulate, for themselves, an academic plan of study that reflects an understanding of the university curriculum?
  * Do advising practices enable students to align their interests with a course of study that will enable them to develop intellectually, socially and morally?

- Implement faculty development opportunities that encourage faculty to recognize and acknowledge the consumerist mindset that many students have and prepare faculty from this mindset to an understanding of the fundamental aims of the college experience. Ask:
  * Do faculty development programs adopt the belief that you should "meet students where they are"? Do pedagogical approaches at your institution reflect the need to move students from passive to active learners?
  * Do faculty development programs reflect the developmental needs of your students?
  * Do faculty feel empowered to experiment and innovate with their pedagogical approaches?

- Engage the campus broadly to discuss varying definitions of student success and explore whether coming to a common definition is possible. Ask:
  * Are there opportunities for university stakeholders to come together to discuss the mission of the institution especially as this relates to student learning? Do university committees, especially committees that have institutional reach, e.g., an Enrollment Management Committee, include and encourage participation from all university stakeholders including students?

- Work with state legislators and other government bodies to consider alternative institutional performance measures for student success other than retention and graduation that align with faculty, staff and student outcomes. Ask:
  * Does the institution have a collegial working relationship with government personnel at the state level?
  * Has the institution identified alternative measures of institutional performance for retention and graduation that substantiate progress and should be considered?
  * Has the institution reviewed the literature on accepted alternative measures being used by other states and institutions?
  * Would the institution be willing to launch a statewide conversation about considering alternative measures for demonstrating institutional performance?

- Incorporate high impact practices into the pedagogical infrastructure by creating student learning objectives combined with experiential learning opportunities that integrates active involvement in the academic, co-curricular and social life of the institution. Ask:
  * Does the institution understand the importance of high impact practices being tied to coursework?
  * Do faculty and staff engage in conversations and planning efforts that focus on experiential learning opportunities?
  * Are there intentional efforts and/or initiatives on your campus that resemble high impact practices?

- Identify outcomes that impact success, tying programmatic efforts to those outcomes, and developing reliable measures of them that may be understood and used by faculty and staff to guide their work. Ask:
  * Do faculty and staff engage in conversations about student success: what it means, how it is demonstrated and how it is measured?
  * Do courses and co-curricular activities have learning outcomes developed? Are reliable measures in place to determine whether sought learning outcomes are achieved?
  * Do faculty and staff understand the role that Student Affairs plays in the learning, growth and development of students?
  * Do faculty and staff understand the complex interplay between cognitive and behavioral growth in students and how, together, they serve as strong predictors of academic performance and student retention?

- Collect data that identifies the students' goals/needs and aligns them with the type, focus, and mission of the institution in such a way that all entities realize success. Ask:
    * Do the student and the institution "match"?
    * Do the student's goals match the mission/focus of the institution?
    * Does the institution "type" fit the type of student attending?
    * Are the programs/course offerings appropriate for the students attending the institution?
    * Can multiple goals be present so that both the institution and student realize success?

- Create collaborative administrative models for student success that include shared responsibilities and accountability for the design, implementation, and assessment of programming for students from a holistic view of student learning. Ask:
    * Are administrative personnel across divisions engaged from the beginning of the planning process for projects related to student success?
    * Does a comprehensive student success plan exist on the campus that was created with broad cross-divisional input and feedback from all stakeholders?
    * Does the student success plan follow the student path from pre-enrollment through graduation and beyond, and include the stakeholders from all touch points along the path?
    * Are top administrators, especially from academic and student affairs, striving to meet common goals related to student success and are they held mutually accountable for their outcomes?

- Ensure that top-level managers have a collaborative mindset and refuse to tolerate behaviors at all levels that stifle collaboration, result in barriers and undermine student success. Ask:
    * Do open, honest conversations take place on the campus around behaviors that result in barriers and undermine student success?
    * Is top management modeling a collaborative mindset that fosters the expectation to collaborate?

* Is collaboration rewarded and celebrated on the campus?
* Are those who exhibit behaviors that stifle collaboration allowed to continue doing so? How might this be addressed?

• Create a comprehensive student success center that reworks the function and relationship of key administrators in both academic and student affairs at an organizational level to support greater collaboration. Ask:
  * Are student success programs and services, especially those services that impact the first year, scattered all over campus?
  * Do students report that navigating the campus infrastructure is difficult or feel that they get "the run around"?
  * Is the institution looking to improve student services' processes and interested in providing seamless integration between one student process and the next?
  * Are front-line staff cross-trained to understand the entire student path so that they can accurately and confidently serve as a resource to students?

• Focus on systemic student success solutions that identify individual student needs, integrate assessment and incorporate continuous improvement to increase the likelihood of campus-wide impact. Ask:
  * Does the student success plan incorporate mechanisms that assist in understanding student needs, including using historical data to predict probability of success?
  * Does the student success strategy include a comprehensive assessment plan that considers not only student participation and student satisfaction, but also specific learning outcomes, and predicted versus actual outcomes?
  * Does the institution formally incorporate what they learn from the assessment process and apply it to make changes, process improvements or discontinue service?

Figure 2a: The Connection between Student Success Barriers and Collaboration Barriers in Universities and Colleges

Student Success Barriers	Resulting from	Staff/ Faculty Behaviors	Resulting from	Behavioral Manifestation of Barriers	Resulting from	Collaboration Barriers in Institutions
Inability to get most appropriate services		Silos Bureaucratic Processes Local processes that trump overall success		Fiercely protecting things that impact meeting goals Attempt to get all needs met within area of supervisory control Overly stringent on supervisees		Fear of not meeting goals
Comprehensive needs fail to get addressed Students segregate themselves to single individual departments or services		Decisions made without considering broad impact Moving forward single initiatives or projects rather than integrating efforts Using band-aid solutions		Inadequate attention to constituent needs Disconnected efforts with opposing aims Redundancy of efforts Inefficient use of resources		Short-term thinking
		Passing up collaborative opportunities and systemic solutions that might shine light on someone else		Short-sighted, isolated decisions, programs and services that sub-optimize system Failure to leverage broader perspective of thought		Fear of losing credit or recognition; someone else stealing limelight

Figure 2b: The Connection between Student Success Barriers and Collaboration Barriers in Universities and Colleges

Student Success Barriers	Resulting from	Staff/ Faculty Behaviors	Resulting from	Behavioral Manifestation of Barriers	Resulting from	Collaboration Barriers in Institutions
		Inability to build healthy organization that continuously improves		Different departmental goals in opposition to one another		Misalignment
		Undermining mission and collective success				
Outmoded programs and services		Poor management relations				
Underserved due to specific needs not identified and addressed		Improper planning		Protecting budgets		Resources
		Improper use of resources aimed at those things that might not be in the best interest of the whole		Protecting headcount		
		Those things most important underfunded				
		Stale processes and programs that meet needs of a bygone era		Resisting new ideas from new employees		Organizational heterogeneity Common belief that the way we've always done it is the best or only way
		Alternatives for improvement not considered				
		Lack of access to data				

The Student Success Conundrum

Figure 2c: The Connection between Student Success Barriers and Collaboration Barriers in Universities and Colleges

Student Success Barriers	Resulting from	Staff/ Faculty Behaviors	Resulting from	Behavioral Manifestation of Barriers	Resulting from	Collaboration Barriers in Institutions
		Information is inaccessible to those who need it Not enough time or resources to process information No strategy for handling conflicting information or understanding different interpretations of info		Transmission barriers: when one group's needs are blocked by another group Assimilation barriers: too much information Failure to promote open dialogue amongst stakeholders		Information flow
Get the run-around Receive inaccurate information Go through motions with lack of true engagement		Poor employee morale Poor performance of subordinates Poor role models for collaboration		Micromanage Failure to delegate Don't trust others with responsibility to carry out tasks (won't be done his/her way or as well)		Culture or Practice of autonomy Fear of losing control or authority Leader believes he/she can go it alone; Do it best and faster on my own
		Good of the whole not met Inefficient, ineffective programs, services and processes that don't meet the comprehensive needs of students		Fiercely protecting organizational boundaries Competitive rather than collaborative nature of interaction Mistrust of horizontal, cross-divisional connections resulting in 'I lose if you gain'		Organizational hierarchy Vertical chains of command heavily guarded and enforced

The Student Success Conundrum

3

INSTITUTIONAL CHANGE: DEVELOPING A STUDENT SUCCESS PROGRAM

Paul Dosal
Vice Provost of Student Success
University of South Florida

Doris M. Ingersoll
Sr. Consultant Advisor
EMAS Pro.

Ronald J. Ingersoll
Sr. Consultant Advisor
EMAS Pro.

CHAPTER 3

Forces in our environment are causing changes in postsecondary education (Ingersoll and Bontrager; Tapscott and Williams, 2010; Thomas and Seely-Brown 2011; DeMillo 2011; Taylor 2010). These changes vary from small changes within department offices to wholesale changes that involve the entire institution. Developing, identifying, implementing and leading this change challenges the skills and knowledge of all senior enrollment managers. They must develop their present skills and knowledge, and look to new areas for their personal development to participate as change agents in the future of their schools.

Successful institution-wide change is exemplified in The University of South Florida, which significantly changed its approach to its enrollment management and student success program. Before going on, reflect a bit on what kinds of concerns or questions you might have if you faced such a change initiative at your school. You may find your institution has similar experiences as The University of South Florida, including many of the important areas senior enrollment managers must address in the future. Some of these factors are highlighted and developed at the conclusion of the project narrative.

THE STUDENT SUCCESS INITIATIVE AT THE UNIVERSITY OF SOUTH FLORIDA

The University of South Florida (USF), located in Tampa, is one of the nation's top 63 public research universities and one of only 25 public research universities nationwide with very high research activity that is designated as "community engaged" by the Carnegie Foundation for the Advancement of Teaching. Established in 1956 as a public university, USF has traditionally operated as a commuter school, serving a place-bound student population. However, in the last ten years, under the leadership of Dr. Judy Genshaft, the University has been transformed into a premier research institution, ranked 44th in total research expenditures and 38th in federal research expenditures for public universities. Enrollment has grown on the Tampa campus to 40,000, and at least 5,000 of these students live in on-campus residence halls, with several thousand more *resi-muters* living in close proximity to the campus.

The phenomenal growth in research activities has been deliberate. President Genshaft has placed USF on a path aimed toward membership in the prestigious American Association of Universities. She recognized, however, that AAU-eligibility requires significant improvements in its student success rates. The University of South Florida, therefore, with first-year retention rates hovering around 80 percent and six-year graduation rates below 50 percent back in 2000, needed to strengthen its research activities as it raised student success rates to the level of its would-be AAU peers, which boast six-year graduation rates higher than 90 percent. As a result of the deficiencies in its own profile, USF leaders embarked upon an ambitious student success initiative designed, at least in part, to ensure that the focus on research growth would go hand-in-hand with student success.

THE STUDENT SUCCESS TASK FORCE, NOVEMBER 2009-APRIL 2010

In the fall of 2009, Ralph Wilcox, Provost and Executive Vice President, and Jennifer Meningall, Vice President, Student Affairs, challenged the entire USF community to make the 2009-2010 academic year "The Year of Student Success." Asserting that "Nothing is more important to our University than the quality of our academic programs," Provost Wilcox and Vice President Meningall jointly convened a university-wide Student Success Task Force (SSTF) and directed it to "explore best practices and strategies for improving our institutional performance and our students' experience: from ensuring the students' preparedness for college, to access and affordability, retention and progression, knowledge and skill acquisition, graduation rates, and competitive placement" (Letter from Provost Ralph Wilcox and Vice President Jennifer Meningall to Members of the Student Success Task Force, October 23, 2009).

The Provost and Vice President issued a broad call for appointments and nominations to serve on the task force, determined that the SSTF include representatives from all units and sectors of USF. By late October 2009, about 100 people had been appointed to serve on the task force, which the co-author of this chapter, Paul Dosal, had the honor to chair. The 2009-2010 Student Success Task Force built on and benefited from at least three previous task forces assigned to study and comment on policies and programs related to student success. One of these task forces, co-chaired by then Vice Provost Ralph Wilcox, recognized the linkage between student success rates and effective student recruitment and enrollment planning, with an explicit charge to develop recommendations "to build a student body by design rather than by chance" ("A Proposed Action Plan to Enhance Student Academic Persistence and Success at the University of South Florida," Report of the Enrollment Management Action Team, Student Academic Progress and Achievement Group, University of South Florida, May 10, 2004). The charge also reflected the growing influence of the Florida Board of Governors over institutional policies related to student success, for the board had approved performance and accountability measures that included retention rates and 4-year and 6-year graduation rates.

While the University had already made significant progress prior to the formation of the SSTF, there was widespread skepticism about the prospects for drafting a comprehensive report and, more importantly, acting on it. Three previous groups had already worked on student success issues, leaving many wondering what, if anything, would be different about this task force. One of the challenges faced by the 2009-10 Task Force, aside from its immense size, was to develop a plan of action that would lead to full and immediate implementation of its recommendations.

The size of the SSTF matched the scope of its charge. Indeed, given the ambitions of Provost Wilcox and Vice President Meningall, both of whom recognized that every unit of the entire University had a role to play in the student success initiative, one may wonder if the task force had enough members. At the inaugural meeting of the SSTF on November 5, 2009, the Provost presented a comprehensive vision of student success:

Successful undergraduate and graduate students will enter USF both academically and personally prepared to complete a rigorous and systematic path of engaged learning that will enrich their lives and contribute to society's well-being. Along that path they will engage in educationally purposeful activities and will be provided the requisite support to ensure their timely progression and attainment of relevant knowledge, skills and competencies essential to contributing to, and competing successfully in, the global marketplace of ideas. By fully engaging with a safe, secure and diverse community of scholars, successful students will develop a high degree of satisfaction and pride in their USF experience and will demonstrate optimal levels of persistence and enhanced graduation rates, so maximizing their opportunities for progression to graduate and professional programs, enhancing career placement and minimizing their financial indebtedness through eliminating excess hours and related strategies.

Toward these ends, Drs. Wilcox and Meningall enumerated the charge to the task force. Reporting jointly to the Provost and the Vice President for Student Affairs, the task force would:
- Develop an operational definition of Student Success for USF.
- Conduct a comprehensive, rigorous and evidence-based institutional assessment through carefully structured Student Success Teams.
- Examine best practices at "like" institutions and conduct a performance "gap analysis."
- Establish goals for USF, 2010/2011 through 2020/2021, framed around policy, practices, programs, personnel and performance.
- Present actionable and prioritized recommendations for radically transforming Student Success at USF by April 15, 2010.
- Include recommendations on how to most effectively engage the broader USF community in taking ownership of Student Success.

The goals of the SSTF, as presented to the task force at its inaugural meeting, were "to achieve institutional behaviors and outcomes consistent with our national peers and to establish a national model of excellence at USF through:
- Continuing our commitment to access and diversity.
- Renewing our focus on academic attainment.
- Improving levels of college preparedness for admitted students through shaping our student profile.
- Enhancing academic progress, graduation rates and time-to-graduation and reducing disparities.
- Reducing excess hours and thus Student Credit Hours to degree.
- Reducing student debt.
- Enhancing student and alumni satisfaction.
- Improving student progression rates to graduate school.
- Improving career placement and competitiveness in the marketplace.

Given such a broad and comprehensive charge, with less than six months to achieve it, the task force was divided into eight teams, each of which received a specific charge, summarized in Table 1. With significant overlapping responsibilities among the eight groups, coordinating the work and recommendations of the work groups became critically important to keep the task force on schedule and to harmonize the recommendations that would emerge from each work group.

Table 1. Charge of the Task Force Teams

Team	Charge
Student Readiness	To examine the extent to which USF students were and are prepared for success in their undergraduate studies.
Student Support Services & Policies	To examine the efficacy of student support programs throughout the university, including but not limited to: orientation or other transitional programs, advising; tutoring; supplemental instruction; and college readiness programs.
Access and Affordability	To examine the extent to which national, state, and institutional financial aid facilitates student persistence and success.
Instruction	To examine the efficacy of instructional methods, support systems for faculty, learning technology, classroom facilities, library resources, and learning outcomes at the undergraduate level.
The Campus Experience	To examine all policies and procedures that require aspects of student life for students to be ready to study, work, be involved and live on campus.
The Graduate Experience	To examine all aspects of the student graduate school experience, including time to degree, curriculum, program offerings, financial aid, career planning, and placement.
The Student Experience	To examine the out of classroom experience and perceptions of USF held by current and former students to identify academic and non-academic areas in which USF can do more to facilitate student success.
The Curriculum	To examine all aspects of the undergraduate curriculum to identify areas of improvement, including academic programs, scheduling, classroom facilities, and other issues that may impede students' progress.

While the tasks assigned to the eight teams could have required time-consuming research and analysis, the senior leadership gave the task force less than six months to complete its report. For academics accustomed to a more leisurely pace for research and analysis, the charge seemed overwhelming and impossible. However, the senior leadership had already concluded that USF already possessed the knowledge and expertise to recommend immediate changes. The six months given to the task force were to be used, not for contemplation and reflection, but for producing a blueprint for action, not another call for further research and reflection.

The SSTF submitted a 161-page final report on April 14, 2010, one day before the deadline (USF 2010). It included about 50 prioritized short- and long-term recommendations framed around policy, practices, programs, personnel, and performance. To accommodate several recommendations framed around space and facilities, the team added a sixth category, physical infrastructure.

The foundation of the report was an operational definition of student success that contained measureable objectives:

> *The University of South Florida will empower students to succeed through educationally purposeful activities, initiatives, and accountability measures that will ensure that students are retained and graduated at higher than predicted rates, with higher degrees of satisfaction and minimal financial indebtedness, and are employed or enter graduate, professional, or post-doctoral programs at high rates, having acquired the skills, knowledge and dispositions to succeed in any of those endeavors they pursue.*

Building on this foundation, the Task Force prefaced its recommendations with three fundamental reforms that it considered prerequisites for the successful implementation of its short- and long-term recommendations:

1. Institutionalize student success as a permanent priority of USF

To carry out the work of the task force and ensure that the University continues to focus on the means by which it can enhance student success, the task force concluded that the process and a scaled-down structure of the Student Success Task Force should be institutionalized. The University should designate a permanent body such as a Council on Student Success, with broad representation (similar to that of the SSTF itself), that would continue the work of identifying means to enhance student success; implement or follow-up on the recommendations in the Task Force Reports; initiate, suggest, or evaluate research related to student success; and recommend appropriate actions and activities that will ensure continued emphasis on student success university-wide.

2. Integrate student success into the institutional culture of USF

The task force concluded that the formation of a Council on Student Success was a necessary but insufficient step toward creating a learning environment more conducive to and supportive of student success. The University also had to change the behavior, attitudes, and values of all administrators, faculty, and staff to accommodate and promote the renewed emphasis on the success of our undergraduate and graduate students. Faculty would have to recognize that they were responsible for teaching and mentoring students as well as conducting research; administrators would have to understand that they too would be held accountable for promoting the success of USF students in attaining career and educational goals; staff would also have to buy into the initiative by recognizing that their work was critical to ensuring the timely progression of students toward their degrees. To promote institutional cultural change, the task force recommended that the University use every opportunity and every available means to create the appropriate institutional environment.

3. Build an institutional research capacity to support student success initiatives

The Student Success Task Force recognized that it lacked much of the quantitative and qualitative data that was required to conduct appropriate analyses to make informed decisions about where to invest scarce resources and prioritize efforts. With additional resources, student success researchers would conduct the qualitative and quantitative research projects required to inform decisions about proposed changes in policies, assist in the development of new or improved programs and services, and provide support for other actions and initiatives designed to improve student success.

Following these three fundamental reforms, the 2009-10 Student Success Task Force presented a prioritized list of short- and long-term recommendations in six general categories. The complete report included many other recommendations, but the prioritized items are listed in Tables 2 and 3.

Table 2. Short-Term Recommendations for 2010/2011

Category	Recommendations
POLICIES	Review and revise academic progress policies to promote student success and progress toward degree completion.
	Compose a team (or hire consultants) to evaluate, study, and recommend means to promote an institutional culture that demands, values, and rewards the highest levels of service.
PRACTICES	Develop a Student Experience Calendar interface to promote greater student engagement with campus activities.
	Encourage students to check the availability of a major at USF that matches their personal interests. Students should be expected to consult with an advisor prior to enrollment to confirm compatibility between their interests and course offerings and requirements in the major.
	Colleges and departments should investigate the causes of low pass rates in courses with high "D", "W" and "F" grades to determine the underlying causes of low success rates and then identify ways to reduce those difficulties.
	Improve the evaluation process for faculty, adjunct instructors, and graduate teaching assistants who assist instructors, in particular, providing increased support for those who teach in the general education curriculum. The evaluation process for anyone who interacts with students, i.e., academic advisors and counselors, should be improved to enhance performance and service.
	Extend office hours and/or expand program offerings that are critical to the student experience.
PROGRAMS	Strengthen academic advising services continuously.
	Ensure that the annual base budget of the library covers (minimally) annual increases in online collection costs (online databases, e-book package, online journal subscriptions) and monograph purchases.
	Provide the resources for the development of a student-centered technology training and multimedia center. This center, located in the library and staffed with experts in instructional technology, will guide and support students in the creation of multimedia, video, digital projects in fulfillment of course objectives.

Category	Recommendations
PROGRAMS (cont)	Collaborate with administrative and student service units on campus to develop on-the-job training and professional development and funding resources for assistantships and/or fellowship opportunities for graduate students.
	Increase support for successful instruction through the C21TE and the library.
	Increase resources of the University Experience program to expand its offerings.
	Strengthen Counseling Center services.
	Strengthen Veteran Services.
	Initiate strategies to increase student financial assistance.
PERSONNEL	Expand on-campus job opportunities for students and create a formalized internship program which develops paid, credit-earning internship opportunities.
	Create a Student Concierge office.
	Designate a person or office to lead a strategic and comprehensive effort to enhance student success.
PERFORMANCE	Repeat the Graduating Student Survey of 2005 to assess if there have been any changes in the attitudes, perceptions, or satisfactions of graduating students.
	Implement an automated exit survey for graduating undergraduate/graduate students as part of a graduation application package to assess if the attitudes, perceptions, or satisfactions of graduating students have been met.
	Develop and implement an alumni survey to assess attitudes, perceptions, and satisfaction of alumni.
PHYSICAL INFRASTRUCTURE	Provide urgently needed physical improvements to buildings and the campus, focusing on upkeep and maintenance of lighting, cleanliness, obstructed views, and temperature control.
	Commit to classroom improvements, including furnishings, to enhance the learning environment.
	Secure a University work order process to report custodial, facility and grounds concerns.

Table 3. Long-Term Recommendations for 2020/2021

Category	Recommendations
POLICY	Review registration policies and consider offering "guaranteed" courses.[1]
PRACTICES	Reform the University infrastructure to facilitate collaboration between student service programs.
	Establish a multi-faceted early warning system to identify students pre- and post-enrollment who exhibit academic behavior that puts them at risk for degree progression.
	Colleges and departments should review their undergraduate and graduate curricula and identify barriers to timely graduation (i.e., for undergraduate, four years of full-time enrollment) and then work to find ways to eliminate those barriers.
	Restructure the first two years of college in the form of a University College, emulating best practices at AAU universities such as the University of Florida.
	Develop strategies to help administrative and academic units that serve students better understand who our constituents are at USF.
	Centralize and strengthen the advising structure within all colleges.
PROGRAMS	Implement Academic Tracking.
	Explore additional methods to expand the emphasis on the development of writing skills for all undergraduate and graduate students.
	Develop three- to six-hour long semi-annual training programs for academic advisors, with program content guided by student feedback.
	Provide the resources necessary for Tutoring and Learning Services to support student success in high risk courses and the most demanding academic programs.
	Establish and properly fund additional living learning communities.
	Provide additional resources to the Career Center to implement programs and services that incorporate the career development process early in the undergraduate and graduate experience.
	Provide additional support to enhance the quality and quantity of distance learning courses.
	Engage in strategies to increase student financial assistance.

---

1. Courses with a guaranteed seat for selected students in need of the course for timely graduation.

Category	Recommendations
PERSONNEL	Ensure that more full-time faculty members teach undergraduate students.
	Decrease the student/faculty ratio to enhance the learning environment and reduce class sizes significantly,
PERFORMANCE	Institute an entrance and exit graduating undergraduate/graduate student survey to assess students' expectations concerning readiness and compile a database that would assist in the further enhancement of undergraduate/graduate student readiness.
PHYSICAL INFRASTRUCTURE	Address urgent structural physical facilities issues.
	Launch a campaign to create a new state-of-the-art Digital Library and Learning Center to enhance the quality of student learning on campus and make a substantial contribution to the intellectual growth and learning of each student.
	Launch a campaign to create a new state-of-the art Wellness Center that would house the offices of Student Health Services, Counseling Services, Advocacy Program, and Campus Recreation in one dedicated facility to best serve students.

The University of South Florida moved quickly to implement the task force recommendations. Provost Wilcox and Vice President Meningall met with the chair of the task force within two weeks to discuss implementation, and the President's cabinet received a briefing on the report in May 2010. On July 1, the Provost appointed Paul Dosal, chair of the task force, as the Director (later Vice Provost) of Student Success and placed him in charge of Undergraduate Admissions, University Scholarships and Financial Aid, and the University Registrar in a newly named Office of Student Success. Dr. Dosal also retained responsibilities for promoting and coordinating the student success initiative and implementing the task force recommendations. The broad portfolio assigned to the Vice Provost reflected a new approach to strategic enrollment planning and management: it was fully integrated—in theory and in practice—into the student success movement.

THE RESULT

The administrative restructuring distinguished USF among research-intensive universities in the United States and reflected a deliberate effort to institutionalize the student success initiative. The President appointed a Student Success Council in August 2010, chaired by the Vice Provost of Student Success and with broad representation from across the university, to carry forward the work of the task force and oversee the implementation of its recommendations. Further, the President allocated $3 million in non-recurring funds to the Student Success Council to fund projects and initiatives recommended by the task force. The Council immediately authorized funding to the Office of Decision Support to hire three additional research analysts, acting on another one of the fundamental reforms recommended by the task force. By the beginning of the Fall 2010 term, just four months after the task force submitted its report, the University had established the infrastructure required to implement the blueprint for student success. It also showed the University community that the senior leadership had indeed made a serious commitment to student success, giving the movement additional momentum as the fall term opened.

One of the first tasks assigned to the Office of Student Success was the development of a new student enrollment plan for the 2011-12 academic year. The President had expressed her displeasure with the academic profile of the Fall 2010 freshmen class. After several consecutive years of enrolling a freshmen class with higher and higher standardized test scores and high school grade point averages, the President insisted that the University raise the academic profile of the incoming class. The Office of Undergraduate Admissions raised its admissions requirements to bring in a Fall 2011 class that would have an average SAT score of at least 1200, which would represent a 24-point increase over Fall 2010.

The new and higher standard formed part of a larger institutional strategy to earn eligibility for AAU membership and promote the student success initiative. Academic preparedness had been the focus of one of the eight teams that constituted the task force, and rightly so. The University could not expect to achieve quick and dramatic gains in its student success rates if it ignored the academic preparedness of the students it enrolled. Critics inside and outside of the University pointed out that high school GPAs were more accurate predictors of success in higher education than standardized test scores. However, USF evaluated and admitted students based on a combination of factors, including standardized test scores, high school grades, and other factors, such as success in Advanced Placement, Dual Enrollment, and International Baccalaureate courses and programs. The University raised expectations in all these areas for admissions, but the 1200 mark for the SAT became fixed as the standard for success for the recruitment and enrollment of the Fall 2011 class.

The recruiting cycle began with high expectations as well as warnings that the University may fall short in other enrollment targets if the highest priority was placed on the academic profile of the Fall 2011 class. The size of the class, projected at 4,050 for Summer and Fall 2011, was feared to decline, with negative consequences for generating student credit hours and housing. The diversity of that class might also change substantially. While USF had high and increasing numbers of Black and Hispanic students, the total number of under-represented minorities in the Fall 2011 class might decline since these students had traditionally scored lower on standardized test scores. Moreover, and perhaps more importantly in retrospect, more of them depended on need-based financial aid to cover the rising costs of college, meaning that yield among these students would decline if, as anticipated, tuition increased and federal and state-based aid declined. Senior leadership, however, decided to assume these and other risks in pursuit of a strong academic class that was poised for success.

The message conveyed throughout the Office of Student Success was to remain focused and disciplined on the SAT score of 1200. That was the goal. College deans and other administrators quickly recognized that it was their goal too, and they had a role to play in the recruitment of the Fall 2011 class. They participated in recruitment events and even participated in a calling campaign in the spring to bring in the desired class. Even the President got on the phone and called prospective students, sending a powerful message to students, families, and the USF community that the University was determined to reach its enrollment objectives.

As it turned out, the average SAT score of the Fall 2011 freshmen class was 1203, 27 points higher than the Fall 2010 class. The average high school GPA jumped to 3.91, up from 3.81 a year earlier. The size of the total 2011-2012 class (including summer enrollment) fell to about 3,600, 500 less than projected and a full thousand less than the previous year. The numbers of Black and Hispanic students in the FTIC class also fell significantly, a reflection of the higher than average melt rates (loss of confirmed students) in the summer. However, the University had set and hit an ambitious target, and USF had just enrolled the strongest academic class in its history. Given the strategic objectives and high institutional aspirations of the university, senior leadership concluded that the drive to raise the academic profile was well worth the effort.

Bringing in an exceptionally talented class would not, in and of itself, improve student success rates at USF. The approach taken in the task force had been to view student success efforts, and strategic enrollment management in general, as part of the entire life cycle of a student, from prospective student preparing for college, through admission, enrollment, progression, and graduation to satisfied alumni. In this effort, recruitment and admission is a critically important part of a larger effort that must include enhancing other areas simultaneously.

Thus, while Admissions, Financial Aid, the Registrar, Orientation, Student Affairs, and other divisions and offices focused on recruiting and enrolling the most academically talented class in USF history, the Office of Student Success and the Student Success Council launched another 16 projects designed to advance the student success movement. These initiatives included the development of a financial aid leveraging model; a course redesign project utilizing teaching technologies more effectively to promote learning gains, to remove barriers to timely progression and to lower costs; implementation of DegreeWorks, a state-of-the art degree audit system; expansion of library study hours and spaces to support student access to collections, services, and study space; placing more math and science tutors in the Tutoring and Learning Center; expansion of living learning communities; promotion of on-campus employment opportunities for students; and the creation of a mentoring office to coordinate and promote the work of mentoring programs across the campus.

As USF moves into the next recruiting cycle (for 2012-13), the institution is restructuring its strategic enrollment management (SEM) process. The 2011-12 campaign, while ultimately successfully, revealed weaknesses in the organizational structure and processes by which the institution plans and manages enrollment. The focus to date had been exclusively on inputs: the recruitment and enrollment of new students (FTICs, transfers, and graduate students). With the institutionalization of student success as a permanent priority of USF, the institution must be equally concerned with outputs: four- and six-year graduation rates as well as year-to-year progression rates, and student credit hours. To develop and manage more effectively, the institution will have to develop a much more deliberate, coordinated, and integrated SEM planning process. Academic programming, for example, had been developed with little to no coordination with the enrollment management team. Fiscal planning, likewise, had been conducted in separate offices, despite the fact that declining state appropriations made the University more dependent upon and sensitive to enrollment, tuition, and student credit hours.

Hence, the next step in the evolution of the student success initiative at USF is the formation of a SEM Policy Council, a high-level deliberative body that will set strategic priorities for enrollment and coordinate enrollment planning with academic program development, facilities planning and construction; housing; student services, fiscal planning, and more. SEM, like the student success movement of which it is a critical part, impacts all areas of the University and so all units must be involved in developing, monitoring, and recalibrating strategic enrollment management. A lower-level SEM Management Team will develop action plans to achieve the strategic goals set by the SEM Policy council, assisted by four or five subcommittees that will monitor specific areas of concern and interest, ranging from marketing to resource development.

This comprehensive and integrated approach to student success, with SEM embedded in it, requires significant changes in administrative structures, attitudes, and behavior. It requires the demolition of administrative silos and all artificial barriers to collaborative work. Student success is not, and cannot be, the exclusive domain of any one unit, and it certainly cannot be separated from effective enrollment planning and management. Indeed, if and when the University of South Florida succeeds in raising retention and graduation rates (which have already jumped 3 points), it will find itself in the position of demanding more students—or at least more credit hours—to generate the revenues it needs to keep enrollment at its optimal overall level of 40,000 students.

To get to this point, the University has had to persuade itself that it could be done. There have been naysayers along the way, and they remain on the sidelines, eager to criticize efforts to change institutional behavior. Yet the movement is so well-advanced that it is difficult to restrain it. Of critical importance has been the steady insistence of the President and Provost that student success will remain the highest priority of the university. There are, to be sure, formidable challenges ahead. Enrollment managers across the country are already terrified by the prospect of losing summer Pell Grant funding. Other challenges will emerge, since factors and forces over which we have little to no control guide so much of what we do in SEM. Those in the profession know that SEM is as much an art as it is a science, despite the data façade that covers much of what we do. By embedding SEM in the student success initiative, we are bringing SEM into a more appropriate administrative structure, a new arena that may serve as a model for enrollment planners and managers at other institutions.

Addressing Serious Institutional Change

The USF experience serves as an example of how a school would go about starting and following through the change process necessary to establish better options and conditions for student success. It was a change that involved the whole institution.

This is a major step in new directions for a school that was doing well. Their enrollment was not a problem before starting this process. Enrollment had been increasing, the image of the school was sound, and there were a lot of satisfied people both at the University and in the environment around them. Certainly students were successful, but this was not the focus of the culture or the programs. The senior staff and the President wanted to move the University to a new level and they were serious. One reason for the change was a set of metrics to guide the University to membership in the American Association of Universities (AAU). This would call for, among other things the improvement of quality and graduation rates. This was a wise decision since many researchers have concluded that the better school will have more options for the future (Tapscott and Williams 2010).

In the future, however, much of the progress of higher educational institutions will have to involve the whole institution. In the USF project, the focus was on student success. The same approach should occur for schools that make a change in missions such as admitting both males and females if the college has been single-sex. Challenges will come from the federal government, state governments, and other groups. The response may require large parts of the institution to collaborate to design and implement the desired change.

Key Success Factors: Skills, Knowledge and Attitudes for Success

The following are the main themes of the change which could guide any institutional change effort.

High level commitment and desire for the outcome: The president and board of a school must be behind any dramatic change initiated by enrollment managers or it is the president alone that drives the process. A project like this demands financial and resource support and the willingness of the faculty and staff to give time and energy to it. The president then needs people on the project who are high energy and committed to the achievement of the goals. The senior enrollment manager's energy and commitment to success must be unyielding.

Specific time frame: The plans should be completed and made available within a short time period. The work of the group developing the project has to be done within a specific time period. The outcome in terms of clarity and quality has to be high and it must contain *implementable* actions at both the strategic and tactical levels. There needs to be a clear understanding of the terms *strategic* and *tactical.*

A clear vision and defined outcomes: The vision statement preceding the working task force must be clear and drive much of the process. The recommendations are to be taken seriously. Suggestions for the vision need to come from the senior staff and be consistent with what the faculty and staff can support. It is present when the "beating of the drum matches the beating of the heart" (Boublil and Kretzmer 2010).

Use a task force that includes all parts of the organization: This is one of the most significant actions to take. This type of cross functional team has members who can work on the project, let people know what is happening and inform the task force about the feelings that they hear and experience at the school. This establishes a communication network for working out recommendations. This also establishes a community of collaboration from the start.

Have clear guidelines and goals: The guidelines for the team must very clear. The vision presented by the Provost and Vice President for Student Affairs was followed by very specific guidelines for the USF task force. The task force should have some training and development in how to work together to accomplish the goal of the project.[2]

Include the culture: The culture of a school is likely to be the single thing that will cause a program to fail. If students are not doing well in a school, it is often that they are in the wrong culture or the focus of the culture is not sufficiently on students. When it comes to change, the culture can very quickly become an obstacle. The use of a cross-functional team is a help in addressing the culture of the school. The team can bring to the table many different views of the way the organization behaves and structures itself around the culture.

---

2. The work of Peter Senge et al. (1994) is a good example of this type of team development.

Define the extent of initial data collection: Getting data together can be time consuming but it is essential to have the data related to where you are and where you want to go. One of the first issues to address is an inventory of what data you have and what data you will need for the project. The project should not get bogged down in the search for data to solve all problems or to show all opportunities. What do you really need? The sources of data should be clear. The University had previous groups address these issues without initiating actions—but the data and information they used was still there. The feeling was that we must have the information we need either in the databases or in the people at the University. For most initiatives the rule would likely be to target the data you need without gathering extraneous data.

"Not Just Another Report": At USF it was made clear from the beginning that there would be action on the outcome of the work of the team. This happened because the leadership championed the effort and the members of the task force and its leader had the energy to work towards a product of high quality in a short period of time.

Determine the basics that must be done: Identify the basic actions needed if the student success initiative is going to succeed. Set student success as a permanent priority; integrate the concept into the culture. Build the appropriate research capacity to support student success initiative. This basically indicates that, without action in these areas, the work of building the student success effort would fail.

Do the right thing: One result of the USF project was the restructuring of the office. This restructuring put the office together in a way that enrollment could be shaped with aspects of it integrated. This structure also included ways to promote change within the faculty and provided links to the external environment for action.

4

CONSTRUCTIVE CONFLICT CULTURES FOR STRATEGIC ENROLLMENT MANAGEMENT

Tricia S. Jones
Professor of Adult and Organizational Development
Department of Psychological Studies in Education, Temple University

Doris M. Ingersoll
Sr. Consultant Advisor
EMAS Pro.

CHAPTER 4

For two years State University participated in a university wide strategic planning process that resulted in what most faculty and staff considered a solid plan for moving forward. The planning process has gotten a very strong involvement from faculty—stronger than any earlier effort. The champion of the strategic plan and process had been the Provost. But, just as the ink was drying on the final plan initiatives, the Provost announced that he was leaving to take the presidency of a prestigious private university. The incoming Provost soon made it clear that she was not supportive of the majority of the strategic plan and wanted to start over. A new series of planning meetings was set and almost no faculty members were present. As the faculty newspaper indicated in an editorial, faculty don't really believe the administration will follow through on this plan either.

ॐ

Justice University was founded with a mission to bring quality higher education to all; and for over 100 years, JU has been consistent with that mission. The university has been known for strong recruitment and support of minority and non-dominant students. Part of this success was a strong commitment to remedial education when needed and innovative financial aid packages. Due to these plans JU has been among the most diverse universities in the country. But, in the last several years things have changed noticeably—so noticeably that visitors to campus often remark on how the student and faculty population looks very different than before. In recent strategic management committee meetings the head of recruitment and the head of financial aid have made strong arguments that, given the current budget situations, there is simply no way the university can continue to maintain the same student profiles of the last decade. In fact, they argued that the budget cuts from state appropriations will force tuition increases which will even further reduce the ability of working class students to attend JU. Many long-time faculty, administrators, and community supporters at the meeting expressed their feelings that money was driving this change—it will destroy Justice University.

⸝⸍

Dr. Gray, Chair of the English Department, has called a meeting with the Director of General Education and the Dean to try and come to some collaborative agreement about what he thinks of as the "the Gen Ed problem." The University General Education program, which was retooled recently to meet the needs of adult students and distance learners, has been working very well. Online courses and weekend/ evening courses have done very well in enrollment and seem to have more demand than conventional courses by far. The Director of General Education is very pleased and is encouraging Dr. Gray to offer the three required English Gen Ed courses in these new formats. But, as Dr. Gray has explained to the Dean and the Director of Gen Ed, it is extremely difficult to get enough faculty members willing to teach these new formats without increasing faculty workload or pay. Dr. Gray does not believe that the English Gen Ed courses should be taught by adjunct faculty, but currently more than 60 percent of those sections are covered in this way. The Dean's response is that he will not fund more full-time instructor or tenure track positions to meet Gen Ed needs—especially at this time with hiring freezes and budget pressures.

THE IMPORTANCE OF CONSTRUCTIVE CONFLICT MANAGEMENT FOR STRATEGIC ENROLLMENT MANAGEMENT

All of the situations presented are common challenges in strategic enrollment management (SEM) and all of them reveal the need for SEM professionals to be aware of and able to handle the regular conflicts that come from enrollment management processes. As SEM evolves into more global and sophisticated processes, the complexity of SEM and concurrent conflict increases. Viewing enrollment management from a holistic approach means appreciating that it is comprised of a variety of interdependent activities such as clarification of the institution's mission, long-range planning, academic program development, marketing, recruitment, retention and career planning (Kemerer 1985). This holistic approach requires the cooperation of all levels of campus personnel, from the president to the faculty, staff and the maintenance department, as Bontrager's (2004) model of SEM illustrates. This means that the SEM leader must model constructive conflict management for SEM to succeed. Kalsbeek (2007, 7) states this most eloquently:

> *A significant part of the job of the SEM leader is educating diverse campus constituencies about the nature, purposes, and outcomes of SEM and building support for the organizational changes SEM typically requires. … Effective leadership also requires effective conflict management . . . If individuals have predictably different ideas of what would characterize an ideal organization, then organizational goals, structures, and purposes preferred by different individuals may not be only different but fundamentally incompatible . . .*

State University, in the example above, encountered a very common challenge—it marshaled the efforts of the university to generate an effective plan and then shelved it because of a leadership change. Though implementation inevitably results in conflicts, discarding promising work generates dysfunctional conflict and discourages personnel from taking the next effort seriously.

One of the challenges for SEM is the identifying a clear mission and the risks of disregarding it (Bontrager 2004). Developing a strong mission can be a double-edged sword; the stronger the mission, the more inconsistency can create negative conflict, as Justice University experienced. While practical realities may force an institution to modify its mission, conflict resulting from the dissonance must be well managed. As SEM processes involve the academic side of the institution to a greater extent, issues of coordination and conflict increase. In their brief history of the SEM field, Wilkinson and his colleagues identify the current emphasis as the age of the academic context (2007, 3):

> *The Age of the Academic Context started in 2005 with Stan Henderson's article "Refocusing Enrollment Management: Losing Structure and Finding the Academic Context." It is in this "age" that SEM branched out to include the academic side of the institution. So far, this "age" has focused on developing and refining the SEM organizational structure and integrating SEM models while being encouraged to reach out to the academic division as SEM partners. The focus is still on increasing enrollment through enhanced*

recruiting models and the use of financial aid packaging and leveraging coupled with establishing a SEM organizational structure within the institution but there is now recognition that academics are important to the overall viability of the process.

However, SEM practitioners frequently site tensions between the "academic-driven" culture of institutions and the "student-centered" culture that underlies effective SEM practice (Wallace-Hulecki, 2009). In the third case study at the outset of this chapter, Dr. Gray and his collaborators, the Director of General Education and the Dean, must manage the current staffing conflicts. The alternative is that relationships and SEM initiatives falter, making the next effort at collaboration even more difficult. Penn (1999) stresses that an enrollment manager must possess the ability to influence, communicate, persuade, lobby, and negotiate with others, as well as secure funding for marketing strategies and departmental needs. The "nuts and bolts" management of SEM decisions for the academic context means that SEM personnel and academic leaders must be able to negotiate effectively and collaboratively to deliver the reality of the plan and vision.

Conflict will happen in all aspects of planning and implementing SEM processes, but this conflict can be very positive if SEM leaders and university members have created constructive conflict cultures to handle these issues well. This chapter is a call for the careful development of constructive conflict cultures to mirror and support the careful planning of SEM efforts. First, we'll present an overview of conflict to introduce some basic ideas that about organizational conflict in higher education contexts. Then we explore the relationship between conflict and change processes central to SEM innovation and explain how collaborative conflict cultures can benefit all aspects of the university as well as enrollment management. And finally, the chapter presents a model of constructive conflict cultures and discusses how university personnel can develop and support these cultures.

THE NATURE OF CONFLICT
Definition of Conflict

Conflict is "the expression of a disagreement between two or more interdependent people about what should be done and/or how it should be done" (Jones, Remland, and Sanford 2008, 254). Kathy Costantino and Christina Merchant (1996), experts who design dispute systems for large organizations, view conflict as the "expression of dissatisfaction or disagreement with an interaction, process, product, or service." Conflict can be handled by a variety of methods, but short of physical violence, conflict management requires highly skilled communication.

Conflict and Interdependence

Conflict only happens between interdependent people—people who come into conflict because they need something from the other person with that need not being met. Bradica (2001) argues that SEM requires the interdependence and cooperation of faculty and staff to ensure sufficient enrollment for organizational success. The recognition of SEM interdependence highlights the value of the following three insights.

(1) *Conflicts emerge when expectations for interdependence are violated.* Conflicts arise when expectations are not met, and the more or greater the expectations, the more likely the conflict and the greater the conflict intensity.

(2) *The more interdependent the relationship, the more likely it is that conflicts will happen.* Consider the relationship between Dr. Gray, the Director of General Education and the Dean. There is a great deal of interdependence and none can make their work successful without the active contribution of the other.

(3) *How conflict is managed impacts the interdependence in the relationship.* If conflicts are managed constructively it may strengthen the relationship, encouraging closer ties and more interdependence. However, if conflicts are not managed well, one or both people are likely to look outside that relationship to get their needs met.

Basically, effective SEM increases the degree and nature of task and process interdependence in the university. By so doing, SEM is a conflict generative activity which can be a very positive thing if appropriate attention is given to how interdependence is structured and how it triggers conflict episodes.

Sources of Conflict

Another aspect of defining conflict concerns the reasons that people have conflicts, or what the disagreements are about. There are many possible sources of conflict:

(1) *Disagreement may be about how to allocate scarce resources.* Scarce resources, as the social exchange theorists say (Roloff 1981), are resources that people value but have less of than they desire.

(2) *Disagreement may be about who has the right to control a situation.* People often perceive interference from the other, sensing that the other wants to exercise unwanted control over some aspect of the situation.

(3) *Disagreements may be about how to treat someone with respect; about whether we are being treated with respect.* Lyndon Baines Johnson, the 37th President of the United States was known for his homey colloquial sayings like, "Never tell a man to go to hell unless you know you

can send him there." LBJ's colorful language should not obscure the wisdom of this thought. When people feel disrespected it is a significant trigger to conflict and emotional escalation. The greater the perceived disrespect, the more intense and irreparable the conflict is likely to be.

(4) *Disagreement may be about the goals or outcomes to be achieved.* Many conflicts occur because people want different things. A college administrator wants to strengthen the communication studies area with more faculty positions but the Dean prefers to strengthen psychology by giving the positions to that department. A Provost (for example, in the State University situation) wants to steer the university in an elite research direction while the faculty wishes to retain traditions as a teaching institution.

(5) *Disagreements may be about the process, procedure or methods to get a desired outcome.* Just because there is agreement on goals does not mean that no conflict will arise. There may be strong disagreements about the best way to make a desired outcome a reality. All parties may agree that the goal is to increase the recruitment of minority students and increase their graduation rates; while some may see the best way to accomplish that as through tailored learning communities, others may see service learning and community outreach programs as the key.

Suzanne McCorkle (2008, 3), an expert in conflict management, recently articulated sources of conflict that she sees in her consulting work with SEM professionals. She notes some sources in addition to those already discussed:

Information. These conflicts relate to who has what data, which data to use, and whether someone is withholding it. The solution is to make sure everyone has the same data and is in agreement about what data will be used.

Relationship. These are conflicts over who we are to each other—boss or friend. The solution is to discuss the situation and agree on boundaries and expectations.

Value. These are conflicts between deeply-rooted issues of faith or philosophy or generational differences. In a sense, these are the most difficult because people care about them so deeply and consider them part of their identity.

Style. Misunderstandings can occur because of different styles in personality, communication, conflict and culture.

Emotion. This type of conflict occurs when people's feelings are hurt. Perhaps they do not think they are getting the respect they deserve or feel entitled to something they are not getting.

Organizations and universities have additional sources of conflict by the nature of their structure and functions. Louis Pondy (1967) noted that all organizations have systems, bureaucratic and bargaining conflicts. Systems conflicts are about coordination between elements of the organization, for example, having recruitment and financial aid working together rather than creating situations the other cannot handle. Bureaucratic conflicts are superior/subordinate conflicts that occur when leaders and subordinates disagree in some way, for example, the Dean and Dr. Gray's disagreement over staffing priorities in the Department of English. And bargaining conflicts are conflicts over the distribution of scarce resources—presumably from a win-lose or competitive frame. The Justice University conflict typifies a bargaining conflict about whether scarce resources of financial aid go to certain kinds of students.

Lewin's (1993) thorough summary of organizational conflict literature links the complexity of structure and process with the presence of organizational conflict. Put simply, the more structurally complex the organization, the more likely it is to experience systems, bureaucratic and bargaining conflicts. Universities tend to be very complex organizations with many silos operating autonomously within units, departments, or colleges (Holton 2008). In fact, many SEM professionals can testify to the tendency of academic and staff components of the institution to be largely ignorant of the presence, process, and mission of the other. The history in many institutions of higher education is to have less communication, and decreased interdependence, among faculty and staff who are very long-term members of the system.

Compounding difficulties in higher education institutions is the process for leadership selection (Detsky 2010). Especially in the case of academic leaders, the selection process is less tied to administrative ability than some other area of expertise and success. Often a department chair or even a Dean may be promoted or selected because s/he is a strong scholar. An academic leader is rarely given thorough training or adequate support in professional development for administrative tasks. And because s/he often comes from and will return to the faculty positions held before administrative duty, s/he may feel constrained to make decisions that will damage those faculty relationships.

Functional and Dysfunctional Conflict

Many faculty and staff have an automatic reaction to "conflict"—that it will be unpleasant and negative. This reaction makes it more difficult for SEM professionals to invite and encourage others' participation in conflict processes to handle elements of SEM change. Thus, one of the initial challenges for SEM is to help others understand that conflict is neither bad nor good, but that the ways a conflict is handled can be destructive or constructive. A destructive or dysfunctional conflict is one in which one or both parties to the conflict are dissatisfied with

Table 1. Dimensions of Conflict

Functional	Dysfunctional
Open	Closed
Honest	Dishonest/Deceitful
Calm/Comfortable	Tense/Uncomfortable
Focused	Proliferated
Flexible	Rigid
Energizing	Draining
Creative	Stupefying
Deescalatory	Escalatory
Tractable	Intractable

the process and/or the outcome of the conflict management. A constructive or functional conflict is one in which both parties are pleased with the process and outcome of the conflict management. There are several dimensions on which functional and dysfunctional conflict differ. Those dimensions are summarized in Table 1 and discussed in more detail in the text following.

Open v. Closed—One of the most obvious signs of a functional conflict is that people trust each other enough to be open with information and freely exchange ideas and viewpoints. It is through this openness that trust is not only demonstrated, but increased. In dysfunctional conflict, people hide information from the other; they disclose little because they assume the other may use this information against them.

Honest v. Dishonest/Deceitful—Simply exchanging information does not mean conflict will be functional. The information has to be truthful and honest as well as available. People may be dishonest by not providing complete information or by knowingly supplying false information. Without exchange of valid information it is extremely difficult to collaborate.

Calm/Comfortable v. Tense/Uncomfortable—When conflicts are managed successfully—functionally—people don't even think of them as conflicts. They feel a sense of companionship, comfort, and collegiality with the other as they address the issue. But people are well aware of the emotional experience of being embroiled in a conflict that has turned sour; dysfunctional conflicts are emotionally tense and agitated.

Focused v. Proliferated—Destructive conflicts may begin with a focus on one issue, but soon the disputants are "reminding" each other of additional issues in the present and the past that were not resolved satisfactorily. Some conflict practitioners talk about this as "throwing in the kitchen sink," but the formal term coined by Deutsch (1973) is "issue proliferation." The more issues proliferate, the harder it is to work through any issue, for, as one person seems to get ahead on an issue, the other shifts ground to an issue with which they may have more success. In contrast, functional conflicts keep the interaction focused on the issues that are germane, with both parties attending to them. The sense is of a manageable level of conflict, and one that concerns the present and future rather than the past.

Flexible v. Rigid—In destructive conflicts, people become more and more resistant to entertaining flexible options and ideas. When a conflict is functional, people remain open to different views of the problem, different ways of dealing with the problem, and different criteria for success in dealing with the problem.

Energizing v. Draining—Dysfunctional conflict is emotionally and mentally draining, can be physically fatiguing and can interfere with the ability to think clearly and complexly. But functional conflict can have the opposite effect; it can energize and empower.

Creative v. Stupefying—Functional conflicts can enhance creativity and constructive change. In organizational and social conflicts these are referred to as generative conflicts (Galtung, 1988). But, in dysfunctional conflict, largely due to emotional arousal, the opposite is true. The more intensely emotional one becomes, the less able he is to process complex information and engage in creative problem-solving (Deutsch 1973).

Deescalatory v. Escalatory—Dysfunctional conflicts tend to escalate on all dimensions. Conflict escalation occurs when the feelings associated with the conflict become more hostile, when the behaviors used in the conflict become more aggressive, when the positions taken in the conflict become more extreme, and when the willingness to adopt cooperative orientations to the conflict becomes less likely (Galtung 1988).

Tractable v. Intractable—We should be cautious not to equate dysfunctional conflict with intractable conflict. Technically, intractable conflicts are conflicts that have escalated to a point where management or resolution is extremely unlikely, if not impossible. Not all dysfunctional conflicts are intractable, or are going to become intractable. But, functional conflicts do not become intractable. Because of all of the other characteristics of functional conflicts we have discussed, the foundation for intractability is never laid.

Climate and Conflict: Toxic Workplaces

Morton Deutsch (1973) suggested that social environment contributes to either constructive or destructive conflict resolution. For example, environments with unhealthy levels of competition encourage destructive conflicts and result in negative consequences for everyone. Conversely, environments with high levels of cooperation tend to encourage constructive conflicts with positive consequences for all. David and Roger Johnson, students of Deutsch and founders of the very influential theory of Cooperative Learning, have found consistent research support for this relationship (Johnson and Johnson 1996). The more competitive or hostile the university climate, the more likely conflict will be dysfunctional; and the more cooperative or supportive the university climate, the more likely conflict will be functional.

SEM professionals have two critical tasks—working with what may already be hostile climates in universities and creating supportive climates associated with their SEM work. Unfortunately, the academic environment has a number of organizational and work features that increase the likelihood of hostile interpersonal behaviors (Keashley and Neumann 2010). Many colleges and universities would be classified as "toxic" workplaces according to Frost (2004) who articulated the seven "Ins" of toxicity, summarized in Table 2.

Table 2. The Seven "Ins" of Toxic Workplaces

Intention: The Role of Malice	Some managers assume that their command of situations and their ability to get results stems from creating pain in their staff. Fear engendered in others is one of their key weapons of control. Their actions are designed to humiliate others and to keep them off balance, undermining people's confidence or self-esteem so that there are no significant challenges to their authority.
Incompetence: Managers with Weak or Inadequate People Skills	Many managers move up through the ranks of their organizations based on their technical skills. They tend not to be evaluated for their "people-handling" abilities. Or, if their people skills are weak or underdeveloped, this lack of competence is overlooked or downplayed by senior management in favor of the other "harder" skill sets.
Infidelity: The Act of Betrayal	Managers who betray their subordinates spread toxins into the system. Employees feel betrayed by their managers when promised promotions or raises do not materialize; when their boss takes their best ideas and presents them as his or her own.
Insensitivity: People Who Are Emotionally Unintelligent	Managers with a high level of emotional intelligence tend to be good "readers" of the way staff members are feeling, particularly when they display symptoms of emotional distress. When managers do not or cannot pick up these emotional cues in others it can harm their staff and the organization.
Intrusion	Charismatic leaders seduce their followers into striving for high accomplishment. However, these same magnetic personalities can draw their followers into such intensive work routines that an unhealthy balance is created between the followers' work and personal lives.
Institutional Forces: Contemporary Corporate Agendas	Toxins flow from company practices that create pain in those who must carry them out.
Inevitability	We cannot avoid some kinds of emotional pain, even if our organizational and management practices are well calibrated to the needs of their membership. They occur inevitably.

Higher education institutions are generally prone to poor climate, but many also have very severe issues with workplace bullying. In a recent study of university employees (Keashly and Neuman 2009), 49 percent of faculty and 53 percent of staff reported having been bullied. Colleagues were more likely to be identified as bullies by faculty (63.4%), while superiors were more likely to be identified as bullies by frontline staff (52.9%). The rates of mobbing (bullying done by two or more people at the same time) differed as a function of the occupational group being studied; faculty members were almost twice as likely as staff to report being the victims of mobbing by three or more actors (14.5% vs. 8%, respectively). And, when bullying/mobbing occurs, it tends to be long-standing. McKay et al. (2008) found that 21 percent of their sample reported bullying that had persisted for more than five years in duration. Without painting too dire a picture, it is important for SEM professionals to realize that they are working in organizations that are ripe for making conflicts dysfunctional and that ongoing dysfunctional conflicts may interfere with the SEM plans and outcomes even if SEM professionals attempt to address them.

SEM processes will work better if supportive climates can be established. Using language that is descriptive, problem-oriented, spontaneous, empathic, equal, and provisional communicates a non-defensive attitude and a respect for the other (Gibb, 1978). Supportive climates are linked with issues of trust; trust breeds support and support encourages trust. The lack of trust may precipitate conflict, while the presence of it may prevent potential conflict from arising (Deutsch, 1973). A cooperative and supportive climate builds trust because it provides an environment that allows all parties to achieve their goals simultaneously. The State University example at the beginning of the chapter underscores how a positive and supportive climate can degenerate and impact SEM efforts. The faculty and staff who devoted themselves to the strategic planning effort that was abandoned now feel disrespected and mistrustful. At State University, as at other educational institutions, it is easier to create distrust than trust.

SEM professionals can take insight from organizational research about the importance of building trust and supportive environments through effective communication. Matthew Dull's (2010) research proves that the relationship between trusted leadership and organizational performance is well established. In one study (Merit Systems Protection Board's Merit Principles Survey of 2005) more than 30,000 respondents reported their perceptions of leadership, communication and trust. Among the key findings were:

- *Job satisfaction*, whether respondents say they are *free to exercise voice*, and the *perceived performance* of respondents' organizations all are positively correlated with *trusted leadership*. If people trust leadership, the agency also typically exhibits high levels of job satisfaction, openness, and a belief among employees that the agency does good work.

- By contrast, *turnover intention and filing of a formal complaint* were both negatively cor-related with *trusted leadership*. Where respondents' trust is low that agency leaders will listen to concerns and act with fairness, they are more likely to report that they plan to leave the organization or even that they have taken formal action, pursuing a job-related complaint.
- Most strikingly, *free to exercise voice* yields a 0.89 correlation with *trusted leadership*. If an agency's respondents report low levels of trust that leadership will communicate clearly and honor commitments, that agency is much less likely to be characterized by frank and reliable internal feedback and deliberation.

APPRECIATING SEM AS A CHANGE PROCESS

As Bontrager's (2004) model of the SEM implementation cycle makes very clear—SEM imple-mentation is a large scale organizational change process. Twelves (2004) used Bolman and Deal's (2003) organizational change theory to study SEM restructuring at the University of Nevada, Las Vegas. Her case study illustrates how SEM restructuring has all of the hallmarks of a change process in large, bureaucratic organizations. And Wallace-Hulecki (2009) studied the impor-tance of engaging academic leaders in these efforts. She found that Deans were involved in three of Bryson's ten strategic planning stages: identifying the organization's mandate and need for change, identifying SEM issues and policy implications, and decisions on what SEM strate-gies to adopt. Deans were also very helpful in communicating a sense of urgency, formulating a vision for the future, forming a powerful coalition with key influencers in the process, and institutionalizing new approaches to enrollment planning and management. This research gives examples of how necessary it is to have academic leadership partnering on SEM efforts. As with all change initiatives, it will generate a great deal of conflict. Whether that conflict is productive or destructive will depend largely on the ability of SEM professionals to lead, and help others lead, for change rather than against change. Leading for change requires that the leader have an appreciation of why change is threatening and how to help other embrace it.

The success of the majority of colleges for the next five to ten years will depend on the abil-ity of each to address change in the school and changes coming from its environment. Only 80 percent of higher education institutions will need to manage radical change quickly; the larger schools that are well endowed and powerful will likely be the least affected, although current economic shifts may force them into change management regardless of their size or prestige. With tough economic times, the advance of technology, the expectations of parents, the fed-eral government, and state governments, the rate of change is increasing and becoming more imperative. The forces for change will likely come from the environment: Federal and State legislation and policy mandates, boards, students, parents, and the places where graduates will be working. The ability to thrive and succeed will depend on the ability of the university to adapt to the forces in the environment.

Monitoring the Environment for Change

Monitoring the environment and translating this to potential agendas for action is an activity of presidents according to Tierney (2008). However, presidents are rarely able to spend the time or energy on this task. Since monitoring requires someone who clearly grasps the concepts and believes in the dynamic nature of the institution and its environment, this is a potential role for senior enrollment leaders and one that could add to the potential for success in the areas of enrollment and student success. The strategic enrollment management area is likely the first line for reacting to outside influences—not just adapting but initially reacting to events. If a strategic model is used, everything from the academic offerings to the treatment of students is of concern to the enrollment group. There is no better place to identify themes for the future.

How an institution responds to change is many times determined by the way the information is brought into the culture. A SEM monitor is aware of both the culture and the goals of the institution. Those two factors determine the data he or she brings in from the environment, and determines the process he or she will use to react to that information and change.

Conflict and Change

Organizational change is often met with resistance, even when monitoring and information infusion is done well. Conrad and Poole (2007) argue that there are several reasons for this resistance:

- Unfavorable experiences with changes in the past
- Organizational goals they don't share
- Changes in productivity demands
- Unfavorable climate created during change
- Loss incurred by change
- Poorly planned change
- Ready, fire, aim change processes
- Change for change's sake

In addition, dysfunctional conflict can happen in change processes because people feel they have lost their identity, have negative emotions about the goal or process and feel basically disempowered. These are the three drivers of all conflict, but especially change-related conflict.

Identity, emotion, and power are intricately linked; effective strategic change is most likely when the SEM professional considers how change processes will impact each of these for participating faculty and staff.

- *Identity Issues in Change Conflict*—Desired and damaged identity lies at the heart of the experience of conflict. Most people are in conflict because they believe someone or something is preventing them from "being who they are" or "who they want to be." Likewise, people in conflict are often ignorant of how their actions are negatively impacting the identity of the other.

- *Emotion Issues in Change Conflict*—Emotions are central to conflict, serving as a metric of how important the conflict is, and emotions provide a way of understanding what needs to change in order for participants to feel better about the situation. Emotions are strongly linked to identity and power. Emotions are "motivation" and, as such, explain why people act in certain ways.

- *Power Issues in Change Conflict*—What is the ability to influence the current situation? That's the bottom line of power. As a corollary, change can disempower people by removing resources or access to channels through which resources can be obtained.

The example of Justice University in the beginning of the chapter shows how a change process can threaten the identity of individuals and the institution; how that threatened identity generates very negative emotion; and how the change is perceived as a means of disempowerment of students, faculty and community members. It is very unlikely that the hypothetical change agents in the Justice University example intended to insult, anger or disempower anyone. Often in change processes there is no intent to do so, but the inadvertent consequences may be the same (Conrad and Poole 2007).

BUILDING CONSTRUCTIVE CONFLICT CULTURES

SEM professionals should adopt an institutional culture perspective in their work; including the culture of an organization as a main thread for improving enrollment and student success. Ironically, when problems arise, the viewpoint of the change agents tends to become narrower, focusing on the event at hand, rather than broader so that the larger cultural influences that are driving the conditions are recognized. In SEM, culture is not a target of energy when a university runs into problems or cannot take advantage of opportunities. And, culture is either the direct cause of many problems or opportunities, or the culture determines whether a particular idea can be implemented or not.

"Culture" is the social glue that holds the institution together. Solutions and adaptation are dependent on the creativity and capacity for innovation which resides within each individual who is part of the culture. The culture is a pattern of meanings and shared assumptions that emerge from both individual and organizational behavior and is matched with the opportunities and threats coming from the environment. To appropriately monitor those threats and opportunities, an institution needs to gather the data regularly.

One of the chapter authors had experience with a public university in the Northeast that demonstrates the importance of monitoring the environment, whose account is reproduced below:

> *This public institution had a very strong President. He believed in the use of data in his programs, so our particular recommendations on the use of data in the Enrollment Management area were accepted with enthusiasm. We met with many of the data folks and detailed what was needed and set some time lines. Soon we realized that deadlines were being missed and there was no discussion about the fact they would be missed and when we asked for clarification of the issues, we were told these recommendations weren't possible. What we found ourselves in the middle of was a culture of data hoarding and control of institutional data analysis. Offices who wanted data could only get their information from IT and in the format provided. New analysis of data was only done when the President asked for specific information, pushing them to get it for him. All VPs were frustrated by lack of data and the Enrollment program was struggling to get new information easily. This problem was only solved when the President met with all of the IT folks and asked if it could be done. The head of IT said "yes, it can, but. . . ." and the President said, "Well, do it!" This was the way our recommendations actually got done.*

One of the challenges with culture, is to define and develop a framework to address the issue. In general, Tierney (2008) suggests that there are two fundamental ways to view culture—as objectivists or social constructionists. *Objectivists* look at facts and figures and take an objective approach. If there are challenges to the institution to be addressed, facts and research are sought to define and correct the problem. Once these have been defined and studied, actions are taken and the problem solved. Many institutions assume they can understand a problem and can arrive at an answer based on a few variables. This is not as dynamic a view as that needed for the complex issues today. *Social constructionists* believe that every school is different—that reality is socially constructed and will vary for all institutions. Because of the

idea that reality is being redefined every day, the following are some helpful guidelines:
- Actions occur on multiple fronts.
- Any issue has multiple solutions.
- Solutions may be fleeting.
- Look for consequences in unlikely places.
- Be aware of any solution that undermines strong or core values.

Characteristics and Benefits of the Constructive Conflict Cultures

Creating a constructive conflict culture means developing a supportive environment in which conflicts within the university are handled in a manner that is functional rather than dysfunctional and that supports SEM efforts. In this final section of the chapter we briefly discuss the characteristics of constructive conflict cultures, detail their benefits, and present a model of constructive conflict management that SEM professionals can use in their institutions.

Institutions that have constructive conflict cultures have the following characteristics in how members handle interpersonal or organizational conflict issues that arise.

(1) Members see conflict as a positive; they do not fall prey to the mistake of seeing conflict as only negative. As a result, they do not avoid conflicts, instead engaging them initially rather than letting the conflict fester and grow.

(2) The values of constructive conflict management are normed, modeled, and rewarded. The principles of constructive conflict are normed in terms of stated expectations that pervade the institution; members know that these are the values of how to deal with conflict. More importantly, these values are modeled by members and especially by organizational leaders. SEM professionals have considerable ability to model the values of constructive conflict management in all aspects of SEM planning and implementation. Most importantly, constructive conflict management is rewarded so that members understand they will benefit from their use of these behaviors, even though they are sometimes difficult.

(3) Constructive conflict cultures emphasize collaboration, although non-collaborative processes may continue to be used. As the model presented in the next section indicates, it is important to have interests-based, rights-based and power-based conflict management processes available.

(4) Responsibility for constructive conflict culture and management is born by all—not just those in conflict. This necessitates the creation of "upstanders" who are willing to approach a conflict even if they are not the central parties to the dispute.

(5) There are clear accountability structures for organizational members who violate norms

of constructive conflict management.

There are many benefits to constructive conflict cultures. As organizational research has indicated, they can achieve the following advantages (Conrad and Poole 2007; Costantino and Merchant 1996; Slaiku and Hasson 1998).

(1) Constructive conflict cultures protect and improve relationships in the institution, especially in times of change due to the increase in trust and perceived supportive environment. These cultures can remove toxins in the workplace that cripple change efforts (Frost, 2004).

(2) Constructive conflict cultures result in higher quality decisions and outcomes to problems. When the quality of the decision is paramount the effort to develop constructive conflict cultures will be very beneficial.

(3) Not only will constructive conflict cultures increase the probability of quality decisions, they also increase the probability that the decision will be implemented with fidelity. The best decision-making process is worth little if the decision never becomes reality.

(4) Since constructive conflict cultures develop supportive climates they increase organizational member loyalty and commitment to organization and reduce absenteeism, poor performance, and job turnover (and associated recruitment costs) (Dull 2010).

(5) Because of these other benefits, the creation of constructive conflict cultures often reduces unnecessary rights-based dispute resolution (e.g., litigation) that can be very expensive and create public image problems in times of organizational change.

MODEL OF CONSTRUCTIVE CONFLICT CULTURE

The following model, presented in Figure 1, illustrates the essential components of a constructive conflict culture that SEM professionals can help develop to ensure constructive conflict management, especially during change-related conflict.

These factors are organized hierarchically, as some are foundational to others. As SEM professionals consider the implementation of this model in their institutions, the hierarchy should help them prioritize and assess where to place initial and subsequent energies.

(1) *Effective Communication*—People have to trust that they are getting accurate information to the right people at the right time and in the way it is most useful; communication processes are strongly related to conflict presence and impact. Communication about conflict itself is critical. If there has been distrust in the institution it is even more important for the SEM professional to make sure that communication networks are intact and are being effectively used by all organizational members. The use of communication technologies for SEM work is very important here (Wilkinson et al. 2007).

Figure 1. Critical Factors in Constructive Conflict Culture

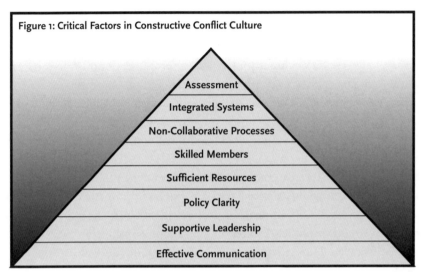

Figure 1: Critical Factors in Constructive Conflict Culture

Assessment

Integrated Systems

Non-Collaborative Processes

Skilled Members

Sufficient Resources

Policy Clarity

Supportive Leadership

Effective Communication

(2) *Supportive Leadership*—It is imperative that leaders provide resources for collaboration, to model collaboration, and to encourage development of collaborative tools. If leaders do not take the lead on this the organization's members will not believe that collaboration is valued or will be protected or rewarded.

(3) *Policy Clarity*—The first aspect of this factor requires that policies be developed and communicated explaining how conflict should be handled. People need to understand policy about when best to use collaborative process and how to access and use the range of conflict processes in the system. Too often organizations develop elaborate designs for dispute resolution but never communicate those plans to the members below the executive level. As a result, the system is not used and the benefits fail to be realized (Costantino and Merchant 1996).

(4) *Sufficient Resources*—As SEM professionals already appreciate, the kinds of organizational changes discussed here are not easy, cheap or fast. As a result, it is important that people have time, training, and support for collaboration and effective conflict management.

(5) *Skilled Members*—To what extent do organizational members have basic skills to collaborate and manage conflict? If constructive conflict management is essential for the SEM implementation, it behooves the institution to consider whether conflict skills training should be provided. Do members know how to communicate non-defensively, to negotiate effectively, and to facilitate group meetings and group problem-solving discussions? If not, providing those skills will increase their ability to participate effectively in change efforts.

(6) *Non-Collaborative Processes*—It is very important for SEM professionals and institutional leaders to recognize that collaboration is not always the best way to handle a conflict. For example, if a university has a bullying problem, it is unwise and counterproductive to suggest that targets "collaborate" with their bullies. All organizations should have effective procedures in place for handling problems that require rights- or power-based approaches.

The different orientations to dispute resolution were laid out in *Getting Disputes Resolved: Designing Systems to Cut the Costs of Conflict* (1988) by William Ury, Jeanne Brett and Stephen Goldberg. As they explained:

> **Interest-based approaches**, which they advocate and lament as less used than they should be, are approaches that emphasize an interest-based negotiation of the conflict between the disputing parties. Interest-based approaches involve direct negotiation between the parties as well as intervention by a third party facilitator, conciliator, or mediator who does not remove decision-making authority from the parties.
>
> **Rights-based approaches** involve the use of external arbitration or adjudication to determine whether someone's rights (provided to them under law, policy or practice) have been violated, by whom, and with what consequence. Rights-based approaches usually include fact-finding, binding and non-binding arbitration, adjudication and litigation.
>
> **Power-based approaches** are generally more difficult to identify because they don't manifest as easily in terms of discrete dispute resolution processes (like mediation or arbitration). Instead, power-based approaches include all means by which conflicts are managed through the exertion of physical, social, economic or psychological power against the other. Thus, power based approaches may include physical confrontation, sabotage, strikes, lockouts, media campaigns, boycotts and civil disobedience, to name just a few.

(7) *Integrated Systems*—Collaborative and non-collaborative processes work together in an overall dispute resolution system. In 1998, Karl Slaikeu and Ralph Hasson contributed their volume, *Controlling the Costs of Conflict: How to Design a System for your Organization.* Slaikeu and Hasson re-introduced Ury et al's (1988) four approaches to conflict management (with slightly different labels). Slaikeu and Hasson introduced the idea of seven critical subsystems that must be properly developed, implemented and maintained in order for the Office of the Dean for Student Development (ODSD) to function: policy, roles and responsibilities, documentation, selection, training, support and evaluation.

(8) *Assessment Processes*—Although assessment and evaluation are often touted, they are rarely done effectively. The constructive conflict cultures created should be regularly assessed to

determine whether they are actually increasing functional conflict management and benefitting SEM initiatives.

These assessment processes can and should be a part of the overall focus on assessment and evaluation as Kalsbeek (2007, 9) has suggested:

> *The most successful examples of SEM in colleges and universities nationwide share at least this element: they are committed to a sustained and systemic process for the creation, dissemination, and use of knowledge, to routine analysis, assessment, and evaluation, to the development of an organizational culture of evidence.*

CONCLUSION

Higher education institutions are living through some of the most challenging times in recent memory. Strategic enrollment management, given its impacts on all aspects of schools' functioning, will play a truly critical role in helping to guide change efforts that protect the institutions and move them into the future. SEM professionals will be better able to achieve these ends if they appreciate and understand the importance of collaboration and creating constructive conflict cultures to support SEM initiatives.

Action Plan

The following are some actions each institution might take to incorporate collaboration and constructive conflict management into the culture of their institution.

(1) The SEM professional ensures that all members of the institution realize that constructive conflict is a positive behavior that should become part of the culture. Conflict will occur in all change; therefore knowing that it can initiate new ideas and promote better problem solving, people will be able to deal with it more effectively.

(2) The SEM professional establishes and makes sure that the communication networks are intact and are being effectively used by all organizational members. If they have not developed effective communication within the institution, begin here. Develop a newsletter; establish an enrollment management team representing a cross section of the institution with a goal to model collaboration within the institution; and commit to regular contacts whether by meeting format or sending out reports and minutes of meetings.

(3) Encourage institutional leaders to provide resources for collaboration, to model collaboration, and to establish development of collaborative tools.

(4) Develop policies explaining how conflict should be handled in the institution including the use of mediation and arbitration if necessary. These policies should be communicated to all members of the organization and used consistently.

(5) Provide training of organizational members to establish and develop basic skills to collaborate and manage conflict.

(6) All organizations should make sure effective procedures exist for handling problems that require rights or power-based approaches since an issue such as bullying in a school cannot be handled with collaboration.

(7) Establish an ongoing assessment process for these action steps to keep the focus on creating the culture of collaboration and effective conflict management.

5

THE COMMUNITY OF SEM

Stanley E. Henderson
Vice Chancellor for Enrollment Management and Student Life
University of Michigan-Dearborn

CHAPTER 5

"GOOD MORNING!": MODELING COMMUNITY

I had a colleague who always gave the obligatory, "Good Morning," when he started a program—and got the usual ho-hum response. "You can do better than that," he would say sternly, "Try it again!" For many in the audience, it was a device that got their attention and engaged them for the presentation to come. However, I noticed from program evaluations that some audience members would react negatively to his tone, taking offense at being lectured. I decided his concept was good, but the implementation left something to be desired.

I wasn't quite sure how to pull my university audiences into an engaged greeting process until I thought about the "call and response" of African-American churches. It's impossible to say, "Good morning," to a Black audience and not get the energy of the greeting back with even more enthusiasm. This sense of community connection made me think about a new way to view our campuses.

Colleges and universities routinely refer to themselves as *institutions* of higher education: "Our institution has a wonderful reputation." Or, "Our institution has an excellent faculty." I wonder how many parents would want their students "institutionalized" for four or five years? When I came to my present university, I felt the phrase "institution of higher education" just didn't fit. The engagement of students in and out of the classroom and beyond the campus had a different feel. I came to see my new campus as a "*community* of higher education."

Using the power of language to convey an image, I could differentiate my campus from others: an *institution* is a passive place where things happen to the people within it. A *community* is an active place with members who participate, contribute, and make a difference. The image of community gave another voice to our expectation that students would practice engaged learning on our campus. And it pledged that the campus was a place where faculty and staff members of our community of higher education supported our student community members. It helped so-cialize new students to our campus culture, and we had a powerful recruitment tool with families who resonated with the idea of their kids coming to a community rather than an institution.

As a result, it became only a small step to pull the energy of a greeting out of the audience. After all, if you are in your home community, or your community of faith, or your community of work, and someone says, "Good morning," you give the greeting right back.

STRATEGIC ENROLLMENT MANAGEMENT AS COMMUNITY

The concept of community in higher education resonates as a new concept of strategic enroll-ment management: the Community of SEM. Throughout SEM's rise we spoke about its role in the "academic context" (Dolence 1993; Henderson 2005). However, if SEM is part and parcel of the Academy, itself a kind of community, there may be community elements to SEM that can help to integrate its many parts. While the campus culture dictates the shape of enrollment management, if part of that culture is a sense of community, should not SEM reflect the com-munity nature of the campus? What would such a Community of SEM look like and how can we reconcile it to existing views of SEM? Perhaps a community approach can provide a new lens for understanding the many facets of SEM on our campuses.

Such a view might be considered a "walk-on-water" approach for SEM. Indeed, on various campuses, SEM works to meet enrollment goals, improve quality, increase inclusion, ensure ac-cess and affordability, increase net tuition revenue, increase retention and graduation rates, and improve student learning outcomes—often in conflict with various factions. Rather than taking the happy path of community where everyone is contributing, in reality, SEM may operate in an environment with clashing factions: everyone may want *better* students; administration in-variably wants *more* students; faculty usually want *fewer* students along with the power to lower enrollment caps and reduce capacity.

THE DECLINE OF COMMUNITY IN THE ACADEMY

Some might suggest that higher education is growing more fragmented instead of becoming more like a community. The notion that SEM might be a higher education "community" is difficult to accept when one considers the accelerating siloization of American higher educa-tion. Many faculty members are more connected through their research to their national and international academic disciplines than to their campuses and students. The anthropology fac-ulty member who is quoted as saying, "Whenever I watch people interacting in a stadium, a subway, a supermarket checkout, I find myself seeing tribal rites or kinship networks," (Hacker and Dreifus 2010) embodies the negative stereotype of the Ivory Tower academic's superiority to his community.

The current recession has brought hard times to higher education communities, making it difficult to think in terms of members of the community pulling together for everyone's success. Endowment assets plummeted in the Crash of 2008. Schools are overleveraged; liabilities are increasing; and assets are drying up while costs continue to rise. Public higher education is seeing searing cuts in state appropriations: state universities are going from state-supported, to state-assisted, to merely state-located. The result is rising tuition as more and more students struggle to find jobs with increasingly expensive degrees. Our students feel the hopelessness of being passive players at an institution where things happen to them. More and more of them are seeing higher education as a value proposition: they simply fail to see the value of being in school. If students fail to see the value of investing more and more money along with the time demands that conflict with the other parts of their lives, they are more likely to drop out or not come in the first place…all because we are functioning more like institutions than communities.

Hossler and Kalsbeek (2009) assert that higher education leaders are convinced that their future is determined by their academic programs and the learning outcomes of their students. This, too, drives a wedge between the academic community and SEM, leaving too many SEM professionals on the outside looking in. Our programs are so strong, some academic leaders say, that if students aren't coming to them, there must be something wrong with the process of recruitment. If too many students fail to graduate, they assume admission standards are the culprit. Decisions are too often based on faculty interests rather than student interests, and the evergreen demand to raise admission standards fails to realize that the bottom quartile of the class will always be disadvantaged because of the wide divide between them and those students in the higher quartiles. Raising admission standards has always been easier than building in the hard slog of retention support to get the bottom quartile to graduation.

THE PROBLEM OF THE ACADEMIC SOLUTION

It would be the rare enrollment manager who has never thought about how there always seems to be an academic solution to every problem on campus. The provost, the deans and the faculty all see issues through an academic lens and formulate resolutions on their terms without regard for others' perspectives.

I'm reminded of the enrollment manager who died and went to heaven where St. Peter was showing her around. They walked the streets of paradise until St. Peter suggested they go into the celestial cafeteria for lunch. They joined the line where people were waiting patiently and quietly, engaging in pleasant conversation. Suddenly a man in a rumpled tweed coat rushed in, shouting, "Out of my way, coming through," and pushed his way to the head of the line.

"My," said the enrollment manager, "who is that rude man?"

"Oh, that's God," said St. Peter. "He thinks he's chair of the Faculty Senate."

In the face of a retention problem, academic departments hire more advisors or staff when SEM or Student Affairs team members could add great insight (and potentially leverage existing staff) to enhance student engagement and success.

Or, the faculty design new programs that will attract a handful of new students while ignoring what SEM has shown to be the sure winners for enrollment growth. Or, the deans say, "We're not getting our numbers. Admissions needs to visit high schools. Enrollment Management, what are you going to do about enrollment growth?"

Or, Deans and faculty chairs ignore the role their decisions have played in enrollment shortfalls and expect enrollment managers to affect change for the better.

COMMUNITY AS SERVICE

Dolence suggests that improving service is one of the key goals of SEM (1993). Forty years ago my mentor at Michigan State University taught that, "They recruit [and we can say today, retain] best who serve best." Then, as today, the school that provides the first response (read: best service) to an admission application had a better chance of enrolling and retaining a student. Questions answered, personalized interactions, timely information that helped to commit the recruit were all examples of exemplary service.

Service is still at the heart of enrollment management success on many campuses, requiring superior business and technology expertise. We want our students to be challenged in the classroom by our faculty, not frustrated by navigating the bureaucracy of the institution.

As a result, traditional, hierarchical organizations and "9 to 5" operations are obsolete, and the current focus on self-service and non-stop service programs is giving way to thinking and planning for cyber-service (Williams 1998), concepts and practices as unknown today as social networking was five years ago. Our future service models will take us in directions we can't imagine, so we should be thinking about them and planning for them today in order to meet students'—and their parents'— expectations tomorrow. Only this proactive approach to service can ensure that our institutions not only survive but thrive.

Service, in its multiple manifestations of meeting student and family needs through marketing, counseling, customer relationship management, technology and pricing, might also be seen as an updated version of the traditional admissions counseling concept of "fit." If the highest quality service also plays a role in the competitive market for student enrollment, universities and colleges must start to think about how to position their suite of services for maximum enrollment impact.

The concept of a Community of SEM is ideally suited to provide context for the best service. The image of a community readily encompasses services. Services are core in a community. In our home communities they might be police and fire, education, shopping centers, utilities, infrastructure. In our educational communities they are faculty, staff, facilities, programming, culture, planning, technology. In either case, they help bind the community members together in a common humanity that ensures their well-being.

THE FACES OF SEM

Likening SEM to a community is not so far-fetched. There has long been a tendency to anthropomorphize SEM when we divide it into its component parts. The SEM "personality" is made up of multiple traits or features that have to be combined into a robust "body" to ensure a campus can achieve its enrollment goals. Consider the three "faces" of SEM: structural management, planning, and leadership (Smith and Kilgore 2006; Henderson and Yale 2008):

- **Structural management**: SEM's structural management side focuses on the departments and functions that carry the accountability of achieving enrollment goals. The emphasis on structure brings together the right combination of offices and staff to provide the services of recruitment and retention, and the managerial component looks for optimal resource allocation to meet enrollment priorities. What will it take to meet marketing and media buys? What is the right mix of need-based and merit financial aid? Do course offerings and scheduling maximize the utilization of classroom stock for optimal enrollment? Can the campus provide efficient, timely service to students? What student intervention initiatives will produce success and persistence to graduation?

  All of these are service modules that enhance recruitment by providing quality, first response, just-in-time inducements, and quality reassurance that lead the right fit of students to enroll in the right numbers. Then structure and management develop services that maximize students' timely movement through the academic curriculum and ensure their success and ultimate graduation in numbers that keep the cradle to endowment continuum going.

- **Planning**: Another face of SEM is the planning process that guides our pursuit of preferred futures by focusing on long-range planning and campus-wide strategy development. This planning process leads to strategic development of new curricula and programs that meet current and prospective student demand. It identifies facilities development and renovation needs and drives investment in technology. Pricing decisions maximize revenue while supporting the necessary mix of aid strategies to ensure access and affordability that will maintain optimal enrollments. The research that is the foundation of good planning will analyze student success patterns and identify interventions to drive retention. Again, this planning side of SEM is about servicing the campus community members by providing the tools to do their work successfully in ways that move them toward their ultimate career and life goals.

- **Leadership**: Without senior executive leadership understanding and involvement in driving SEM, its success will be limited. Yet top-down leadership alone, while necessary, is not sufficient. Leadership at multiple levels, spreading like arteries through the campus, provides the lifeblood of getting SEM done. If leaders at the top, leaders in the academic community, and leaders in the enrollment structure come together with a common sense of purpose, they can gain trust and prompt action around a common mission of enrollment health. This environment will motivate the campus to set goals, develop strategies, and undertake assessment of outcomes to form a feedback loop that moves the campus to its optimum enrollment and then maintains the optimal levels.

The successful enrollment management program integrates these three components—"faces"—of SEM into something that is greater than the sum of its parts. Blending the three faces of SEM requires an understanding of the complex dynamics that shape the university's enrollment environment.

Figure 1: *The traditional funnel approach to enrollments* (Henderson and Yale 2008) builds from the population of all college bound students into increasingly smaller components of prospects, applicants, deposits, and enrolled. It has failed to provide the comprehensive approach required by SEM.

Figure 1: The Traditional Funnel Approach to Enrollments

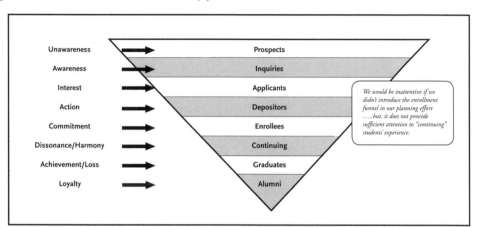

Figure 2: Traditional Enrollment Perspective

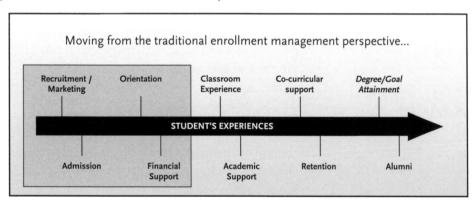

Even turning the funnel on its side to show a continuum (Figure 2) (Henderson and Yale 2008) from prospects through to alumni has the inherent weakness of failing to account for the view of SEM as a "cradle to endowment" enterprise. Here the traditional view of enrollment as recruitment, which makes a handoff to the rest of the campus, fails to position recruitment as the beginning of retention.

A true continuum is seamless and all-inclusive (Figure 3) (Henderson and Yale 2008). The campus, to be successful, must envision the student in all the phases of her relationship with the institution in order to help her reach eventual success as a happy alumna willing and able to give money to her alma mater.

Figure 3: The SEM Perspective

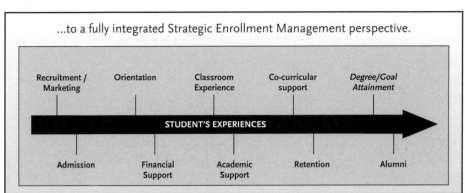

The "three faces" concept of SEM provides a more integrated approach to enrollment management than the more specialized perspectives from the past. The concept embeds market forces into the academic context under a new umbrella: a service ethic that makes us see curricula, teaching, research, facilities and engagement all as ways we serve—and advantage— the student members of our community of SEM. The three faces of SEM give our communities of higher education a framework for planning and leading to a common end—optimal enrollments—through the vehicle of service in the academic community.

COMMUNITY: THE FOURTH FACE OF SEM

Community, then, is the fourth, and integrating, face of SEM—a truly human face. Consider how the power of language can shine a different light on what we see and change our understanding: In an institution, someone always has a policy, a rule, a faculty culture, or an answer. In a community, we must look beyond the policies and the history to find what benefits individuals and the community as a whole.

The community of SEM is about building relationships. In traditional SEM, we often say that there is no template for how to do SEM. The enrollment manager, we say, needs to get to know the culture of her campus. However, the "culture" is really the "community" and its members. Understanding how to create and then nurture relationships in the campus community—whether with faculty, staff, or students—will help the enrollment manager to structure, plan, and lead SEM on her campus. If she also ensures that she is serving not just the external markets of prospective students but also the internal campus community members, she can be assured of success.

The community of SEM can harness the broader culture and reshape the academic solution syndrome by ensuring that there is a human face in each of SEM's traditional components:

Structure should facilitate seamless service, create open channels for feedback, and foster creativity. The structural face in a SEM Community should be less about organizational charts and more about creating an environment that allows people to do what they need to in order to work for students' *academic* success. For both faculty members and student service professionals, our goal is the academic success of our students. In the SEM Community, structure should allow for intersections between academic and student service units. Structure in a SEM Community will be the servant and not the master of success.

Planning should understand that data are critical only insofar as they improve service and contribute to the "cradle to endowment" concept of student success in finding and meeting their academic goals. Planning is strategic as well as collaborative in the SEM Community. Planning makes it possible for higher education community members to bring all viewpoints to bear, to understand that the enrollment manager, the student affairs professional and the financial services director all will have contributions to make to the well-being of the academic context.

If campus leadership in a SEM Community models the community message consistently in large and small ways, it will embed a sense of participation and support into the culture of the place. Such an integrated leadership at all levels of the campus community will overcome the traditional silos of the academy and provide a kind of "community center" for the work of enrollment management. Like the other faces of SEM, leadership in a SEM Community is really about service—in this case, *servant* leadership. As such, leaders in the SEM Community must be willing to lose themselves in followership. In describing the best kind of leaders, Lao Tzu wrote, "When the job is done…the people will say, 'We have done it ourselves.'"

The greatest—and easiest—failure of leadership is to fall into the Woodrow Wilson Syndrome. Wilson, as a visionary, knew exactly how the League of Nations should be structured and implemented after World War I and was unwilling to compromise with the U.S. Senate. As a result, the Senate rejected the Treaty of Versailles, the U.S. never joined the League, and World War II became inevitable.

The greatest—and most difficult—lesson for a visionary leader is to learn to turn over the vision to others, knowing the final outcome will not match his or her original spark. A community leader must also deal with change. The visionary leader will know that change withers in the face of day-to-day work. Change has to be nurtured by success, and it advances only by fits and starts. Change must be the prime directive of visionary leadership that is committed to the inclusion of ideas, of people, of cultures—in short, committed to the community.

THE HEART OF THE COMMUNITY OF SEM

Have we really hit on what is at the heart of the Community of SEM? The real definition comes in response to the realities we face each day in our work. Consider some examples of the face of the SEM Community:

ଌ

Even within the same division an institutional, passive world view can foster the development of silos rather than the integrated service model of a community. When we undertook a blended approach to student success in our Enrollment Management and Student Life division at the University of Michigan-Dearborn, we had four separate, but related, offices that rarely, if ever, referred students to another office. We used the Academic Support, Career Services, Counseling and Disability Services, and the Women's Resource Center offices to create the Student Success Center. In the new SSC we adopted a case management concept: getting a better idea of what students need right away by looking at the resources other offices in the SSC could offer. We cross-trained staff to understand the other offices, in order to make intelligent referrals. Instead of telling a student in Academic Support Services, "You should do some career exploration in Career Services," staff would walk the student to a Welcome Center to sign her up with a career advisor.

We began providing retention services to student groups academically at-risk according to the expertise of each office: Career Services worked with undecided students. Counseling worked with students who had been coming for therapy. Disability Services worked with students registered for accommodations. The Women's Resource Center worked with returning adult women in a Transitions Program that could pull in services from the other offices. Instead of treating students from a single office perspective, the focus shifted to providing the student with whatever support was needed to help her see the value of staying in school.

ଌ

A SEM Community perspective can lend a hand to another community member by leveraging existing resources instead of creating redundant positions. Because of significant growth in one of our colleges, advising resources were stretched thin. The dean's budget request for additional staff was going nowhere. Enrollment Management and Student Life offered an advisor from the Student Success Center. Still centrally held as our budget line, she was locally placed in the college advising office with day-to-day supervision there. In return, we gained an on-site advisor who could work with undecided students and other Student Success Center targeted groups and teach the college advisors about the services of the Center.

80

The community expectation that calls for participation and collaboration on all levels led to a grassroots academic initiative in financial/logistical partnership with Enrollment Management. Our Student Success Center had partnered with a chemistry professor to start Supplemental Instruction in his class. After the semester was over, he came to my office with a colleague, with a proposal to reach all of the gateway courses in the Natural Science department, some 1200 students per semester. They had already lined up faculty support, had identified students to be study session leaders, and had thought out a marketing plan to reach students enrolled in the classes. All they needed from me was money. "Darn," I thought, "Just when you get a good thing going, the faculty want to take it over." Then I thought, "Wait a minute, this is what you wanted to happen!" By the end of the meeting, they had their money. And, a year later, we were celebrating spectacular success with the program, including a four percentage point improvement in the fall-to-fall retention for students who participated in Supplemental Instruction over those who did not.

80

The community drive for joint action led to new relationships between our Enrollment Management division and the colleges. One of the Student Success Center directors came to me and said, "Advisors are putting students in the wrong classes, and I'm going to change their schedules."

"Well," I replied, "What do you think the advisors will have to say about that?"

"They won't change the schedules, so I'm going to do it."

"Let's take another approach first," I coached. "Why don't you go to the advisors and show them the transcripts of these students and ask if you are correct that the students are in the wrong classes? The advisors will say yes, and then you can suggest that they authorize you to make the changes on their behalf."

"They'll never agree to that."

"Humor me."

After he met with the advisors, he called. "I can't believe it. They agreed to have us make the changes."

Conventional wisdom would have suggested that the advisors would resist any involvement in "their" business by "outsiders." Instead of confrontation, my director pitched collaboration. Using data provided by student schedules, he gained agreement from the advisors that the students were taking classes that were a recipe for failure for a variety of reasons—not following prerequisite requirements, choosing courses without advisors, too many courses given work schedules, etc. Then he presented a solution to the problem: The college advising offices could delegate to the Student Success Center the job of correcting the students' schedules. We were in essence working for the advisors. They maintained academic control, but we were saving students.

This led to the additional delegation of follow-up to Early Warning alerts from college advising offices to the Student Success Center. When a faculty member reports a student is not doing well in her class, the SSC staff work with the student to determine the best course of action: getting a tutor, participating in Supplemental Instruction, taking a study skills seminar or dropping a class. The SSC interfaces with a variety of offices in working with Early Warning: Financial Aid to ensure students will not take action that will cause Satisfactory Academic Progress difficulties, various academic support programs in the colleges, even working with parent notification for those students who have given a FERPA release.

Perhaps most significantly, a SEM Community face can help to move students out of a passive institution where things out of their control happen to them into a community place where people work with them to meet their needs. A group of Muslim students was charged with violations of University Center policies and sanctioned. A Muslim colleague pointed out there was a disconnect between the university's punitive approach and the students' life experiences. They had come of age since 9/11 and experienced discrimination as a community and as individuals. Where the university wanted accountability, the students wanted to be treated with respect and have their grievances heard. Punishment felt like the disrespect they encountered on a regular basis in their community. Service to these students required rethinking how to respect them. For many of us who grew up in the Civil Rights era, the similarities between Black students of mid-twentieth century and Muslim students of the early twenty-first were uncanny.

CONCLUSION: MAKING A DIFFERENCE

The relationships, the partnerships, the alliances that we build and the services we provide come together to provide a human face to the Community of SEM, and that, in turn, can give life to our SEM work in structures, planning, and leadership. The lens of the SEM Community brings data and research to bear on work that respects the academic ethos of every campus while ensuring enrollment health through student success. Inculcating a culture of service that emphasizes participation, collaboration, and contribution in SEM can take our campuses to new levels of robust enrollment health that the traditional, institutional facets of enrollment management cannot achieve. In our Community of SEM, as in our life's communities of home, of faith, and service, we can make a difference.

Robert Kennedy said, "Few will have the greatness to bend history itself, but each of us can work to change a small portion of events, and in the total of all those acts will be written the history of this generation." (1967)

As we structure and manage, as we plan, as we lead, may we work in the Community of SEM to change our small portion of events on our campuses…and truly make a difference.

6

FINANCIAL AID: PAYING THE BILLS

Guilbert Brown
Assistant Vice President for Planning & Budgeting and Chief Budget Officer
George Mason University

CHAPTER 6[1]

There is perhaps no area of higher education finance that is more complex or controversial than the realm of student financial assistance or financial aid.[2] Both the complexity and potential for controversy surrounding these programs begins with the fact that the practices collectively referred to as "financial aid" serve a broad range of potentially competing financial, institutional and public policy goals. Scholarships are used to entice athletes and promising scholars to attend institutions with little or no out of pocket costs; grants and gift aid are combined with loans to assemble aid "packages" that make costs of attendance appear affordable even though they may be greater than the student's family's annual income; and increasingly, nonresident students at public universities are given tuition discounts to encourage them to enroll at a price that is less than the published ("sticker price") tuition, but still significantly higher than the tuition resident students pay to attend the same institution. Different program, mission and financial goals of the institution are addressed through financial aid practices, and both the goals and practices can vary dramatically based on institutional identity, legacy and budgetary circumstances. The terminology used to refer to various forms of financial aid reflects these varying purposes and can be confusing to those outside higher education professional circles.

In the context of strategic enrollment management (SEM), financial aid facilitates "paying the bills" for both students and the institutions they attend. Without financial aid many students

---

1. Portions of this chapter will appear in the author's unpublished master's thesis to be submitted in 2012 to the Higher Education Program at George Mason University. The author has granted full rights for publication and use of this manuscript to the American Association of Collegiate Registrar's and Admissions Officers.

2. In this chapter "financial aid" refers to the full range of governmental aid (Federal and State), institutional and private sources of grants, scholarships, loans, gifts and work opportunities made available to students as means to financing their educations.

simply could not afford to attend college or would choose to attend a lower cost institution; similarly, without the enrollment revenues provided by those same students, many colleges and universities could not afford to pay employee salaries and other operating costs. Besides their use to shape enrollments, provide access and make college more affordable, *financial aid programs are fundamental to the financing of both private and public institutions of higher education.*

It is important to note that in the case of discounts, remissions or institutional "gift" aid, *all forms of financial aid result in the realization of payment for some combination of goods and services provided by colleges and universities.* Consider the following scenarios describing how, over time, millions upon millions of individual students manage to pay for college:

1. *Gail decides to attend a private college when she receives an academic scholarship covering half her tuition costs for four years, provided she maintains at least a 3.50 GPA.*

2. *George didn't think he could afford to attend college but learned at a financial aid workshop he might qualify for a Pell Grant that would cover tuition at his local public college.*

3. *Sid received a financial aid package that included a combination of Federal grants, subsidized and unsubsidized loans, college work study and institutional grant funds equaling the full costs of attendance.*

4. *Alice received an athletic scholarship covering full tuition, books, room and board for five years provided she remained academically eligible to play on the college basketball team.*

5. *Jill qualified for a state financial aid award, based on her income, that covers about one-third of her tuition costs. Combined with family savings, money from her part-time job and living at home, she is able to afford to attend her regional public university without loans.*

Each of the cases above describes forms of "financial aid" yet reflects differing purposes of those programs. For the students in the examples, financial aid plays a significant role in how they plan to pay for college. The students themselves likely know little about the institutional legacies, funding models or policy decisions leading to their respective awards; or the academic, financial, extracurricular and public policy objectives reflected by the specific aid programs from which they financially benefit. Cases 1 and 4 are typically referred to as "merit aid" designed to encourage students, through favorable pricing, to enroll at a specific institution. Merit-based awards are typically offered to prospective students who possess some quality or skill (and thus receive the offer through individual "merit") that is desired by the institution to meet a programmatic goal, and who presumably would be less likely to attend without the scholarship offer.

In case 1 above, the academic scholarship might be funded from private gift support to the institution, in which case the institution will still realize 100% of its published tuition rate from Gail's enrollment, with half of the funds coming from Gail or her family and the other half from a private gift source. Alternately, it might be an unfunded tuition discount, in which case the institution has made a determination that the institution (including Gail's classmates) will benefit programmatically from having a student of Gail's qualifications as a member of the student body, and will still meet its operating costs with one-half its published tuition rate.

Similarly, in case 4 the actual funding for Alice's scholarship may come from athletic boosters in the form of donations for scholarships, from charges made to other students in the form of student fees supporting intercollegiate athletics, or through some combination of these sources, athletic department income or institutional discounting. In either case the university will realize revenue for tuition, room and board,. As in Gail's case, the institution has made a decision that having a competitive basketball team is sufficiently important (to university life, or donors, or legal compliance with Title IX requirements) to provide scholarships, including one for Alice, for this purpose. Merit awards may be given for musical talent, on the basis of past achievements such as National Honor Society membership, for academic merit based on test scores or high school grade point average, or other distinguishing characteristics that an institution wishes to have reflected in its student body.[3]

The other cases noted above (2, 3 and 5) are examples of "need-based" financial aid. As with merit-based aid, the actual sources of funds for need-based awards can vary, depending on the specific program providing the financial aid award. By definition, need-based aid is means-tested, that is, students must demonstrate that their financial means are such that the aid is required to meet the costs of attendance. This is most commonly achieved through completion of the Free Application for Federal Student Aid (FAFSA) used to calculate an Expected Family Contribution (EFC) based on family income and similar factors. For the purposes of awarding institutional need-based aid, institutions may require additional information not used for the FAFSA calculation of EFC, such as home equity. In each of these cases the financial aid programs—Pell Grants, subsidized loans, institutional grant aid, state need-based aid—exist to make higher education affordable for students whose financial means may otherwise preclude college attendance.

---

3. cf. Breneman (1994) who describes how institutions that could fill their classes with full paying students instead opt to increase diversity of talent and background via tuition discounting.

Financial aid policies and practices thus serve multiple institutional objectives: "need-based" financial aid makes college affordable to students whose financial resources might otherwise prevent their attendance, and the market pricing effects of "merit-based" financial aid drive students to make decisions to attend one institution over another. While financial aid programs make it possible for many students to attend college, those same programs have been linked to the increasing costs of higher education.[4] The traditional financial aid model - with heavy dependence on student loans—is being called into question, particularly as changes in American student demographics suggest higher rates of growth among historically underrepresented populations, with relatively diminished ability to pay college costs.[5] As the basic business models of American higher education are scrutinized, criticized and ultimately evolve over time, the core economic relationships of the aid/loan model supporting most public and private colleges and universities are similarly coming under the microscope of policy makers. Governing boards, legislators and public policy advocates are asking: Do escalating Federal student aid grant program awards (e.g., Pell grants) inflate college costs due to institutions treating these as "entitlements"? Does paying for a bachelor's degree over several years still make economic sense to individual students as more careers require advanced or ongoing professional education? With tuition increases already outstripping price inflation in just about every other major sector of the economy, how will higher education manage to serve the developing market demographic of students requiring increased levels of program support services and showing higher levels of financial need? Is higher education's current business model sustainable?

In considering these questions surrounding student financial aid, this chapter considers higher education's business model in the context of the fundamental economic attributes of colleges and universities, including critiques of that model and SEM practices. Two alternative paths are proffered to address current and anticipated financial challenges confronting both students and higher education institutions. One path is to increase direct subsidies to higher education through public policy decisions, in order to maintain or increase financial support as enrollments and programs expand. This strategy reflects the original Morrill Act purposes of land grant universities, serving the public goods of fostering economic development and an educated citizenry while simultaneously promoting the private goods of personal enrichment and

---

4. An excellent analysis can be found in *The Tuition Puzzle: Putting the Pieces Together* (Washington, DC: Institute for Higher Education Policy, 1999), http://www.ihep.org/assets/files/publications/s-z/TuitionPuzzle.pdf

5. See the discussion in Bob Bontrager, ed., *SEM and Institutional Success: Integrating Enrollment, Finance and Student Access* (Washington, DC: AACRAO, 2008)

career development through education. This approach has traditionally relied upon significant levels of public funding in support of the public goods served by higher education.

Lacking sufficient levels of public funding, an alternative path is to utilize the tools and techniques of SEM to optimize financial contributions from students on the basis of willingness and ability to pay—reflecting the private good to be realized by individual students—while continuing to serve the historic public purposes of higher education, including access to affordable and high quality educational programs. In this latter context of diminishing levels of subsidies for public colleges and universities, reflecting the recent experience of public institutions of higher education, financial aid programs are fundamental to achieving individual, institutional and societal goals.

A key question concerning financial aid policy is whether providing subsidies directly to students is a more effective strategy than subsidizing institutions to serve those same students. The economics of higher education and use of SEM to generate tuition revenues in support of institutional mission is exhaustively treated in the AACRAO publication *SEM and Institutional Success: Integrating Enrollment, Finance and Student Access*, portions of which are incorporated in the following discussion. Public policy preferences for "market-like" approaches to public goods (such as public higher education) favor the approach of providing aid directly to students, and this approach folds neatly into SEM practices that support the use of pricing to address a broad range of institutional goals including access, affordability and quality as gauged by both student characteristics and the adequacy of financial resources to support institutional operations.

HISTORY AND CONTEXT: A CHANGING FINANCIAL AID LANDSCAPE

Society has a significant interest in efficient colleges and universities. The total societal economic investment in higher education institutions includes tuition payments from students, tax subsidies from years past as well as the present, philanthropic gifts—again, past and present—and a broad range of other fees for goods and services ranging from athletic event tickets to research grants to health care payments. Focusing on undergraduate instruction, in a recent survey financial reasons were cited as the single greatest reason for students leaving college (NCES 2010), and college costs and tuition inflation increasingly dominate headlines and state legislative funding discussions. Public higher education institutions typically tie increasing tuition rates, and the resulting demand for more financial aid, to reductions in public subsidies. At the same time scarce institutional financial resources are being diverted away from mission-critical activities and toward revenue-generating activities (Rhoades and Slaughter 2004). Ultimately, public higher education institutions might argue, increased subsidies serve to reduce reliance on revenue-generating strategies and thus save the non-mission related costs of generating those revenues.

The rising cost of higher education over the past few decades has precipitated a number of studies to examine institutional financial aid practices (Breneman 1994; Baum 2008), the economic characteristics of higher education (Winston 1997), resulting societal distribution of subsidies through both philanthropy and public appropriations (Winston 1997 and 2001a), and the impacts of changing finances on affordability and access (Brittan 2003; Baum and Lapovsky 2006). For public institutions in particular, changing funding landscapes have brought issues of access and affordability head-to-head with existential challenges concerning the public and private purposes these institutions simultaneously serve (Zemsky 2003; Brittan 2003). Understanding the underlying dynamics of higher education finances requires a comprehensive view of all institutional activities (Ehrenberg 2006). A comparative study of instructional costs concludes that there is no relationship between the cost of teaching courses and the tuition charged to students (Middaugh 2005).

While the facilities and grounds of most colleges and universities may create the impression that higher education costs are driven primarily by expenses other than labor, personnel costs typically comprise 70-80 percent of operating budgets for public and private institutions alike and it is not unusual for salary and benefit expenses to make up 90 percent of academic department budgets.[6] In addition to faculty, colleges and universities employ numerous support personnel ranging from general office staff to highly specialized laboratory assistants, research administrators, financial managers, and information technology professionals, to name a few specialties found in a typical college workforce. Facilities are typically funded by private gifts, public appropriations, or bonds paid over terms of twenty or more years.

For decades, public institutions have been growing in numbers of students, and instructional and research expenditures, while government support for instruction has not kept pace with

---

6. These ratios vary significantly at different institutions; deductions such as depreciation expense and interest on debt service can significantly reduce this ratio in institutional financial statements. The author bases these ratios on experiences at diverse public and private research universities. At George Mason University, a regional public institution with enrollment of approximately 30,000 students, for the 2009-2010 fiscal year 78 percent of education and general operating costs were budgeted for salaries and related benefits. Operating budget funds are those most significantly impacted by revenue streams such as tuition and state appropriations. An issue paper titled "Frequently Asked Questions About College Costs" released at the request of Charles Miller, Chairman of The Secretary of Education's Commission on the Future of Higher Education begins with these phrases: "1. Why does college cost so much? Colleges are labor-intensive. a. On average, 75 percent of the costs to run a college are related to personnel expenses, including benefits." Retrieved June 1, 2010 from http://www.ed.gov/about/bdscomm/list/hiedfuture/reports/dickeson2.pdf.

increased levels of institutional spending (SHEEO 2010). Tuition and other revenue sources have been left to pick up the slack (Hossler 2004). Beyond personnel costs, colleges and universities face a mix of expenses similar to those one would find in the private sector: a long list of regulatory compliance costs, rising energy prices, litigation and risk management costs, and overall inflation on goods and services (Common Fund 2010). For many institutions the costs of information technology involve not only equipping students and faculty with the most current networking, software, and computer technologies, but also with access to online library resources including specialized databases, periodicals, and instructional resources. Ongoing improvements in instrumentation and computer simulation technologies require continuous investments to maintain research laboratories. Finally, there is the increasing cost of institutional financial aid in the forms of scholarships and tuition discounts.

Both public and private colleges and universities have similar economic structures characterized by diverse revenue streams, including subsidies (Winston 1997). Public institutions by far educate the greatest numbers of undergraduate (over 63%) and graduate students (over 50%) in the United States (NCES 2010). These institutions are more reliant on direct subsidies from state legislatures (Winston 1997) and their mission statements frequently compel these institutions to attempt to serve a growing population of students (Zemsky 2003).

The spiraling tuition and fee increases higher education institutions have experienced over the last several decades can be traced to decreases to subsidies, enrollment growth and increased infrastructure costs associated with revenue-generating activities. Supplanting subsidies with "earned" revenue introduces layers of inefficiency that result in higher overall costs for achieving the same set of goals. The interplay of enrollment growth, static or declining state subsidies and cost inflation results in tuition rate increases that are exponentially larger than expense increases. The financial complexities surrounding externally-sponsored research, together with its related infrastructures also serve to increase costs and ultimately impact tuition prices. Is enrollment management an example of infrastructural investment that is required to generate revenue in lieu of state subsidies, which in turn has produced by-products in the form of merit aid that further fuels tuition price inflation? How can financial aid programs be used to achieve the same public policy objectives as direct subsidies to higher education, and what is the role of enrollment managers in optimizing the benefits of financial aid to their respective institutions?

HIGHER EDUCATION'S ECONOMIC STRUCTURE: HOW ENROLLMENT GROWTH AND DECREASED SUBSIDIES DRIVE TUITION INCREASES

Through the last quarter of the 20th century and beginning decade of the 21st, major sectors of the United States economy have experienced fundamental transformations. For public higher education institutions, these transformations have included reductions to public funds supporting instruction, changes to federal policies impacting cost reimbursements for research and medical training, the shifting of student aid programs to emphasize loans over grants, and a shifting of the burden for paying for higher education from governmental support to students and their families (College Board 1999; SHEEO 2010). Concurrent with these changes has been a significant emphasis on entrepreneurial initiatives in public colleges and universities that hold as their objective the generation of revenue to support the mission-critical institutional programs of instruction, public service, discovery or creation and subsequent dissemination of new knowledge (Slaughter and Rhoades 1997).

Explanations for the high costs of higher education have generally compared and contrasted its cost and revenue structure with more familiar business models in the general economy (Bowen 1967, Winston 1997). In 1997 Bowen describes higher education as an inherently labor-intensive enterprise with a finite potential for efficiency gains, reflecting the Baumol Effect or "cost disease" similarly attendant to the labor-intensive performing arts; when subsidized, labor-intensive enterprises expand, either subsidies must increase as well or prices will inflate (Baumol and Bowen 1996).

In 1998, a comprehensive attempt to address college costs was the focus of the National Commission on the Cost of Higher Education, which included numerous public hearings and sessions to attempt to define and explain the reasons for escalating tuition rates. Precipitated by public pressure over tuition rate increases and "the cost of college," the primary contribution of the report was to proffer a common taxonomy to describe the complex phenomena surrounding collegiate finances from public policy, institutional and student perspectives. The commission report considers several alternative interpretations of the term "cost" before settling on a distinction between *cost* as what institutions spend, *price* as what students pay and *subsidy* as the difference between cost and price, supplied in the forms of state appropriations, charitable gifts, investment income and revenue earnings from unrelated business activities. The Commission contrasted the economic structure of higher education with that of private industry, explaining that in commercial enterprises, price is typically higher than cost, and the difference is profit (Winston 1997). For those enterprises, increasing volume results in higher costs, higher revenues and increased profit. For higher education, increased volume means costs exceed revenue by even greater levels than before, and so increased subsidies are needed (Winston 1997). If those subsidies are not forthcoming, tuition prices must increase or spending per student must decrease. What has happened in fact is the former. In the period 1970 to 2005, public college and university spending increased by 31 percent, adjusted for inflation, yet state support (also adjusted) increased by only 7 percent (Lingenfelter, 2008). Tuition increases made up the difference.

A series of simple tables illustrates the dynamics of these interrelationships. Assume that an institution enrolls 1,000 students and charges $4,108 tuition per student, the national average for public institutions in 2009 (SHEEO 2010). In addition the institution receives a $6,928 per student subsidy from its state, also the national average amount for 2009 (SHEEO 2010). Assume further that all revenues and expenses are increasing by 3% and enrollments are level, that is, not increasing or decreasing. Approximately 80% of expenses are for salaries. The resulting two-year finances for the institution might resemble the figures shown in Table 1.1:

Table 1.1: Steady State Institutional Finances —1,000 Students

Item	Year One	Year Two	$ Change	% Change
Revenue				
Tuition	$ 4,108,000	$ 4,231,240	$ 123,240	3%
State Support	$ 6,928,000	$ 7,135,840	$ 207,840	3%
Total Revenue	$ 11,036,000	$ 11,367,080	$ 331,080	3%
Expense				
Salaries	$ 8,828,800	$ 9,093,664	$ 264,864	3%
All Other Expenses	$ 2,207,200	$ 2,273,416	$ 66,216	3%
Total Expense	$ 11,036,000	$ 11,367,080	$ 331,080	3%
Total # of Students	1,000	1,000	-	-
Avg Student Tuition	$ 4,108	$ 4,231	$ 123	3%
Cost per Student	$ 11,036	$ 11,367	$ 331	3%

Table 1.1 illustrates how, in a uniform steady state condition—with no increases or decreases to enrollments, and all revenue sources and expenses growing together—tuition increases, salary increases and total spending (cost) per student would increase at comparable rates based on uniform cost and price inflation. While simple, the mathematical relationships in this model make intuitive sense and represent a common sense understanding of how tuition might be expected to increase over time. With enrollments remaining constant and revenues and expenses increasing 3%, the average tuition charge also increases by 3%. Both students and faculty benefit directly from the increased subsidies as average costs per student increase by $331 funded primarily through increased subsidies ($208) and only partially by increased tuition ($123) and faculty receive salary increases for teaching the same numbers of students.

Conversely, when subsidies do not keep pace with increased enrollments, both students and faculty pay the consequences. Average post-secondary state appropriations per student peaked in 2001 and since then have declined by 13% after adjustments for inflation, while during the same period tuition has increased by 25% in real terms (SHEEO 2010). As a result, and when combined with enrollment growth, funding per student from the combination of tuition and state appropriations actually *declined* from $11,239 in 2001 to $11,036 in 2009 (SHEEO 2010) when adjusted for inflation. The long term trends of declining subsidies combined with enrollment growth result in significant tuition increases without corresponding increases to spending per student.

Even without adjustments to inflation, as subsidies fail to keep up with enrollment growth, the Baumol Effect results in dramatic increases to tuition rates without corresponding increases in per-unit spending. Changes to enrollments and state support from 2008 to 2009 are illustrated in Table 1.2. In this one year period, public enrollments grew by 3.4% and state appropriations per student declined by 4%. *Changing only these assumptions* in the second year of the previous example, total tuition revenue must increase by *three times* the rate of expense increases to balance the budget. Even if no additional costs associated with the increased enrollments are assumed, for example hiring additional faculty, tuition revenue must increase by 9.3%. Of the increased tuition, the new enrollments (volume) would account for about 3.6% of the revenue increase and average tuition charges per student (rate) would need to increase by 5.7%.

For continuing students, a 5.7% tuition increase may exacerbate financial pressures to the point of having to withdraw from school, increase borrowing or increase work hours. Despite the 5.7% tuition rate increase, the institution will be spending slightly less per student than during the prior year, as a portion of the tuition increase is funding a portion of the average cost for new students that would otherwise be provided by increased subsidies (state support). As a result, continuing students pay an additional $234 on average with $43 less spent on their

Table 1.2: Increasing Enrollments and Declining State Support

Item	Year One	Year Two	$ Change	% Change
Revenue				
Tuition	$ 4,108,000	$ 4,490,070	$ 382,070	9.3%
State Support	$ 6,928,000	$ 6,877,010	$ (50,990)	(0.1%)
Total Revenue	$ 11,036,000	$ 11,367,080	$ 331,080	3%
Expense				
Salaries	$ 8,828,800	$ 9,093,664	$ 264,864	3%
All Other Expenses	$ 2,207,200	$ 2,273,416	$ 66,216	3%
Total Expense	$11,036,000	$11,367,080	$ 331,080	3%
Total # of Students	1,000	1,034	34	3.4%
Avg Student Tuition	$ 4,108	$ 4,342	$ 234	5.7%
Cost per Student	$ 11,036	$ 10,993	($ 43)	<0.1%

education. Similarly for the faculty, 3% salary increases leave no funds available to increase the size of the faculty, so that with enrollment growth, classes will be larger and demands for grading, office hours, advising and other instruction-related activities will increase (by about 3.4%, the size of the enrollment growth).

The Consumer Price Index, against which tuition increases are frequently compared, is based on a basket of goods and services that bear little relationship to the costs of operating a college or university, precisely *because* higher education is so labor intensive and its costs are driven primarily by labor market considerations (SHEEO 2004). Eventually, faculty will need to be added, further pressuring tuition. When multiplied over many years of enrollment growth and declining subsidies, the Baumol Effect contributes to significant price increases without corresponding per-unit cost increases.

Tables 1.1 and 1.2 illustrate how the economic structure of public colleges and universities can, in the context of decreasing subsidies, simultaneously reflect rapidly escalating prices in the form of tuition increases, modest increases to the overall expenditure base, decreased spending on a per-student basis and increased workload from a faculty perspective. As these exhibits illustrate, given salary costs in the range of 80%, subsidies in the range of 60%, and modest changes to both variables combined with enrollment growth, tuition rates increase by multiples of the base cost of inflation. The simple reality is that public higher education has been expanding enrollments, while subsidies on a per-student basis have declined. Increased enrollments without corresponding increases to instructional programs reduce course availability, program quality and affordability. Institutions are also called upon to provide extracurricular (non-instructional) support services to an expanded student body. Despite increasing at nearly twice the rate of expense growth, the tuition rate increases illustrated in Table 1.2 result in *less* spending per student while creating new financial barriers to access based on price.

Faced with these difficult challenges—realizing sufficient revenues to maintain or enhance program quality while at the same time increasing access through more affordable pricing structures—public higher education institutions have invested in, and turned to, pricing and aid strategies informed by enrollment management practices.

THE COST IMPACTS OF ENROLLMENT MANAGEMENT

California State University, Long Beach, facing its first enrollment decline in 1978, established task forces to develop recommendations on recruitment, marketing and outreach activities. Quickly, the college came to the realization that increasing efforts to recruit more students from a declining population of potential students would not solve the problem. Instead, the college elected to redefine its enrollment goals through enrollment management, which is viewed by the college as a "concept," a "process," and an "outcome." (Kreutner and Godfrey, 1981)

According to Kreutner and Godfrey, the concept of enrollment management means that through systematic and sensitive planning and coordinated execution, the university can control its future (Mabry 1987).

Enrollment management strategies have grown in scope and sophistication over the past several decades to include in their objectives the realization of both institutional mission and students' educational goals (Bontrager 2008). The core principles elucidated by Kreutner and Godfrey (1981)—marketing, enrollment, retention and research (to improve on subsequent marketing, enrollment and retention activities) continue to be reflected in outcome-driven "strategic enrollment management" activities (Hossler and Bean 1990). Whether enrollment management leads to the realization of the institutional mission and students' educational goals as Bontrager argues, or to the further stratification of educational opportunity as Slaughter and Rhoades (2004) suggest, there is little question that the practices of enrollment management lead to increased costs for merit-based financial aid (Davis 2003) and that the institutions engaging most frequently in those strategies are private research universities, which have experienced the most significant growth in tuition prices fueled largely by competition for prestige, high profile students and resources (Clotfelter 1996; Wellman 2006; Winston 2001b).

The resulting higher education business model described as "academic capitalism" (Slaughter and Rhoades 1997) necessitates new organizational structures and processes to support revenue generation. These structures consume significant financial resources, the argument continues, and instill regulatory and bureaucratic cultures that reduce the efficiency of mission-critical activities. For Slaughter and Rhoades (2004, 295-6) strategic enrollment management (SEM) is an example of this more generalized trend, focusing "on maximizing yield rates and quality, and minimizing tuition discounts and financial aid. This approach has become the focus of annual meetings and several publications sponsored by the American Association of Collegiate Registrars and Admissions Officers (AACRAO). It has also become a cottage consulting industry." Numerous studies suggest that the leveraging strategies of SEM provide the greatest financial benefit to students who could otherwise afford to pay while driving up costs in a recruiting "arms race" to enroll the "best and brightest" students.

In contrast to this characterization, in his examination of selective liberal arts colleges, Breneman (1994) describes how institutions that could otherwise maximize revenues by admitting only those capable of paying undiscounted tuition rates, instead elected to discount tuition to attract students of diverse backgrounds and abilities. SEM practitioners would argue that tuition discounting and financial aid are tools used not only to recruit high profile students, but also to realize socioeconomic, gender and ethnic diversity in the student body, and that the tuition revenue gains from the practice of SEM facilitate increased levels of institutional financial aid to traditionally underrepresented groups (Bontrager 2004). Even the use of merit aid to drive net revenue-producing enrollments can advance goals of affordability and access. Applying SEM principles in public institution settings frequently results in using merit aid to recruit nonresident students who pay significantly more than their own costs of education, in effect supplementing or supplanting subsidies (and making possible lower tuition rates, and thus diminished financial need) for resident students (Bontrager 2008).

As Table 1.2 illustrates, untangling the tuition pricing implications of increased operating expenses in environments of increasing enrollments and decreasing subsidies is not a simple matter. In contrast to a commercial environment where increasing volume might be expected to result in lower per-unit costs, in labor-intensive colleges and universities increased numbers of students without corresponding increases in external subsidies give rise to escalating per-student costs. Lower prices would be realized under the historical funding model whereby external subsidies provided directly to institutions increased with enrollments and program offerings. On the revenue side, SEM strategies establish differential pricing achieved in part through the use of financial aid (or "discount," or "leveraging") strategies both to achieve lower prices for students who otherwise cannot afford to attend and higher prices for students willing and able to pay. SEM strategies address the tuition rate compounding of the Baumol Effect by selectively increasing the *average* tuition price. At its highest level, Winston's higher education economic model compares average price to average cost and finds price to be lower, on average, by the amount of the average subsidy. Yet some students pay more than the average price and even more than the average cost of their educations. SEM and the blending of financial aid, scholarship and recruitment strategies is specifically concerned with how a broad range of institutional goals as described by Bontrager can be simultaneously addressed.

On the cost side, the extent to which revenue-generating infrastructure in the forms of personnel, marketing, consulting and other costs add to the overall cost base can be readily identified. The extent to which that infrastructure provides critical support to the public mission of colleges and universities (e.g., through the equitable distribution of opportunity via tuition discounting) is more difficult to establish. Comparisons of need- and merit-based aid trends beyond the student level do not readily capture the net revenue consequences of discounting the highest tuition prices paid by students by large percentages or amounts, for example. At many public institutions the resident tuition price does not cover average costs while the nonresident price is significantly higher than the average cost. Providing merit aid to nonresident students still yields net revenue that serves to subsidize resident students. The financial reporting structures of colleges and universities do not readily facilitate combining this student level analysis with cost accounting for the overhead related to the administration of SEM. Furthermore, to the extent SEM plays a role in equitably distributing the scarce commodity of postsecondary educational opportunity among prospective students, the costs of enrollment management may serve public institutional missions beyond the generation of net revenues and recruitment of qualified students. As the preceding discussion shows, increasing enrollments without increasing subsidies—a circumstance many public higher education institutions assume will be the "new normal" for years to come—creates substantial budgetary pressures on current programs and services.

What is clear is that there are limited revenue sources available to fund such costs. If the cost is not borne by public subsidies, or private philanthropy, or other income streams such as indirect cost recovery for research or auxiliary enterprise sales and services, the funds required to balance the budget will come from tuition charges. To the extent that revenue-generating infrastructure actually succeeds in generating new revenues, as opposed to consuming revenues that could be allocated to new programs or other mission-critical activities, diverting resources away from that infrastructure might erode revenues. The challenge for SEM practitioners is to demonstrate in both general and specific manners how their activities effectively support and enhance their institutions' missions in comparison to alternative uses for funds invested in SEM-related activities, including financial aid.

7

RUNNING AHEAD: METRICS

Darin Wohlgemuth
Director of Research for Enrollment and Director of Budget Research & Analysis
Iowa State University

Jonathan Compton
Senior Research Analyst, Office of the Registrar
Iowa State University

Ann Gansemer-Topf
Assistant Professor in Educational Leadership and Policy Studies,
School of Education
Iowa State University

CHAPTER 7

INTRODUCTION

The summer vacation trip was about to begin. The mini-van was packed with a map and set of directions ready for the long drive. There was anticipation and excitement as everyone jumped into the vehicle. Less than an hour into the trip the enthusiasm faded, marked by the familiar question . . . "Are we there yet?"

Enrollment management resembles a long road trip. Ambitious recruitment and retention goals are set, policies and personnel are aligned to meet the goals, and a new admissions cycle begins. A month or two into the cycle, colleagues begin asking, "How are the numbers?" "Will we meet the goal again?"

One solution to road trip boredom is to track milestones: as each is passed, it can be checked off the list. GPS devices, maps, and calculating miles per hour based on speed can inform progress. Monitoring progress towards enrollment goals is more complex, but enrollment managers can use a variety of tools and techniques to track progress, warn of potential hazards, and identify milestones yet to be attained.

Using Metrics in Strategic Enrollment Management

Simply stated, a metric is a quantitative measurement. A metric can be used to measure performance, progress toward a goal or the quality of a certain process or operation. The use of metrics in enrollment management is not new; metrics such as enrollment numbers, tuition revenue, retention, and graduation rates are commonly used and understood (Bontrager 2004a). Institutions provide metrics for federal reporting purposes, and parents, students, legislatures, and governing boards review these metrics as indications of institutional quality. These types of metrics are used primarily to measure performance: Was the university successful in meeting its enrollment goals? How does a college's graduation rate compare to that of another college?

In addition to using metrics as performance measures, metrics can be used for purposes of planning and management (Brinkman and McIntyre 1997). Enrollment management metrics often use the student as the unit of measurement. As Bean (1990) stated, "Enrollment management has a particular concern for the size and character of the student body, and therefore, part of the vision for enrollment management needs to include students as benchmarks of strategic success" (42). Will we meet our new student enrollment goal based on the number of students in our applicant pool? How many prospective student inquiries are needed to reach our enrollment targets for specific majors? Are there specific segments of the population (i.e., first generation, low income, etc.) that behave differently than others?

This chapter will focus on developing metrics for strategic enrollment management (SEM). In his article describing SEM, Bontrager (2004a) grouped SEM metrics into four categories: recruitment metrics, marketing and communication metrics, retention metrics, and financial metrics. This chapter will not cover all these areas, but will provide examples detailing the process of developing metrics: how metrics can be used in predicting and planning new and continuing student enrollment, and how metrics can be used for strategic planning—especially for monitoring such things as academic progress, student persistence and graduation rates. The case studies and examples have been developed to provide a context for the larger discussions on metrics. The chapter will close with suggestions on how institutions can align personnel and resources in ways that support the development and use of metrics. Through case studies, examples, and discussion, the goal of this chapter is to assist those interested in SEM gain a clearer understanding of the use, applicability, and importance of metrics.

USING METRICS FOR PLANNING AND PREDICTING NEW & CONTINUING ENROLLMENT

Case Study University

Case Study University (CSU) is a regional, public institution with an average incoming freshman class of 3,000 students. CSU's enrollment primarily consists of students from within a 200 mile radius of campus. The number of high school graduates in that area is projected to decline over the next five years, which will likely impact CSU's enrollment. Three years ago CSU began expanding its recruitment efforts to other geographic areas in anticipation of the decline in its key market. The efforts have resulted in increased enrollment from these areas. CSU has published "admissions reports" (counts of applicants, offers, deposits) the first of each month for several years.

As enrollment goals are developed for the upcoming year, three questions need to be addressed:

- How many inquiries, applicants, and admitted students are needed to reach the enrollment goal of 3,000?
- Based on the current number of prospective students and past trends, what will be next year's new student enrollment?
- What metrics should be developed to monitor the progress toward this goal?

Using Metrics for Recruitment Planning

Strategic enrollment managers frequently utilize the admissions funnel as a way to visualize and describe the admissions cycle. The admissions funnel describes the various stages students pass through in an institution's admissions process. It begins with a large pool of prospects and then narrows down to inquiries, applicants, offers of admission from the institution, deposits from students to signify enrollment, and finally, enrollment. "The funnel captures the rates of movement of prospective students toward enrollment at key intervals, such as the percentage of admitted students who enroll" (Noel-Levitz 2009, 3). However, as Bontrager (2004b) points out: "In reality, recruiting and retaining students is more like climbing a mountain. It requires careful planning, effective execution, and technical skill" (10). Metrics can be used to assess the various stages of the admissions process.

For this chapter the following terms are used to describe the stages of the recruitment cycle:
- Prospects – Students who will be invited to apply to the institution
- Inquiries – Prospective students who contact the institution
- Applicants – Prospective students who submit an application
- Offers – Prospective students who are offered admission
- Deposits – Prospective students who have paid their enrollment deposit
- Enrolled – Students who are counted as enrolled on the official census date

Enrollment managers need to examine the recruitment cycle from both sides – looking at the number of prospects needed in order to enroll a certain number of students, and projecting enrollment based on a certain number of prospects. In planning the recruiting cycle, with the enrollment targets in hand, they can determine the number of applicants (or any other stage in the recruitment cycle) required at any specific point in time within the recruitment cycle. This method provides planning metrics as benchmarks to know how many prospective students are required at each stage to achieve the enrollment goals. Conversely, during the recruiting cycle, using the number of applications received to date compared to this point last year is used to predict enrollment this year. In either case, the metrics use the past to predict the future. Specifically, the metric assumes that the ratio of enrollment to applications (or any stage of the recruitment process) in the future entering class will be comparable to the same ratio at the same point in the recruiting cycle of one or more previous years, as shown in Equation 1.

Equation 1: $\dfrac{Enr_i}{X_{i,j}} = \dfrac{Enr_{i-1}}{X_{i-1,j}}$

where

Enr_i = Enrollment in Year i

X = count of Inquiries, Applicants, Offers, Deposits

i = year

j = month within cycle

So $X_{i,j}$ defines the count of prospective students at any stage of the recruitment process for entering year i and at a particular point in time within the cycle, j. This can be for a particular sub-group of students or the entire entering class as required by the need of the institution and enrollment manager, and after careful analysis of the behavior of sub-groups as discussed later in this chapter.

Planning for New Enrollment

In the case study of CSU, "admissions reports" (counts of applicants, offers, deposits) were published at the first of each month for several years. Internal data also capture the number of inquiries each month. Table 1 shows the admissions counts for two groups of students for the past two years (completed) and the current year (incomplete) at selected points in time within the recruitment cycle. These counts are metrics in and of themselves when the past is compared to the current recruiting cycle. While this example is for an institution that has a rolling review process, the method of computing these metrics apply generally to any admissions processes, assuming the recruitment and admissions processes are relatively consistent from year to year.

Working toward the enrollment target of 3,000 new students, new enrollment is broken down into sub-groups, with two groups of interest here: 2,400 Group 1 students and 180 Group 2 students in addition to other groups. These goals were established after careful review of the demographics, recruiting pipeline and the institution's strategic plan. Before the class is recruited or begins to apply, the enrollment manager can determine how many inquiries, applicants, offers, and deposits are required each month to meet the goals, using the historical behavior of each group. Equation 2 shows the number of year i applications (one possible X)

Table 1: Selected Monthly Admissions Reports for Group 1 & Group 2.

GROUP 1							
	Aug.	Nov.	Jan.	Mar.	May	July	Census
2 Years Back (Fall 2010)							
Inquiries	8,971	10,445	11,961	12,035	12,244	12,276	12,223
Applications	147	1,362	2,790	3,644	3,919	3,980	3,981
Offers	13	846	2,259	3,303	3,625	3,692	3,695
Deposits	2	301	905	1,722	2,286	2,371	2,340
Enrolled							2,297
1 Year Back (Fall 2011)							
Inquiries	9,502	10,644	12,190	12,313	12,464	12,282	12,230
Applications	120	1,688	2,679	3,789	4,084	4,027	4,039
Offers	69	1,282	2,385	3,327	3,764	3,713	3,730
Deposits	22	452	1,059	1,706	2,353	2,366	2,369
Enrolled							2,373
Current Recruiting Class (Fall 2012)							
Inquiries	9.820	10,696	11,866				
Applications	209	1,937	2,980				
Offers	127	1,228	2,499				
Deposits	42	477	988				

GROUP 2							
	Aug.	Nov.	Jan.	Mar.	May	July	Census
2 Years Back (Fall 2010)							
Inquiries	3,371	4,171	6,646	6,710	6,756	6,786	6,779
Applications	8	163	450	614	653	664	666
Offers	1	64	353	556	591	607	608
Deposits	0	11	48	105	148	164	161
Enrolled							149
1 Year Back (Fall 2011)							
Inquiries	2,899	5,632	6,027	6,101	6,121	6,123	6,127
Applications	17	229	470	739	776	789	790
Offers	6	138	374	578	688	706	707
Deposits	3	23	47	95	131	146	145
Enrolled							137
Current Recruiting Class (Fall 2012)							
Inquiries	2,878	6,081	6,656				
Applications	23	322	667				
Offers	14	167	492				
Deposits	1	24	68				

required in each month j, based on the most recent enrollment cycle (i-1) as of each month j. Applications can be substituted for any other stage in the recruitment cycle, X.

Equation 2: $\quad X_{i,j} = \text{Target\_Enr}_i * \left(\dfrac{X_{i-1,j}}{Enr_{i-1}} \right)$

Alternatively, in some years the current recruiting cycle is more appropriately benchmarked by the recruiting cycle of 2 years ago (i-2), so that the count of any stage of the recruitment process (X) required to meet the enrollment target is shown in Equation 3.

Equation 3: $\quad X_{i,j} = \text{Target\_Enr}_i * \left(\dfrac{X_{i-2,j}}{Enr_{i-2}} \right)$

Computing an average or weighted average of the past several years may be helpful since a multi-year average tends to smooth out year-specific differences and capture the underlying trend.

Equation 4: $\quad X_{i,j} = \text{Target\_Enr}_i * \left[\dfrac{w_1 \left(\dfrac{X_{i-1,j}}{Enr_{i-1}} \right) + w_2 \left(\dfrac{X_{i-2,j}}{Enr_{i-2}} \right) + w_3 \left(\dfrac{X_{i-3,j}}{Enr_{i-3}} \right)}{(w_1 + w_2 + w_3)} \right]$

Determining the best weights (w_1, w_2, w_3) can be done by testing various weights with complete data (such as predicting last year with the three prior years) to see what set of weights comes closest to predicting the actual $X_{i-1,j}$. It is not necessary that each sub-group or month within the cycle use the same weighting scheme. Table 2 illustrates different weights and terms that describe those weights. In practice, the authors tend to start with a (2, 1, 1) weighted average that weights the most recent cycle twice as much as the previous two for each stage and point in time. These weights can serve as a baseline and the "reasonableness" discussion can examine alternative weighting schemes as appropriate.

Table 2: Weights for various weight average calculations

Description	w_1	w_2	w_3
Three-year average (no weights)	1	1	1
Weight most recent year twice as much as the last two	2	1	1
Weight the 2nd year twice as much as the other two	1	2	1
Two-year average	1	1	0
Two-year weighted average (twice most recent)	2	1	0

Using CSU's data provided in Table 1 for the two previous years, the planning enrollment metrics ("the math") for the current recruiting cycle can be computed for each stage and month of the recruitment process, shown in Table 3. Recall that the Group 2 enrollment target is 180 students (an increase from 137 the previous year and 149 two years prior). The calculations below use a two-year weighted average (2, 1, 0):

Table 3: Required count of Group 2 students to achieve enrollment target = 180 at each stage and month of the recruitment cycle — "The Math". Using a two-year weighted average for Group 2 metrics.

	Aug.	Nov.	Jan.	Mar.	May	July	Census
Inquiries	3,897	6,613	7,955	8,046	8,082	8,096	8,097
Applications	18	266	593	895	943	958	960
Offers	6	147	470	730	841	863	864
Deposits	3	25	60	125	174	194	192

Knowing the market for Group 2 high school students, the enrollment manager realizes that increasing the inquiry pool by 1,500 to 2,000 is not feasible.[1] Resources and additional recruiting efforts will focus on increasing the number of similarly qualified Group 2 applicants and maintain the offer and yield rates with the larger pool of applicants. The metrics provided to the recruiting staff, shown in Table 4, are the maximum number of inquiries from the last two years combined with the two-year weighted average number of applicants, offers, and deposits.

Table 4: Required count of Group 2 students to achieve enrollment target = 180 at each stage and month of the recruitment cycle for recruitment planning.

	Aug.	Nov.	Jan.	Mar.	May	July	Census
Inquiries	3,371	5,632	6,646	6,710	6,756	6,786	6,779
Applications	18	266	593	895	943	958	960
Offers	6	147	470	730	841	863	864
Deposits	3	25	60	125	174	194	192

---

1. The discussion of market share later in this chapter will provide additional understanding of how a particular sub-group of students within a geographic region can be examined to make such a decision.

Because the goal is to increase enrollment by increasing the number of applicants, it will be important to carefully watch the "offer rate = offers / applicants," another metric discussed later in this chapter. The overall goal of increased enrollment will not be accomplished if the growth in applicants is from students who are less likely to be admitted.

As the recruitment process moves forward in time, the recruiting staff shifts focus to metrics further into the process as well (from Inquiries to Applicants to Offers to Deposits). The highlighted cells illustrate when the focus would shift to the next stage. Early in the recruiting cycle the most meaningful measure of Group 2 students is the number of inquiries. Once applications begin arriving in a sufficient number (November in the above table) the recruiters will watch both the number of inquiries and the number of applications received, but not offers. Generally, trying to generate more inquiries late in the recruitment cycle will have little impact on increasing enrollment, so it is important to make sure there are enough students at each stage of the sequence.

Predicting New Enrollment

Once the recruitment cycle is under way, comparing the actual counts of prospects to the metrics above will let the enrollment manager know if their campus is on track to meet the goal. However, it is also possible, using the same historical data and the current counts, to forecast enrollment. It may make more intuitive sense in some contexts to report the size of the incoming class based on the applications in hand to-date and relative to past trends. In this situation, a basic forecast of enrollment this year requires three pieces of data: The number of applications received by a particular month, j, for the current year and the previous year, as well as census enrollment for the previous year, as shown in Equation 5.

$$\text{Equation 5:} \quad Pred\_Enr_i \; = \; X_{i,j} \; * \; \left(\frac{Enr_{i-1}}{X_{i-1,j}} \right)$$

As before, the single year forecast can be based on data from any particular year (i-1, i-2, etc). Alternatively, it may be helpful to use the two or three most recent years simultaneously to forecast enrollment using an average and weighted average of several years of history. To compute an average over the last three years, set all weights equal to 1. A weighted average might give more significance to the most recent year with 2 and the other two with a 1, as shown in Table 2. Since the recruitment process is continually changing both internally and externally, no single weighting scheme will be perfect. Building flexibility into the process, by having the weights appear as parameters in a spreadsheet that can be easily changed, allows several weighting scenarios to be tested.

Equation 6: $$Pred\_Enr_i = X_{i,j} * \frac{\left[w_1 \left(\frac{Enr_{i-1}}{X_{i-1,j}} \right) + w_2 \left(\frac{Enr_{i-2}}{X_{i-2,j}} \right) + w_3 \left(\frac{Enr_{i-3}}{X_{i-3,j}} \right) \right]}{(w_1 + w_2 + w_3)}$$

Any stage of the recruitment cycle and any point in time within the cycle can be used to forecast enrollment; however, if the counts are too small, the enrollment forecasts will be very unreliable. Earlier in the recruitment cycle, especially before applications are processed, the number of inquiries is used. In March, April and May, leading up to the national candidates' reply date, is often a point when the number of deposits serves as the best measure of predicted enrollment of new direct-from-high-school students. However, transfer students typically have a shorter recruitment cycle, as many often apply later than new direct-from-high-school students —in April through July for an August start. Comparing the actual enrollment from last year with the forecasted enrollment at various points in time within the previous recruiting cycle will show when the forecast is meaningful.

Using the data for August in Table 1, the forecasted Group 1 enrollment using a two-year weighted average (2, 1, 0) is: 2,473 using inquiries; 3,844 using applicants as of August; 10,392 using offers; and 19,099 using August deposits. Therefore, at this point in the recruitment cycle the inquiry and applicant numbers will provide better data on which to forecast enrollment.

It is also important to decide if enrollment forecasts will be made on the entire applicant pool or if forecasts should be made on sub-groups and then added up. Possible sub-groups to consider are:

- New direct from high school/new transfers
- Resident/nonresident (for public institutions)
- Local/regional/out of state
- Major feeder high schools or community colleges
- Minority/majority/specific ethnic groups
- Academic ability groups
- Pell eligible or expected family contribution (EFC) ranges
- Gender
- Choice of college (within the institution) or major
- Type of first contact with institution
- New direct from high school students with college credit

A sub-group should be considered when: there are significant behavioral differences in the recruitment process (e.g., yield of local students is 75%, while yield of regional students is 40%

and out-of-state students is 20%); there are differences in retention or time to degree; or there is interest in a particular sub-population of students (e.g. the strategic plan includes increasing enrollment of Group 2 students).

Behavioral differences can be identified by comparing several metrics. There are differences in the timing of students moving through the recruitment cycle. This can be measured by the cumulative percentage of applications (or other stages) received by a given point in time within the recruitment cycle. Using Table 1 and the data from "1 Year Back" (Fall 2011), it is observed that Group 1 had 78% of the inquiries in-house by August (9,502 of the 12,230), while Group 2 only had 47% (2,899 of the 6,127) of the total inquiries in. Similarly, in November, 42% (1,688 of the 4,039) of Group 1 applicants had applied, while 29% (229 of the 790) of Group 2 students.

Yield is a widely used and important metric to measure the effectiveness of the later stages of the recruiting cycle. Additionally, three other conversion measures can benchmark effectiveness of other stages of the recruitment process and are helpful in understanding differences across sub-groups.

- Yield = Enroll/Offers
- Application Rate = Applications/Inquiries
- Offer Rate = Offers/Applications
- Deposit Rate = Deposit/Offers

Table 5 shows conversion rates for Group 1 and Group 2 students in the "1 Year Back" (Fall 2011) recruitment cycle. Splitting out Group 1 and Group 2 allows the significant differences in the final application rate (33% vs. 13%) and final deposit rate (64% vs. 21%) to be considered separately.[2] Allowing for the differences in these rates across groups when building the enrollment forecasts or planning metrics are particularly important when there are focused efforts to increase the pipeline and/or enrollment of specific groups, such as Group 2.

While it may seem optimal to divide the population into several sub-groups, keep in mind that *projecting several small groups will generally increase the error of the overall projection.* There is a delicate balance of accounting for differences in behavior of the sub-groups and having sub-groups that are so small the projections become too volatile. Early in the recruiting cycle, fewer groups may be used and these sub-groups split later in the cycle when the counts of students are larger.

---

2. "Census" percentages are highlighted, however, the differences go back through the recruitment process.

Table 5: Conversion Rates for Group 1 and Group 2 students

1 Year Back (Fall 2011)	Group 1						
Application rate	1%	16%	22%	31%	33%	33%	33%
Offer rate	58%	76%	89%	88%	92%	92%	92%
Deposit rate	32%	35%	44%	51%	63%	64%	64%
Yield							64%

1 Year Back (Fall 2011)	Group 2						
Application rate	1%	4%	8%	12%	13%	13%	13%
Offer rate	35%	60%	80%	78%	89%	89%	89%
Deposit rate	50%	17%	13%	16%	19%	21%	21%
Yield							19%

Statistical models that predict the probability of an individual enrolling based on individual characteristics are common now, using approaches such as Probit or Logistic regression models (Wohlgemuth 1997; DesJardins et al 2006).[3] New data mining techniques and propensity scoring matching models also provide likelihood or probabilities of enrolling (Guo and Fraser 2010). If the institution knows the probability of enrolling for each inquiry, offer, or deposited student, then an additional metric to watch is the expected enrollment or sum of individual probabilities of enrolling within a group. It would be important to update the individual's enrollment probability as prospective students progress through each stage in the recruitment process. For example, two students may have a 15% probability of enrolling as an inquiry, but one may have a 40% probability of enrolling as an applicant and the other may only have a 20% chance of enrolling as an applicant.

Moving to the next stage in the recruitment process is a significant indicator of interest in the institution. Using an inquiry model or probability for a student offered admission does not take into consideration the significant signal of interest the student made in applying. It is also true that with each subsequent stage, the information available is more detailed and usually more accurate (e.g. consider the wealth of individual and family information contained in the FAFSA). Thus, it is important to build separate models for each stage of the recruitment process to take full advantage of the additional information.

---

3. Partnerships with faculty in departments such as Economics, Statistics, Psychology, or Higher Education Research and Evaluation may be a way to build internal models of the probability of enrolling.

Table 6: College Transition Matrix, Fall Census Year 1 to Fall Census Year 2

	YEAR 2 College A				College B			
	Fr.	Soph.	Jr.	Sr.	Fr.	Soph.	Jr.	Sr.
Coll A								
Fr.	76	415	49	1	1			
Soph.		50	439	48				
Jr.			76	573			1	
Sr.				266				
Coll B								
Fr.	1	6			38	242	7	1
Soph.			2			47	280	19
Jr.				1			23	295
Sr.								198
Coll C								
Fr.	18	26	2		4	5	1	
Soph.		8	17			1	1	
Jr.			2	2				
Sr.				3				1
Total	102	536	604	912	50	312	316	517

(Row group label: YEAR 1)

Predicting Continuing Enrollment

Strategic enrollment management emphasizes total enrollment and includes the area of retention (Bontrager 2004a). As a result, enrollment managers are asked to provide predictions for total enrollment to compute tuition revenue and course demand. Well-established metrics that are used in this context include total enrollment, retention rates, continuation rates, and graduation rates.

The next step, given the previous discussion of new student enrollment projections, is to predict continuing student enrollment based on previous year's data. This section describes a model of developing total enrollment forecasts that utilizes components that can also serve as metrics themselves. The formula used for predicting new students can be applied to continuing students, but now includes the complexity of dealing with the movement of students between departments/majors, or colleges, out of the institution, or on to graduation.

YEAR 2

	College C				Grad	Left CSU	Total
	Fr.	Soph.	Jr.	Sr.			
Coll A							
Fr.		4				86	632
Soph.			2			48	587
Jr.			1	1	22	47	721
Sr.					618	36	920
Coll B							
Fr.	4	15				55	369
Soph.			2			30	380
Jr.					9	7	335
Sr.				1	284	16	499
Coll C							
Fr.	191	791	103	4		149	1,294
Soph.		106	709	63		62	967
Jr.			128	760	4	44	940
Sr.				580	790	33	1,407
Total	204	951	957	1,418	2,750	1,764	11,393

(YEAR 1 — vertical label along left side)

The projection of continuing student enrollment uses the "College Transition Matrix." This counts enrollment by combining multiple years of data to track students from one year to the next. The rows of the matrix show the college and classification (freshman, sophomore, junior, and senior by accumulated credit hours) of students in the base year, while the columns show the status of the students in the subsequent year. Table 6 shows a sample college transition matrix for CSU, which has three academic colleges.

Multiple years of census enrollment data and data on graduating students can be combined using the "VLOOKUP" function in Excel or using analytical software tools such as Stata, SPSS, or SAS. The dataset contains a single row per student enrolled in each base year. Columns or variables include both the base year and "next year" characteristics of each student (such as the college and major, classification, residency status, or other important student group classifications). The status of the next year would be either enrolled, graduated, or not enrolled and would be another column in the dataset. Once the data are compiled, the matrix can be created using simple pivot tables in Excel.

Caution when selecting attributes to include in the matrix is once again important so that the size of the college transition matrix does not become too large. For example, if there are five colleges and four different classifications, the matrix is 20 rows x 22 columns (adding additional columns for graduating and not returning)—a total of 440 cells. The number of cells grows to 1,680 when residency (in-state or out-of-state) is added (40 x 42). Each additional variable increases the likelihood of error in the model.

College transition matrices for the three most recent years are created. Next, the counts are turned into percentages that show the flow of students from one year to the next: 76 of the 632 (12%) freshmen in College A remained as freshmen in College A, 65.6% (415 out of 632) of the freshmen in College A in the base year were classified as sophomores in College A. Creating the row percentages for each of the three previous fall-to-fall transitions allows a three year weighted average college transition matrix to be computed.

Computing metrics (in this case enrollment forecasts by college and classification) using the college transition matrix three year weighted average percentages is simply applying the cell percentage to the observed base-year row totals from the most recent years. For example, if prior data shows 65.6% of the College A freshmen became College A sophomores, and there were 690 College A freshmen in the current fall census, then the expected number of College A freshmen that will become sophomores is 453 = 65.6% * 690. Expected enrollment of continuing students by college and classification is the sum of the columns.

Since adding variables to the model can increase the likelihood of error, consider both a forest and trees approach. The "forest" looks only at broad categories; for example, predicted enrollment by residency (in-state vs. out-of-state) and year in school without considering college. Then the "trees" looks at more detailed college-specific projections that can be tempered up or down to match the "forest" view.

The versatility of this projection procedure can be applied to many different circumstances. A projection of course demand could be done by looking course enrollments for the past two or three years broken down by the students' year in school and whether they are new or continuing. For example, if there are 3,000 new freshmen this year, and the weighted average of the past three years shows that 80% of new freshmen take English 101, the course demand for English 101 from new freshmen can be calculated with reasonable accuracy to be about 2,400. Similar ratios would be needed for the continuing students enrolled in English 101, perhaps by year in school, in order to compute the total demand for the course. This process, of course, works best for high-demand courses and can fluctuate depending on changes in courses, program requirements, and majors students enroll in. For example, an increase in the number of Chemical Engineering majors will increase the demand for advanced chemistry courses more than a comparable increase in English majors. It is especially useful in course planning when enrollment is growing or shrinking because course demand will vary from past experience.

Another way to predict new and continuing student enrollment using the above methods is to predict financial aid expenditures within the recruitment cycle. Institutions routinely award more dollars in financial aid than are available because some proportion of those students will not enroll. The dollars awarded to particular sub-groups at various points in time this year and in past financial aid cycles, compared against the actual aid distributed at the end of the academic year, is used to forecast how much aid will be distributed at the end of the current academic year. Additionally, developing separate financial aid forecasts based on admission status (offers and deposits separately) at each point in time will improve the accuracy of the metrics used to forecast financial aid expenditures. When multi-year financial aid commitments are made to new students, the future commitments to continuing students can be estimated using the continuation data, similar to the college transition matrix, for each award.

For instance, suppose a four-year award is contingent upon maintaining a certain grade point average. The forecast of the award expenditures this year can be made using the number of current students and the ratio of students that kept the award from Year 1 to Year 2 in the past. Similarly, the continuation rates for Year 2 to Year 3 and Year 3 to Year 4 of the award will help forecast the expenditures on this aid program. Sub-groups within financial aid forecasts can include data from the FAFSA or the institution's financial aid application when it is available (such as Pell eligible, EFC groups, etc.) (Compton et al. 2010).

It is important to remember that these projections assume that behavior is consistent from year to year. Rarely is this the case. There are usually changes that an institution makes, such as a new marketing campaign, new outreach events, changes in tuition or academic programs. There are also local, regional, national, and global changes in the economy and recruiting environment that influence the enrollment and persistence decisions of students and families. Systematically adjusting for the various factors that change each year is beyond the scope of this chapter. In practice, it may not be feasible to predict how students will respond to a new campaign or a change in the national economy. As mentioned previously, the authors generally start with "the math" based on a three-year weighted average and then gather a team of knowledgeable and experienced enrollment and financial aid staff for a "reasonableness" discussion. This team may make adjustments to "the math" that account for the observed changes that influence the recruiting process, yield of financial aid, and enrollment decisions year to year.

USING METRICS IN THE STRATEGIC PLANNING PROCESS

In addition to being useful for planning enrollment, metrics are also used to measure progress toward long-term goals, such as the institution's strategic plan. Let's return to CSU.

During CSU's strategic planning process, two enrollment goals surfaced. The first was to increase the enrollment of Group 2 students by 10%. The second was to increase the four-year graduation rate by 5%.

To provide input into the strategic planning process on the first issue, CSU enrollment researchers began with a study of the potential market share of Group 2 students. The metric "market share" is the ratio of the number of students in a group that enrolled relative to the overall population of students. When computing the market share, enrollment managers need to take time to accurately define the population of students.

Table 7: Market Share of Groups A and B

	Total	Not Eligible	Trio Eligible
Enrolled	2,200	2,000	200
HS Grad	30,000	26,500	3,500
Market Share	7.3%	7.5%	5.7%
ACT Tested	18,000	16,560	1,440
Market Share	12.2%	12.1%	13.9%
Admissible	11,000	10,340	660
Market Share	20.0%	19.3%	30.3%

Suppose CSU enrolled 2,200 students from their local region and that the population can be split into distinct groups based on student characteristics of 2,000 Group 1 and 200 Group 2 students, shown in Table 7. Some specific examples include the student's eligibility for one or more of the Federal TRIO programs which broadly defined are: first-generation students (neither parent has a 4-year college degree), from low-income families[4], or under represented ethnic minorities. Other groups might be academic ability-based or composed of nationally recognized students, such as national merit scholars. Independent of the characteristics used to form the groups, the small number of enrolled Group 2 students is the reason behind the interest of the strategic planning committee.

Using data from the State Department of Education on high school graduates by district, CSU researchers were able to determine that the number of last year's high school graduates from the region was 30,000. Additional data provides an approximation of student characteris-

---

4. The authors have not found a well-accepted definition of "low-income." Common measures include Pell Eligible or an income that is one to two times the federal poverty level for a given family size.

tics. The results split the graduating class into approximately 26,500 students in Group 1 and 3,500 in Group 2. As shown in Table 7, CSU's market share of the high school graduates was 7.5% for Group 1 and 5.7% in Group 2.

Digging deeper into the data, using tools such as ACT's Enrollment Information Services (EIS) or the College Board's Enrollment Planning Service (EPS), the researchers were able to determine that 18,000 local students took the ACT test, which is a factor in the admissions decision at CSU and other schools within the state. Both of these tools provide detailed information on the population of test takers, so that an approximate split by Group 1 and 2 can be determined (16,460 and 1,440, respectively). Notice that 62% of Group 1 high school graduates took the ACT test (16,560/26,500) and only 41% of Group 2 high school graduates (1,440 / 3,500). Because of the differences in the students' choice to take the exam, CSU's market share of Group 2 that are seeking to enter a college like CSU (signaled by taking the ACT or SAT) is modestly higher for Group 2 students (13.9% for Group 2 vs. 12.1% for Group 1).

Finally, using the EIS or EPS tools, the researchers entered minimum academic credentials to be offered admission and documented that "the population" of admissible students was reduced to 11,000 (split 10,340 and 660). Similar to above, 62% of the Group 1 students that took the test would meet minimum academic standards (10,340/16,560) compared to 46% of Group 2 students (660/1,440). The market share of Group 2 students who took the test and meet minimum standards for admission is 30.3% compared to 19.3% for Group 1 students. Thus, the market share of Group 2 students who are admissible to CSU is 11 percent higher than Group 1 students.

This data was used to shift the focus of the strategic plan away from simply growing enrollment of Group 2 students to a much larger and longer term vision of increasing the pipeline of Group 2 students in the local area. This can be accomplished by participating in discussions with policy makers and practitioners at secondary schools as well as conducting research that seeks to explain the differences in college going behavior of the two groups.

Operational Metrics Case Study: Academic Progress

Another goal of the CSU strategic plan was to raise the four-year graduation rate from 65% to 70%. The strategic planning committee recommended improving the one-year retention rates as the means of improving the graduation rate. Table 8 below shows the actual retention and four-year graduation rates for CSU. In this year there were 1,000 students in this cohort: 85% were retained one year and 65% graduated within four years. In order to determine what would need to be done to improve the four-year graduation rate by 5%, the CSU enrollment researchers calculated the year to year "Continuing Ratio." This is the percent of students retained from one year to the next. For example the continuing ratio for two-year retention is 800/850 (as opposed to the retention rate which is 800/1,000).

Table 8. Retention and Four-Year Graduation Rates at CSU

	Cohort	1-Year Retention	2-Year Retention	3-Year Retention	4-Year Graduation
Number of Students	1000	850	800	775	650
Cohort Retention Rates		85.0%	80.0%	77.5%	65.0%
Continuing Ratio		85.0%	94.1%	96.9%	83.9%

The one year continuation ratio makes it possible to begin doing calculations and simulations to determine the change in retention rates needed to get to the desired four-year graduation rate. In this case, an increase of 6.5% is needed in the one year retention rate in order to achieve a 70% four-year graduation rate (Table 9). This is assuming, of course, that the students that have been retained in the first year continue to be retained through to graduation at the same rate as the current cohort. In helping the committee understand a 6.5% increase in the one-year retention rate, it was pointed out that CSU initially lost 150 students in the first year (1,000 - 850 = 150). In addition, 6.5% of 1,000 is 65, so CSU must keep 43% of those who initially left (65 / 150). It will take a significant campus wide effort to keep nearly half of the students that usually do not return for their second year at CSU. Thinking of changes in retention in terms of the percent of initial leavers who have to be retained is a useful exercise to help set realistic strategic goals for retention and graduation and to understand the resources required to accomplish those goals.

Table 9: Retention Rates Needed to Achieve a 70% Graduation Rate

	Cohort	1-Year	2-Year	3-Year	4-Year
Number of Students	1000	915	861	834	700
Cohort Retention Rates		91.5%	86.1%	83.4%	70.0%
Continuing Ratio		91.5%	94.1%	96.9%	83.9%

Cohort retention and graduation rates metrics are common and the standard for federal reporting and institutional accountability. An alternative metric to consider is student progress toward a degree or what could be called a "Continuation Report." This metric includes four classifications: progress, no progress, left CSU and graduated. This model, shown in Table 10, provides a more detailed look at the progress of students from year to year within an academic unit (major, department, or college) without the constraint of an entering cohort. This continuation report can be used by deans and department chairs to measure the academic progress of students who were in their academic programs last year as opposed to the traditional retention model which places students into cohorts based on their first major. The column entitled "No Progress" represents those students who were freshmen in the previous year who have not earned enough credits to be classified as sophomores after one year. The report looks at whether students progress from one classification to the next because lack of progress toward a degree is as bad as or worse than leaving the university (Kalsbeek 2008). The report also reduced competition between academic units because the focus is not on staying within an academic unit, but rather student persistence at the institution. Institutionally, the goal can be to minimize the number of students that leave CSU. The basis for the continuation report is the college transition matrix discussed earlier in the continuing enrollment forecast section of this chapter.

Table 10 : Continuation from Fall 2009 to Fall 2011 for CSU Academic Unit X

	Progress	No Progress	Left CSU	Graduated	Total
Freshman	88	16	20		124
	71%	13%	16%	0%	100%
Sophomore	115	9	28		152
	76%	6%	18%	0%	100%
Junior	143	17	30	9	199
	72%	9%	15%	5%	100%
Senior		53	17	151	221
	0%	24%	8%	68%	100%
Total	346	95	95	160	696
	50%	14%	14%	23%	100%

In addition, this model can be used to track progress of certain sub-groups of students, such as first generation, ethnic minority students, or low-income students within academic units. Reporting metrics that show the enrollment counts and shares by these student characteristics for the several years at the university as well as broken down by academic units provide a way to measure the progress of each unit toward achieving the institution's goals.

Developing and Supporting a "Metric-Centered" Organization

This chapter has primarily focused on "how" to develop enrollment management metrics. However, for institutions that are just beginning to create a "data-driven" culture, it is important to address the questions of "who", "what", "when" and "where."

Who will develop the metrics? In many instances the first hurdle in the development of metrics is to figure out who will be responsible for developing the metrics and providing the data to support the metrics. Who at your institution possesses the ability to develop and analyze metrics? Does this person have adequate time to devote to this task? In what area of the institution is this person located?

Given the increasing need and reliance on data in decision making, some institutions have created positions within the Office of Admissions, Registrar, and/or Financial Aid that are focused on analyzing data and metrics. This is perhaps the most ideal situation in that it symbolizes the importance of using data in decision making. It also allows for more seamless communication and integration between the data, research, and the individuals who utilize the data. However, if institutions do not have the ability to hire full-time staff within the enrollment management area, they may partner with other colleagues across campus. Staff members in the Office of Institutional Research or faculty or graduate students in areas such as statistics, economics, psychology, mathematics, business or education can provide expertise and assistance in developing metrics. If an institution has the luxury of having more than one individual devoted to enrollment research and metrics, access to data is even more important. This includes the IT systems that allow shared access to stored files and standardized naming conventions for data files and variables. It is also very helpful to have a common set of analytical software tools that the team agrees to use. Most importantly, it requires a shared understanding and knowledge of the various data elements and data structures.

What data is needed to create metrics? The previous discussions of metrics assume that institutions have easy access to usable data. This is not always the case. Although institutions collect a significant amount of data, it is not always easily extracted from the database or the data is captured in a way that is not easily interpreted. Not all data may be housed in the same place. Institutions may have one database for their student enrollment records, another place for transcript data, and yet another for their financial aid data. Most enrollment management decisions require information related to all three areas but one person may not have access to all of the necessary data. Alternatively, a person may have access to different data sets but the data are stored in different formats which make it difficult to combine into one larger data set. Before metrics can be developed, a significant amount of time needs to be dedicated to the basic yet critical task of gathering data and ensuring that the data is accurate and consistent across different databases. Keep in mind that all data gathering programs (or queries) must be re-run and saved on a regular schedule, such as weekly or monthly snapshots. Current and historical data need to be accessible to the individual(s) working on the metrics.

When will metrics be available? Metrics require the use of past data. Therefore, institutions that are just beginning to collect data need to recognize that it will not be possible to develop usable metrics until the following year. This is not always the ideal situation when one is interested in making decisions "now" but unfortunately there is no other substitute for time when historical records are not accessible.

Where will metrics be used? When data becomes accessible and someone is identified who can analyze the data, it is often easy to want to continue to expand the number and complexity of metrics. A simple enrollment projection metric, for example, may be expanded to include enrollment metrics by gender, by race, by race and gender, by academic major, by financial need, by academic major and financial need, etc., etc. While some metrics may be important, too many metrics will be confusing and therefore, counterproductive. Simply because you have the ability to create another metric does not mean that it is useful to do so. Keep in mind where the metrics will be used and resist the temptation to create metrics that will not be useful: Can this metric help staff in the Office of Admissions impact enrollment? Will academic affairs administrators use this metric to make decisions regarding course availability? Focusing on the questions that metrics are intended to answer will optimize the time and resources used for metrics and create useful and usable metrics.

CONCLUSION: METRICS ARE DRIVEN BY DATA

There is no shortage of metrics. By way of summary, Figure 1 shows metrics for various stages of the recruitment and enrollment process from market share to conversion rates from one stage to the next. The chart illustrates the various measures used to plan for and predict enrollment by examining cohort retention rates and year to year continuation rates, and finally the cohort graduation rate and time to degree. This chart identifies the start and end points used for each metric and enables enrollment managers to compare trends or use benchmarks at specific points within the cycle to predict the final enrollment counts.

Figure 1: Conversion Metrics

	Market Saturation (Brand Awareness)	Market Share	Response Rate	Enrollment Rate of Inquiries	Offer Rate	Deposit Rate	Yield
Population (HS Graduates)	●	●	●				
Academically Qualified Pop.		● ●	●				
Search Mailings				●	●		
Inquiries	↓ ↓		↓				
Applications		↓ ↓			●		
Offers of Admsn					↓	●	●
Deposits						↓	
Enroll		↓ ↓		↓			↓
1 Semester Retention							
1 Year Retention (2nd Semester)							
2nd Year Retention (4th Semester)							
3rd Year Retention (6th Semester)							
4th Year Retention (8th Semester)							
4-year Graduation Rate							
5th Year Retention (10th Semester)							
5-Year Graduation Rate							
6th Year Retention Rate							
6-Year Graduation Rate							

	Melt	Projecting New Enrollment	Enrollment Planning	Cohort Retention	Rate	Continuation Rate	Time to Degree
Population (HS Graduates)							
Academically Qualified Pop.							
Search Mailings		•	↑				
Inquiries		•	↑				
Applications		•	↑				
Offers of Admsn		•	↑				
Deposits	•	•	↑				
Enroll	↓	↓↓↓↓	••••	••••	•••	•	↑↑↑
1 Semester Retention							
1 Year Retention (2nd Semester)				↓		↓•	
2nd Year Retention (4th Semester)				↓		↓•	
3rd Year Retention (6th Semester)				↓		•	
4th Year Retention (8th Semester)				↓		•	
4-year Graduation Rate					↓		•
5th Year Retention (10th Semester)							
5-Year Graduation Rate					↓		•
6th Year Retention Rate							
6-Year Graduation Rate					↓		•

Note that no metric spans from recruitment stages through initial enrollment to retention or graduation. While it is true that admissions officers are asked to recruit students that will be academically successful, it is not reasonable to benchmark the one-year retention rate of students offered admission because only those that enroll have any chance of being retained one year out. Similarly for graduation, any metric beyond the initial enrollment is conditional on enrolling and must start there.

Because metrics are based on observed data, this chapter has highlighted the importance of data driven decision making in SEM. Having access to data from each unit under the enrollment management area is critical—including data from admissions, orientation, financial aid and office of the registrar. A key ingredient in any metric is data—whether it is historical data, trend data, academic quality, or current counts. You cannot determine where you are today without having some benchmark to compare against. These data points become part of the enrollment management "GPS"—they provide information on where you are, where you are going, and what else you need to do so that you reach your destination.

8

GETTING IT RIGHT: DATA AND GOOD DECISIONS

Scot Lingrell
Vice President for Student Affairs and Enrollment Management
University of West Georgia

CHAPTER 8

In some of the seminal texts of the strategic enrollment management (SEM) profession,[1] SEM practitioners have outlined the role of the enrollment manager in the organization. The enrollment manager has the unique role of being a connecting link between the "art" of collaboration among many offices and the coordination of many functions, and the "science" of data analyses resulting in prediction, projection, and decision making.

Many practitioners have written about using data in SEM. In fact, the profession of enrollment management, although certainly based on relationship development, collaboration across the institution, and implementing best practices, focuses upon how enrollment managers can make effective decisions to guide their institutions in ways that enhance or manage enrollment. Data is the key: The decision making process and determination of practices to pursue depends upon proper data and information. Data and information brings the "strategic" into SEM. Enrollment managers must make effective decisions using all available data and information to understand the political, social, demographic, economic, and environmental inputs and impacts to direct institutional enrollment programs and practices appropriately.

The successful enrollment management enterprise must be able to produce good data (or extract it from good sources), analyze it, and turn it into information that can be used to make viable decisions. Without data, enrollment managers are relegated to making decisions based on intuition, anecdote, and conjecture.

This chapter will review the importance of using data in decision-making in a SEM organization from a practical rather than theoretical standpoint. The many contexts in which the effective enrollment manager makes decisions, or influences others to make decisions, will

---

1. SEM practitioner authors include Hossler (1984), Dolance (1993), Dixon (1995), Binder & Aldrich-Langen (1995), Black (2001) and Bontrager (2004).

be discussed. Finally, the types of data and information necessary for the effective enrollment manger will be addressed, along with data acquisition and analysis skills enrollment managers need to develop and hone to provide guidance for institutional decision makers, including the effective use of analytics.

USING DATA IN ENROLLMENT MANAGEMENT DECISION MAKING

Data is everywhere. Technology in our current age has allowed us to generate and provide access to a tremendous amount of data. Such access can be a blessing and a curse for the enrollment manager. The enrollment manager's job depends on data and information, with a sound strategy on how to acquire and use the data. Otherwise, the enrollment manager can get lost in the minutiae of the data and lose the bigger picture about how it can help them, and campus leaders, to make better decisions. We should not collect data for data's sake.

Enrollment managers are constantly making decisions that guide the institution towards optimum enrollment. The decisions are both tactical and strategic, but the goal for all decisions is to produce the conditions by which the institution succeeds and meets its enrollment goals and by which students succeed. The data that is useful for enrollment managers to make decisions are varied and voluminous. It ranges from specific student profile information, to other types of local institutional data, to state, regional, national, and international data. It includes data about people, programs, systems, services, competitors, market share, financials, risk, and a myriad of other variables.

STRATEGIC DECISIONS

The most important decisions an enrollment manager makes are the strategic decisions that guide the entire organization. Strategic decisions require data that guide the enrollment manager to make projections and predictions about the future, which, in turn, give direction on what to do now to secure that future. Some examples of important data and information useful to the enrollment manager in making strategic decisions are:

- Market share, market penetration, and [awareness] information (success relative to peers and competitors)
- Census and population projection information
- Current and prospective Student Profile trend data
- Competitor information
- State graduation and college-going rates

- Potential market analysis (such as per capita income)
- National/State financial information
- Institutional data (space availability, program capacity, etc.)
- Other institutional key performance indicators

Sources from which to acquire such data can be found later in the chapter in Table 2 on page 167. Although this data and information can be used to project enrollment, these same elements are useful for many other strategic decisions. In the future we will need better data to understand and react to a great many complex scenarios. This type of data allows the enrollment manager to analyze the past, assess the current situation, project the future state, and develop tactical actions or interventions that will keep the enrollment goals on track.

OTHER DECISION MAKING AREAS

Although many Enrollment Managers would love to spend the majority of their time in the strategic realm, the reality is that most of their time is spent on other decisions. Because they also have their hands in many institutional functions, processes, and services—both within their direct authority and outside of it—enrollment managers must gather data and information to assist with many other decisions. Enrollment managers need data to make sound decisions, namely in the areas of staffing and personnel, collaborative relationships, budgeting and re-source allocation, technology, financial aid leveraging, data analysis and interpretation, strategic planning, assessment of programs and services, and others. In the future the enrollment man-ager will be even more involved in academic and service decisions.

Because of this growing responsibility, enrollment managers must have accurate data from a variety of sources and about many different areas so as to effectively manage their area. Such sources include:

- Institutional key performance indicators
- Unit level data from a student information system
- Caseload /Staffing levels
- Productivity and efficiency
- Space utilization
- Satisfaction with services
- Personnel evaluations
- National/Regional salary studies
- Budget analysis
- Utilization of services

- Return on Investment
- Operating resources/budget
- Outcomes/Assessment
- Student satisfaction
- And many, many more

THE FUTURE

The future of Enrollment Management is Data and Collaboration. Data provides information to develop collaborative relationships to solve complex institutional problems and develop appropriate services and interventions for student success. Data is going to be more important as issues and options are more complex.

Enrollment Management will rely upon gaining access to data; having the analysis skills to turn it into information; and using relationship-building and collaboration skills to disseminate it to appropriate decision makers. The Enrollment Manager's job is to be the eyes and ears of the institution, gather the proper data to explain the internal and external environment, and to then be the internal consultant for institutional leaders so they can make better decisions to lead to institutional and student success. The institution should embrace the world and learn to adapt to it.

The decisions of the future are going to be more important and difficult. Our society and our institutions are becoming more and more complex. To be competitive in the future, institutions will need to embrace and manage change—change that will come much more quickly and have much higher expectations and consequences. What data do you need to make change? How do you get access to it? Where do you store it? How do you make it available to others? How do you know it is accurate?

The future will require knowledgeable Enrollment Managers. Data is a way to that knowledge. We can certainly buy some data and knowledge—but, beyond that, the EM needs to be able to extract that which is relevant to their enterprise, and to sustain this effort. In addition, organizations, specifically EMs, that continually develop data sources to gain new knowledge will be more competitive and more agile as our society becomes more complex. They will be more successful in weathering the changes necessary, and be able to notice the conditions for change and understand the direction and necessity for change.

In higher education we have many complex systems that collect and generate data: the institutions that use it to understand their work, their students, and changing dynamics will be far ahead in the future.

Many institutions only use the data for reporting purposes. Institutions use their systems to gather the information to report to the state and the federal governments for regulatory and compliance purposes, or simply to have an efficient method of processing students through the enrollment funnel. In the future those institutions that develop a more analytical purpose for their data will be more successful in all aspects of the academic enterprise. The savvy enrollment manager will be able to use the data to more accurately shape the class, defining with greater and greater accuracy the types of students the institution desires and can serve effectively. The Enrollment Manager as institutional monitor will play a key role in institutional success if he or she becomes proficient in data acquisition, analytics, and knowledge generation and dissemination—gaining a better understanding of the environment and the student/institution fit.

ADDRESSING MYTHS

At this author's institution, people were making many important decisions based on myths and anecdotes. We were throwing around a lot of higher education clichés that provided excellent cover, and understandable excuses about why our students weren't succeeding. Some of the more effective clichés were about the percentage or number of first-generation students we attracted and enrolled; or, about the commitment of our students because we were not their first choice institution; or about the amount of hours our students worked outside of the institution. All of these "myths" have roots in the literature about retention rates and graduation rates. It is true that first-generation college students, those that are not very committed and those that work extensive hours outside of the institution are less likely to be retained and less likely to graduate on time (or at all). However, it was this limited, conceptual knowledge that at worst detrimentally guided our decisions about our intervention strategies and our programs and services, and at best gave us excuses as to why we could not affect change.

To combat this myth on our campus, a survey was developed called the New Student Profile. Similar to more commonly used national instruments, it is administered at Summer Orientation (prior to students attending class in the fall), and asks very simple questions to get at the reality of our students' experience and perceptions. The questions get at the heart of what we need to know to provide quality, focused services to students.

The data we collected on this survey revealed that we *do not* have a very high percentage of first-generation students; we *do not* have a high percentage of students that consider us their second or lower choice; and we *do not* have a lot of students who plan to work extensive hours outside of the university. Those were myths perpetuated on campus, allowing us to discount our institutional responsibility for helping students succeed. Debunking these myths is an example of how data can affect cultural perceptions, and help focus the dialog that leads to more complete and collaborative decisions. Not only has this led to individualized intervention plans, but it has also focused institutional resources on the things that really matter in our effort to increase student success. Additionally, the survey data has helped us to develop a collaborative culture that is focused and supportive of each other. Personnel and decision makers from many different campus offices have used this information independently and collaboratively to make change. Student activities, academic advising, auxiliary services, multicultural services and others have used this data to adjust and modify their student services. They can now provide customized, personal interventions with students who self-identified a need through their answers on the survey. Good data promotes collaboration and better results.

Although this is only one in a series of strategies, since the implementation of this survey (and the associated interventions it fosters) our retention rate has gone up six percentage points, and our graduation rate has jumped nearly seven percentage points. Having the appropriate data in the decision making process can dramatically affect the quality of the decision and program success.

ANALYTICS

Analytics is the process of coming to an optimal decision based on existing data. This process is accomplished by gathering and storing data; employing data-mining techniques to retrieve the data in a form that, through various techniques, can be turned into information; and using that information to make decisions.

From the earliest texts on enrollment management, authors have described the role of the enrollment manager as one that uses available data to inform practice (Hossler, 1984; Dolence, 1993). For the most part, however, much of the data that has been gathered and used by enrollment managers has been for transactional purposes—reporting what has already occurred rather than informing future decision making. Tremendous amounts of energy and time go into developing student profiles, fact books, and preparing data for national and state reporting requirements. Less time, though, is spent organizing and analyzing data for important decision making tasks. The rule of practicality says if you cannot think of a way to use the data, don't collect it.

Analytical approaches are much more comprehensive processes that not only analyze the past, but also provide insight and information to explain the present and prepare for the future. Analytical approaches help provide different ways to produce and use data. In their book *Analytics at Work: Smarter Decisions, Better Results*, Davenport, Harris, and Morison (2010) approach analytics as a way to answer key questions. Their assertion is that by answering key questions, an organization can project with precision those practices that can most positively affect organizational success. They suggest that businesses can undertake these practices in key areas to create efficiencies and improve performance, and outperform their competition to become industry leaders.

Although the authors' approach to analytics makes no mention of higher education, there is great relevance to this approach in higher education and in the enrollment management organization. Enrollment management has as its core institutional effectiveness and performance including competition for "customers," competition with other organizations on other factors, revenue expectations, and institutional growth.

In truth, higher education may be better positioned to take advantage of analytics than many businesses or industries. The regulatory and compliance environment that surrounds higher education requires us to collect, store, and report vast amounts of data on all aspects of our organization and industry. Not only is this information available at the institutional level, it is also readily available at the state and national levels. Virtually anyone with a computer can access and analyze data on any aspect of an institution. Those within an institution with analytical skills can answer many key questions about not only his or her institution, but also about the competition, peer institutions, role model institutions, state systems, and the national system at-large.

Davenport, Harris, and Morison (2010), outline the types of information an institution needs to know about itself to make the best decisions. They developed a matrix that applies specific questions to two dimensions—innovation and time frame (see Table 1 on page 164). The dimension of *innovation* speaks to how the information gained from the key questions is used. The levels are Information and Insight (indicating the nature of the eventual uses of the data). *Time frame* indicates whether the question concerns the past, present, or future. At each intersection of the matrix the authors provide specific questions that are addressed by analytics. Although the questions are important, the real value of the matrix is as a model that decision makers can use to define the data needed to make an effective decision. Different analytical techniques are necessary for each cell of the matrix; and different types and levels of data are necessary to adequately answer the questions.

Table 1: Key Questions Addressed by Analytics

	Past	Present	Future
Information	What happened? (Reporting)	What is happening now? (Alerts)	What will happen? (Extrapolation)
Insight	How and why did it happen? (Modeling, experimental design)	What's the next best action? (Recommendation)	What's the best/worst that can happen? (Prediction, optimization, simulation)

Davenport, Harris, and Morison (2010)

ACCESSING AND EMPLOYING DATA

Before you can participate in analytics, you first must have, or gain access to, good data. The most important term here is "good" because even if you have great access to data, and are the world's foremost statistical genius, and the data is not good, then the presumptions you generate from the data will be flawed, as will the decisions you make based upon it. We will revisit this concept of data integrity and quality in a later section. In this section we explore access to data and the ways and means the savvy enrollment manager must employ to get it.

For most enrollment managers, the data that is easiest to access is from their own institutions. Not only is the home institution data most accessible, but it is also the data source that is the most important in terms of information that is actionable. It is amazing how much information is available that can help the enrollment manager define institutional problems, understand the barriers to enrollment, and that can help them guide institutional decision makers to make better decisions.

The richest data source at any institution is its Student Information or Enterprise system. Although there are many different enterprise systems, with many advantages and disadvantages, the core feature of all systems is that they collect and store data and information about individual students, faculty, courses, and departments, so that when mined, they can provide endless information for decision makers. Additionally, institutions employ financial systems, many times either directly integrated with the student data or linked in some way, that provide enrollment managers with important cost and revenue information so that they can participate in discussions and decisions about the financial aspects of enrollment management. Enrollment leaders need to be certain they are involved in budget making and decisions about tuition, fees, and use of institutional resources such as financial aid.

Some common ways institutions gather information include the admission application, transcripts from transfer students, standardized test score reports (including profile information), other admission documentation, registration and enrollment processes, scholarship applications, housing applications, graduation applications and degree audit paperwork, and many other processes and functions. Recently, institutions have implemented more and more external data gathering processes, programs and services that generate tremendous amounts of data that can be helpful to the enterprising enrollment manager. Such national surveys as the National Survey of Student Engagement (NSSE), Community College Survey of Student Engagement (CSSE), Beginning College Survey of Student Engagement (BCSSE), Making Achievement Possible Works (MAPWorks), CORE Alcohol Survey, Foundations of Excellence, and innumerable others, all help the enrollment manager gather valid, clean data that guides him/her in the daily tactical decisions as well as the more strategic long-term decisions necessary for effective enrollment management.

Enrollment managers, in cooperation with others at the institution who have direct access to students and the programs and services with which they interact, should also find specific touch points where students engage with the programs and services—and then develop ways to gather information at the point of interaction. A successful example from our campus involves attendance at campus events and appointments. We have employed software that uses swipe card technology to capture student attendance via student ID swiping at campus events, certain campus services (i.e., Student Recreation Center), and support services appointments (tutoring, advising, etc.). Then data from multiple systems are combined to create a master file of student engagement—and further synchronized with profile, demographic, and academic information to develop a comprehensive engagement profile of the student's experience and success. We have been able to analyze the data to determine the characteristics of successful vs. non-successful students in regard to campus engagement—thereby providing information for program redesign and resource allocation to those events and services that are most important to student success on our campus.

Another example of using "touch points" to gather information is one that provides qualitative data regarding student preferences to guide our development of programs and services. One term, we used the registration process to gather information from students about the types and genres of music they prefer. We inserted a "pop-up" screen into the registration process so that when the student clicked on the link to register, the screen came up and asked them several questions about the types of entertainment they prefer. The student had the option to "opt out" of the survey, but many (if not most) completed the survey. This, then, gave us valuable qualitative information that helped us define what type of entertainment we should provide to keep students on campus over the weekends—a factor that has been shown in the literature to increase engagement and integration with campus, thereby increasing the likelihood of retention and on-time graduation. This technique was not disruptive (we received no complaints), and provided valuable information that assisted decision making.

Local institutional data gives the enrollment manager the most contemporary data possible to make assumptions about the institution. Many state and national databases hold data that is several years old, thereby requiring the enrollment manager to make decisions based on assumptions that may actually be different because society has changed so rapidly. Additionally, using the institution's local data gives the enrollment manager the best chance to affect the local situation. Each institution is unique, and must develop local interventions based on its situation. Although the national or state situation and general "best-practices" are important to monitor to determine the efficacy of institutional decision making, it is only by analyzing local data that enrollment managers can identify the most appropriate strategies for generating the greatest success at the institution.

Finally, it is with local institutional data that the enrollment manager has the most influence and control. Although the enrollment manager must capitulate to outside authority when using outside data, within the institution he/she may have influence on factors such as data definitions, methods of collection, quality, quantity, and format of the data, and access, control and security of data. This, though, is assuming that the enrollment manager has some direct control of the collection, storage, and access of the information. If that is not the case, then it is important that the enrollment manager gain access to the data and influence its collection by developing excellent collaborative relationships with the "owners" of the data and/or creating professional links with institutional researchers or institutional effectiveness personnel.

Beyond local institutional data, there are many sources of information that may be helpful for the enrollment manager. Most of these sources aggregate the data at the institution level, but still provide the enrollment manager with accurate, quality data which helps with strategic decision making. To take advantage of this data, the enrollment manager will need to have some data acquisition and analysis skills—but more and more, many of the data sources have their own analysis tools that allow the enrollment manager to manipulate the data and analyze it in multiple ways. Table 2 provides the names and internet pages of some of the most common sites for data access. A point of caution though—because of the length of time it takes for these sites to collect or gain access to data, the data is often a couple of years old. For instance, the data at CollegeResults.org is two years old at any given time.

Table 2: Common Internet Sites for Data Access

Data Source	Web Site	Description
ACT, Inc.	www.act.org/research/	ACT (formerly American College Testing) issue briefs, case studies, and research and information services
Bureau of Labor Statistics (BLS)	www.bls.gov/data/	Government data about labor and employment
The Chronicle of Higher Education, Almanac of Higher Education 2011	http://chronicle.com/section/Almanac-of-Higher-Education/141/	Information and data about higher education
College Board	professionals.collegeboard.com/data-reports-research	College Board, provider of the SAT®
The Education Trust	www.collegeresults.org	Compare colleges on multiple dimensions
Education Week	www.edweek.org	Data about K-12 education/trends
U.S. Department of Education	www.eddataexpress.ed.gov	Access and explore high-value, state-level education data
National Center for Education Statistics (NCES) Data Lab	nces.ed.gov/datalab/	Simple data tables as well as advanced statistical techniques based on IPEDS data
Southern Regional Education Board (SREB)	www.sreb.org/page/1075/education_data.html	Interstate comparisons and trends in education
Postsecondary Education Opportunity	www.postsecondary.org	Newsletter site with a tremendous amount of data
U.S. Census Bureau	www.census.gov	Population QuickFacts and much more
Western Interstate Commission for Higher Education (WICHE)	www.wiche.edu	Research and policy data including population projections

WHAT DATA IS THE MOST IMPORTANT?

The data you need is dependent on the problems you have, the questions you need to answer, the decisions you need to make, and the assumptions you make about the behavior of the students. However, more important than the data you need to have on hand is the ability to access the sources of data that you need quickly. In fact, having too much data on hand is sometimes nearly as paralyzing as not having enough data. Beyond the data that you need to answer some common questions (see below), it is more important to spend time honing your data acquisition, manipulation, and analysis skills rather than fixating on collecting pieces of data that you may someday need. It is much more important that you acquire data once you have narrowed the focus of your investigation—leading to data that is more relevant to your current problem.

In many applications, the data simply will not exist in the format that is necessary for you to utilize for important contemporary decisions. In these cases, the enrollment manager's data skills are even more important due to their role to both create the methodology for generating the data, and to analyze it for helpful use in decision making. The more data-driven your institution becomes, and the more you drill down into the organization to make data-based decisions, the more you must develop specific data collectors for those specific areas. Aggregated data at the institution level simply will not yield answers for specific departments or sub-populations. To the extent that this level of data is necessary for overall institutional health, the enrollment manager will want to find standardized ways of collecting data and disseminating information. This is another place where a good relationship with the Institutional Research or Institutional Effectiveness office will yield great dividends.

Another important decision that the enrollment manager must make is what type of data to pursue. In most cases, to make good decisions the enrollment manager will rely on both quantitative and qualitative data, as well as a variety of analysis techniques, to squeeze as much information as possible out of the data. The more complete the information, the better the decisions.

Although many enrollment managers have a working knowledge of the statistical techniques used with quantitative data, it is important for them to use qualitative data to make the knowledge gained from quantitative data more meaningful. Such qualitative techniques as listening sessions or short answer surveys can provide a depth of information that cannot be gained through quantitative techniques. Answering "how" and "why" questions is very important, especially in times when resources are short and enrollment managers need to make discriminating decisions about projects on which to allocate resources. Qualitative data helps fill in the gaps that naturally surround quantitative data and to see the "on the ground" impact of some of the inconsistencies and trends you see in the data.

STEPS TO BECOMING MORE DATA DRIVEN

The organizations that take steps to become more data driven, and use analytics to their greatest advantage, will be the ones able to adapt more quickly to the changing environment and be more successful. Enrollment managers can lead in this process, but it is important to follow some basic steps in the quest to become more data driven. The following outline provides some practical guidance and specific considerations as you move your organization towards a more data driven culture.

Start small:
- Find one important decision and define what data/information you need to make the decision.
- Find already collected data or arrange your business processes to collect that data.
- Analyze the data to find if it helps decision making.
- Share the decision and process with university leaders.
- Implement the decision.
- Assess the results.
- Share the results and process.

Create divisional/institutional discipline to make data-based decisions:
- Make sure you collect data that is useful in decisions around your top problems/questions.
- Share the process of generating information from data and making decisions (see first section above).
- Example: Identify at-risk students for intervention—what data do you need to accomplish this? How do you get it? What do you do with it?

Hold managers and leaders responsible for their decisions:
- Ask, "What is the evidence to support that decision or direction?"
- Don't accept any answer that does not include verifiable data.

Close the loop:
- Complete and assess the process to validate decisions and to modify them over time.
    * Example outcomes: gender-specific housing, preferred method of contact in admissions changed from in-person to social media, etc.

COLLABORATION AND DISTRIBUTED DECISION MAKING

Most institutional problems or opportunities that are encountered by the enrollment manager are complex and cross multiple institutional functional areas. It is extremely important for the enrollment manager as institutional connector to develop strong relationships with a diverse set of individuals and offices across campus.

The word collaboration is overused in today's business and leadership literature. In its most basic form, collaboration is two (or more) areas "co-laboring" together to reach the same goal or purpose. It is more than each partner completing their individual part of the process; it is working together, creating dependence on each other, for the greater benefit. In our complex organizations, leaders seem to understand that it is important to get more than just their area involved in solving organizational problems; but they often do not have the understanding of how to manage such relationships and may not fully appreciate how the contributions of each partner creates a synergy for the institution that is greater than the sum of its parts.

Many of the problems that plague the enrollment manager are also the problems that perplex other institutional partners. Collaboration between institutional partners helps focus attention on these complex problems, and brings greater resources to bear to solve them. It is within these relationships that true institutional growth is generated. In the future, institutions that experience true collaboration, with divisions and offices working together, will be the most competitive and succeed.

Data is one dimension where the enrollment manager can "make friends and influence people." As an expert on the institution's data, the enrollment manager can help departments gain access to data and generate information to solve their problems. Some enrollment managers take this role very seriously. Craig Cornell, Associate Vice Provost for Enrollment Management at Ohio University, suggests that an effective enrollment manager never go to a meeting without some data in hand. He suggests to fellow practitioners that the data should apply to the issue under consideration by the office that requested it, and that being the "go-to" data expert enables the enrollment manager to open the door for collaborative relationships between institutional offices (Cornell and Lingrell 2011).

CONCLUSION

In a speech to the Harvard School of Public Health Leadership Council, Dr. Larry Summers, former President of Harvard said, "I suspect that when history is written two hundred years from now, [a trend] will emerge as something very important that happened in human thinking during the time when we were alive, and that is that we are becoming rational, analytical, and data-driven in a far wider range of activity than we ever have been before" (Summers 2003).

Analytics and data-based decision making is here to stay, and it is vital to the successful Strategic Enrollment Management organization. Those that do it well will succeed at greater and greater levels; those that do not will be less and less competitive and relevant. Enrollment managers that become proficient in data acquisition, interpretation, and dissemination are poised to become strategic leaders on their campuses, to use data to improve student experience at their institutions and to outpace the competition.

The importance of good data management can be summarized as follows:

1. Good decisions depend on having good data from which to draw information and conclusions.

2. Strategic Enrollment Management requires tremendous amounts of data from many sources. It is the collection of data from disparate sources that, when combined and synthesized, paints the big picture. Enrollment managers need the big picture to develop strategies to solve the big problems.

3. Data is a great tool to create mutually beneficial relationships between multiple campus units. It is at the nexus of these collaborative relationships that enrollment managers gain the most benefit and solve the hardest problems.

4. Invest time and effort to gain access to, and knowledge about, the data that is most relevant to you. This effort will give you the most payout and help you answer the most compelling questions.

5. Becoming more data-driven over time will help organizations be more competitive in this rapidly changing environment. Organizations proficient in analytics will be at the forefront of the higher education community, well ahead of the competition.

9

SEM IN THE POSTBACCALAUREATE CONTEXT

Monique L. Snowden
Associate Provost for Academic and Enrollment Services
Fielding Graduate University

CHAPTER 9

INTRODUCTION[1]

The tensions between institutional values and market realities in American higher education are ever present. Massy (2004) argues that "to discharge their value delegations, universities must have enough financial strength to balance mission with market" (25). To this end, colleges and universities are advancing their educational offerings in order to increase enrollment revenue, subsidize mission-centric academic offerings, and extend institutional reach into corporate and global marketplaces (Bok 2003; Weisbrod, Ballou and Asch 2008). Consequently, postsecondary education is neither confined within institutional walls nor constrained by national borders. To the contrary, efforts to expand institutional capacity, meet student demand, and maximize net tuition revenue have effectively blurred traditional boundaries between the academy and higher education market. Furthermore, the commercialization of academic enterprises such as university-spinoffs (Shane 2004), and the commoditization of academic credentials (Collins 1979; Zemsky, Wegner and Massy 2005) reminds us that:

> *Higher education started in the Agora, the market place, at the bottom of the hill and ascended to the Acropolis on top of the hill.... Mostly it has lived in tension, at one and the same time at the bottom of the hill, at the top of the hill, and on many paths in between.* (Kerr 1988)

---

1. Paragraphs 1-3 contain text and ideas from M.L. Snowden, "Enrollment Logics and Discourse: Toward Professionalizing Higher Education Enrollment Management" (unpublished PhD diss., Texas A&M University, 2010).

All roads up and down the hill are part and parcel of a complex infrastructure, which, analogous to modern Athens, rests upon the triumphs and ruins of fragmented institutional missions and the unintended consequences of individual and collective actions in the marketplace. In *Remaking of the American University*, Zemsky et al. (2005) underscore the historical and inherent tensions between institutional missions and the market. The authors suggest that espoused institutional missions and underlying institutional values are increasingly becoming functions of market competition. However, responding to the market does not oblige colleges and universities to subordinate mission to market (58). Alternatively, and as suggested by Zemsky and colleagues, being mission-centered can indeed be a function of an institution's capacity to be market-smart.

The watchword "no margin, no mission" renders a distinguishable divide between the academy and market as both a mythical and idealistic notion. The *myth* is partly dispelled by the endemic cross-subsidization of academic offerings and the reality that "no current student pays the full costs of his or her education" (Winston 1993, 231). The *ideal* becomes less plausible when mission-driven initiatives and associated decisions are perceived as barriers to maximizing a college or university's net tuition revenue. Between myth and ideal, institutional dependency on tuition revenue suggests that mission attainment is inextricably tied to market-driven student enrollment (Bontrager 2008).

In *The Chosen*, Jerome Karabel argues that truly understanding the foundations of American higher education necessitates unpacking the enrollment histories of the Big Three (Harvard, Yale and Princeton). Moreover, Karabel emphasizes that chronicles of postsecondary enrollment at U.S. colleges and universities is intrinsically tied to the social movements and associated circumstances that constitute American history. That being said, this endeavor to explicate graduate, professional and continuing education (hereto, "postbaccalaureate education"), from a strategic enrollment management (SEM) perspective, is an abridged history of selectively relevant and significant past actions of pioneering and notable crafters of U.S. higher education. In addition, this chapter is an exposition of the contemporary state and undetermined future outlook of U.S. postbaccalaureate education.

Kohl and LaPidus (2000) point out that "the term *postbaccalaureate* has become strongly associated with practice-oriented or professional education" (4). Although "postbaccalaureate" rarely refers to academic programs that yield doctorate degrees, for the sake of brevity, I make use of the term to connote postsecondary degree and non-degree offerings that advance the baccalaureate degree—including master's, doctorate (i.e., PhD), professional doctorate (e.g., EdD, MD and JD) degrees; graduate-level certificates; graduate-level freestanding courses that are credit bearing; and non-credit graduate-level professional development courses.

Chapter Overview

The ambitious agenda for this chapter includes:

- Information about what constitutes SEM in the postbaccalaureate context.
- Illuminating some intrinsic similarities and connections between baccalaureate and postbaccalaureate foundations of postsecondary education.
- Inciting thoughtful consideration—from a learner-centered SEM orientation that is necessarily shaped by adult learning theory—of postbaccalaureate collaboration and constituent relationships.

To this end, the chapter is organized into three sections, followed by a conclusion. Altogether, this text calls attention to the salient enrollment matters of attracting, supporting, teaching, and graduating adult students—many who reach the threshold of postbaccalaureate education while moving toward, resting on, or surpassing a middle ground in their personal lives and/or professional careers.

The first section locates the emergence of U.S. postbaccalaureate education in American history. It seeks to provide a germane foundation that sufficiently informs readers' understandings of the theoretical and practical underpinnings that guide our thoughts about why and how postbaccalaureate education is sought out, experienced, delivered and assessed. The juxtaposition of adult learning in undergraduate vis-à-vis graduate education is laid out to accentuate linkages and fractures of convergent and divergent enrollment issues.

The second section begins with a foundational question: *What does it mean to consider SEM in a particular context?* Historically, enrollment management was perceived as an integrated organizational design that could be employed to attract and retain sufficient numbers of students "during a period of possible national enrollment declines" (Maguire 1976, 16). Contemporary SEM, however, is described as *integrating* within the institution; *embedding* into institutional planning; *fusing* with the academic enterprise; *blurring* the boundaries between administrative and academic units; and *morphing* institutional roles and structures (see Black 2004a, 38). Conceptualizing SEM as an institutionalized profession, and not simply an organizational construct, creates space for introducing diverse scholarship and practice. When Henderson (2001) proclaimed that enrollment management was "on the brink of a profession," the professional potential of SEM and the role that professional associations proffer was clarified in that the related collection of occupations was moving from a "point of adolescence" toward a profession.

The third section acknowledges and builds on what has been learned and achieved, in respect to SEM in the baccalaureate context. To this end, nuances of postbaccalaureate education offer lenses from which alternative viewpoints of SEM structure, process, practice and profession can emerge. Moreover, contemplating SEM from a postbaccalaureate standpoint—well-grounded in adult learning theory, scholarship, and practice—can conceivably stimulate dialogue and actions that shed light on commonalities and distinctions of extant baccalaureate vis-à-vis postbaccalaureate education enrollment issues. In this section, theoretical conceptions and practical applications of student development, adult development, and adult education are taken up. The section also promotes a learner-centered SEM orientation, from a standpoint that contemporary adult learners come to postbaccalaureate education with common, but also distinct, educational rationales, expectations, and needs—in comparison to the archetypal undergraduate student who enters graduate or professional education immediately or soon after earning a baccalaureate degree.

The concluding section places a clarion call to enrollment management professionals engaged in postbaccalaureate contexts to lend their voices, knowledge and experiences to write about and share their expertise in order to expand the current enrollment management lexicon. This chapter aims to stimulate interests and dialogues that can enhance the work performed by individuals who apply the form and function of SEM in postbaccalaureate contexts. Resting on this point of introspection is reflective; while moving forward may be innate to SEM professionals, it is a challenge nonetheless:

> *The writer knows her field—what has been done, what could be done, the limits—the way a tennis player knows the court. And like that expert, she, too, plays the edges. That is where the exhilaration is…Now gingerly, can she enlarge it, can she nudge the bounds? And enclose what wild power?* (Dillard in Ellingson 2009, 190)

THE EMERGENCE OF U.S. POSTBACCALAUREATE EDUCATION

Nineteenth century thoughts on the distinction between a college and university created discursive space in which the teaching and scholarship debate surfaced. The emergence of U.S. postbaccalaureate education, however, made the division more apparent as the distribution of knowledge through scholarship and research, not solely by way of teaching, began to take form. Up until this era in U.S. postsecondary education history, there were only four established "professions" —clergy, law, medicine, and arguably the military—that required some "formal study or instruction"; all other "vocations," categorically, were learned "on the job" (Rudolph 1990, 339). Additionally, the dawning of postbaccalaureate education signified an eventual end to occupational apprenticeship systems—which were common in professions such as law—and set the stage for discipline-based academic departments, specialized scholarship, and perhaps most significantly, scholarship as a *bona fide* profession (Cohen and Kisker 2010).

Despite its notable European origin, in 1643, the master's degree emerged at Harvard College as "an empty token of minimal accomplishment" and would not flourish until the 20th century (Spencer 1986, 1). On another related front, U.S. postsecondary education existed for almost two centuries before concerted efforts to develop the doctorate degree became more pronounced. This particular development in U.S. higher education history was stimulated by the Germanic ideal of learning and teaching, which emphasized the diffusion and advancement of knowledge through scholarship and research—not merely teaching and promoting *arts and letters*. This paradigmatic shift in U.S. postbaccalaureate education began to take shape as American administrators and educators gained valuable experience with German universities. In contrast to baccalaureate education delivered by extant colleges that adopted the English (Oxford) learning model, the Germanic educational form promoted a university model that placed foci on cultivating specialized disciplines and offering graduate seminars and lectures.

In 1860, Yale University—through its Department of Philosophy and Arts—became the first U.S. institution of higher learning to offer a doctorate degree; a year later, Yale awarded the first doctorate degrees in the U.S.—specifically, 3 students were awarded PhDs in American history. These early beginnings notwithstanding, the foundations of U.S. graduate and professional education, as we know it today, can be traced to trailblazing free-standing graduate universities and the founding presidents that led them—e.g., Johns Hopkins University (1876, Daniel Gillman), University of Chicago (1892, William Rainey Harper), and Clark University (1889, G. Stanley Hall). Johns Hopkins University, where a faculty-centered model of the modern university was advanced, is widely recognized for playing the most significant role in shaping the research tradition and "commitment to the scholarly idea" that exists today (Rudolph, 1990, 269). In fact, Charles William Eliot—the twenty-first and longest tenured president of Harvard (1869-1909)—publicly credited Johns Hopkins University with establishing a model for postbaccalaureate education that "forced" Harvard's faculty to develop its doctoral program, which did not thrive until almost two decades after its initial offering in 1870 (Lucas 2006; Rudolph 1990).

As private universities were developing and promoting the pursuit of scholarship and learning, public universities in Michigan, Nebraska, Kansas, and Wisconsin—endeavoring to fulfill their aspirations of becoming renowned research centers—established graduate schools that were separate and distinct from their undergraduate offerings. At the University of Wisconsin, the idea that universities were the most viable institutions to "contribute to the work of societal advancement" took hold and manifested into the "spirit of social service" that became known as the "Wisconsin Idea" (Lucas 2006, 182). As evidenced by the omnipresent service mission of modern public universities, and the social justice/action ethos of some private universities, the idea was diffuse. Moreover, scholarship for the public good began to flourish—in terms of focused attention and resource allocation. Brown (1995) points out:

> *What began in the 1890s—as a coincidence of the needs of large public and private organizations, select wings of professions, and the immediately preceding actions of college administrators to satisfy students and otherwise bolster their enrollments—became by 1900 a more orchestrated constellation of occupational and collegiate actions.* (Brown 1995, 9-10).

In 1907, the University of Wisconsin advanced the "extension of educational programs to address the relevant social, economic, environmental and cultural issues of its citizens" (University Wisconsin-Extension 2010). Borne out of the inspirational leadership of then-University President Charles Van Hise and Governor Robert LaFollette was the establishment of community-serving "extension" agencies at public universities and the eventual formation of postsecondary continuing education schools. Van Hise and LaFollette—and other extension enthusiasts of their time—understood and strongly believed that U.S. institutions of higher education, particularly public universities, have immense responsibilities to provide accessible and relevant education to its citizens. Through their commitment and efforts to serve "every young man and woman in the state," the University of Wisconsin was the vanguard for providing "education for people where they live and work, with practical applications for their daily lives."

In the span of three decades, the modern American university emerged with an expanded mission—teaching, research, and service—and heightened foci on the professionalization of various disciplines. The promising growth of graduate and professional education was accompanied by an associated expansion of careers constituting "new professions" previously viewed as non-professionalized vocations (Rudolph 1990). One of the second-order effects of universities offering more formal study and instruction in the "old professions" was the displacement of longstanding apprenticeship systems; many of these systems were supplanted by discipline-focused professional schools. As remnants of the Jacksonian movement, institutionalized professional schools are the contingent byproducts of egalitarian influences in higher education. Furthermore, professional schools promoted educational equalities that marked an era of new professionalism. This new professionalism blurred vocational and professional distinctions that had historically perpetuated meritocracy and educational privilege, in terms of educational access and career equity.

In the 1950s, the revived and budding master's degree emerged with attentiveness to postbaccalaureate educational offerings that promoted "specialization, professionalization, application, decentralization, and depersonalization" (Spencer 1986, 1). Spencer notes, however, that at its inception the "scorned and lowly" (1) master's degree was "the supreme triumph of academic inutility, an archaic and obsolete diploma which served a useful purpose only in the most limited circumstance and at the most marginal institutions" (2). Conversely, the contemporary master's degree conveys perceived value in terms of "improving professional practice" and preparing students to be "leaders and change agents in their profession" (Kohl 2000, 6).

Presently, the rapid advancements in web technologies and services enable asynchronous academic delivery that renders postbaccalaureate education more accessible and malleable. Non-didactic approaches to eLearning aid shifts in academic services, technology and content. Furthermore, multifaceted academic foundations and ever-expanding institutional perimeters give way to the postmodern "multiversity" (Kerr 1995). The multiversity is a pluralistic institution that "is not really private and it is not really public; it is neither entirely of the world nor entirely apart from it" (1). Moreover, the multiversity is neither constituted by a "single, unified community" nor does it possess a "discretely defined set of consumers" (103).

Cutting across the landscape of higher education, postbaccalaureate education is delivered in different modalities at predominantly undergraduate institutions (pervasive model); free-standing professional schools (e.g., Thunderbird School of Global Management); free-standing graduate universities and institutes (e.g., Claremont Graduate University, Fielding Graduate University, Pacifica Graduate Institute); university-affiliated continuing studies/professional and extension schools (e.g., Harvard Extension School, NYU School of Continuing and Professional Studies, Northwestern School of Continuing Studies); and public university extension agencies (e.g., University of California-Extension, University of Wisconsin-Extension, Texas AgriLife Extension Service). Organizational configurations and educational delivery models abound, and akin to baccalaureate education, there is a phenomenon that remains a constant for postbaccalaureate education: *Enrollment matters.*

STRATEGIC ENROLLMENT MANAGEMENT IN CONTEXT

Extant literature suggests that "context" entered the enrollment management lexicon in the 1990s, when Michael Dolence proclaimed that optimal enrollment goals should be "defined within the academic context of the institution." What does it mean, however, to consider SEM in any particular context? The *Oxford English Dictionary* defines context as "the circumstances that form the setting for an event, statement, or ideas, and in terms of which it can be fully understood." Hence, contemplating SEM in a postbaccalaureate context connotes positioning oneself in the milieu of postbaccalaureate education, in search of understandings about the conditions that drive and impact adult student's exploration, choice, persistence, completion, and on-going evaluation of postbaccalaureate academic offerings.

Context notwithstanding, Kalsbeek (2007) suggests that SEM orientations—academic, administrative, student-focused, and market-centered—signify how we perceive, understand, and appropriate SEM in a collegiate setting. Conceptually, the interconnected trilogy of perception, orientation, and appropriation (Ollman 1971) facilitates our interpretation of SEM in context. Whereas perceptions shape our heuristic frames, orientations ground understandings that stimulate actionable frameworks. Simply stated, a particular orientation emerges from one's perception, which then yields an appropriated response that is grounded by our subsequent actions. Perception connotes our immediate reaction upon coming into contact with SEM—as structure, process, practice and profession—followed by what we come to know about the rationale and significance of enacting an enrollment agenda that might be achieved by appropriating some SEM configuration and plan.

That being said, ubiquitous perceptions of SEM are largely influenced by the structures, processes, practices and professions that constitute SEM in a baccalaureate context. Since the emergence of enrollment management at Boston College in the mid-1970s, our understandings of how to achieve enrollment goals and support student success have necessarily evolved. However, SEM frameworks that reinforce normative—acceptable—and mimetic—good or best—enrollment strategies, tactics, and outcomes are principally constructed and construed within the sphere of baccalaureate education. Thus, recognizable SEM frameworks and associated institutional approaches that are most familiar, well-understood and broadly diffused, are insufficient in addressing postbaccalaureate education enrollment matters.

Since the storied beginning of enrollment management, in the wake of a Boston College student strike against a sharp tuition increase, the average ages and associated experiences of students seeking postsecondary education have shifted dramatically. In addition, online and distributed programs are inducing enrollment challenges for institutions that have historically and primarily offered campus-bound baccalaureate and postbaccalaureate education. On one hand, U.S. higher education remains principally oriented to "traditional" undergraduate students, whose engagement with faculty, fellow students and staff is by and large face-to-face and didactic. On the other hand, the contingent effects of emerging and immersive technology on postsecondary education teaching, learning, services, and economies present both challenges and opportunities, in terms of reconceptualizing SEM in alternative contexts.

Once again, context notwithstanding, the enactment of a SEM paradigm often begins by first articulating institutional purpose, proceeded by identifying enrollment priorities that augment mission clarity and coherence (Hossler and Kalsbeek 2008).[2] Conversely, Kalsbeek and Hossler (2009) argue that "enrollment management must begin by assessing the dynamics that create the competitive market context which in real and measurable ways prescribes and circumscribes the range of strategic futures an institution in all likelihood has to choose among" (4). The former approach is mission-centered; while the latter is market-centered. Each approach, however, connotes certain assumptions, perspectives, referent structures, and organizing principles that result in different instantiations and thus organizational appropriations of SEM.

Appropriating SEM in a postbaccalaureate context focuses on the significance and role of faculty, in terms of achieving and sustaining institutional and programmatic enrollment success. Enrolling and retaining new undergraduate students, at any particular college or university, is generally enhanced by faculty involvement in recruitment, matriculation and retention activities. Kraft (2007) identifies conditions that might incite undergraduate faculty to participate in campus-wide SEM efforts at a highly selective, public, mid-sized teaching university. The study showed that faculty was more likely to participate in SEM activities when they viewed their involvement as a contribution to promoting the reputation and achieving the goals of their respective college, department, and/or program. Faculty felt most rewarded by the "positive energy they received from students, an opportunity to get to know professional colleagues with similar philosophies, and the ability to explore their professional curiosity as educators" (111).

Achieving new and sustaining current enrollment targets for postbaccalaureate education is highly dependent on a particular program's faculty—if not for their active participation in enrollment-related activities, then to leverage faculty disciplinary reputation vis-à-vis the eminence of faculty in competitor programs. Likewise, faculty credentials—denoting scholarship and practice relevant to each prospective student—are key attractors for individuals seeking postbaccalaureate education. An academic program's faculty members are key influencers of postbaccalaureate recruitment and retention. In the end, the actions of faculty are central to each student's college/program choice and academic persistence.

What we know about student choice has been primarily ascertained from research in baccalaureate education, beginning with the simple decision funnel (Kotler 1976). Of saliency to postbaccalaureate studies, Kallio (1995) investigated the influence factors affecting the college choice decisions of graduate students, and noted that the top five (5) academic factors are: 1) *reputation of faculty*, 2) *quality of teaching*, 3) *diversity of course offerings*, 4) *value of degree from particular college/university*, and 5) *particular field of study availability*. Noteworthy, however, is

---

2. This paragraph includes text and ideas from Snowden (2010)

that those surveyed indicated that the ability to continue working in their "current" job was a major non-academic decision factor. Poock & Love (2001) found that in addition to faculty reputation, general senses of faculty "friendliness" and positive engagement with students were determinant factors in graduate program choice. In addition, program reputation and time-to-completion were significant choice factors. Both of the aforementioned studies indicated that in choosing a program of study, students sought out high quality programs and faculty, and optimal flexibility, to effectively balance their academic and work lives.

Understandably, there are common choice factors that influence most prospective students seeking higher education (e.g., cost, location, financial assistance). However, faculty-centric dispositions and work-influenced expectations of adults seeking postbaccalaureate education call for distinct marketing and recruitment strategies and tactics that differ from those used for baccalaureate education. The choice and consideration sets of prospective students exploring postbaccalaureate education tend to be narrowly defined by, aligned with, and focused on more specific career goals than those of traditional undergraduate prospects. This assertion is best exemplified when professional and continuing studies schools appropriate SEM from a strong market-centered orientation that targets career-sensitive prospects. In praxis, professional and continuing studies schools generally demonstrate a deep understanding and effective strategies for promoting and affecting their brand equity in an increasingly competitive postsecondary education marketspace.

Brand equity connotes that institutional, school/program, and faculty reputations matter. Perceived reputation is a relational concept that influences how one entity fairs in juxtaposition with another. To that end, the era of heightened media-induced social networking calls for institutional marketers and enrollment management professionals to better understand and respond to the significance of *promoters* (the most loyal constituents), *passives* (those satisfied, but unenthusiastic constituents), and *detractors* (dissatisfied constituents at the highest risk of defection who produce negative word-of-mouth). Moreover, it is becoming critical for colleges and universities that aim to grow and sustain their student enrollment to understand that strong reputations are not built on what institutions, school/programs, or faculties *intend* to do, but what they actually accomplish.

Rather than relying on speculative claims, postbaccalaureate prospective and enrolled students look and call for evident proof points. Prospects and students, demand assurance of consistent and persistent institutional and program performance that unequivocally delivers on multiple brand promises. While managing institutional and program brands may be the work of an institution's marketing professionals, delivering on institutional and program brand promises necessitates the successful integration and interdependence of indigenous and exogenous skills and expertise. On one hand, skills signify knowledge in action and context. On the other hand, expertise connotes possessing *and* sharing specialized knowledge to advance certain skills and generate new knowledge.

The Field and Professions in Context

Mastenbroek (1993) asserts that "we are confronted by a paradox: in order to integrate better, we must first differentiate well" (143). In other words, functional efficacy achieved by way of specialized skills is a necessary and sufficient condition of better integration. The sharing of differentiated skills, however, enlarges the expertise needed to ensure sound interdependence of functions. Kalsbeek (1997) emphasizes "by its nature, enrollment management relies on an interdependence of many departments, functions, and processes" (157). However, that interdependence is not contained within institutional boundaries. A burgeoning "enrollment industry" (Hossler, 2009) forces us to acknowledge that SEM is an exterior and interior administrative approach that operates on numerous borders.

An industry is "a population of organizations operating in the same domain as indicated by the similarity of their services or products —but adds to this focal population those other and different organizations that critically influence their performance, including exchange partners, competitors, funding sources, and regulators" (Scott 2008a, 86). Thus, an industry's organizations comprise the organizational field "that, in the aggregate, constitute an area of institutional life: key suppliers, resource and product consumers, regulatory agencies, and other organizations that produce similar services or products" (DiMaggio and Powell 1983, 148).

Some constituent field organizations that influence—and in some cases control—a broad array of complex and nuanced postsecondary education enrollment issues can be classified in four broad categories: 1) enrollment management consulting services and related vendors, 2) the student loan industry and related services, 3) rankings and college guidance publications, and 4) postsecondary educational institutions and nonprofit professional associations (Hossler, 2009). In addition, institutional theory suggests that "feeder" organizations offering pathways to postsecondary education, and entities that regulate and evaluate institutional/program viability and education quality, respectively, are key field constituents.

Undoubtedly, there is significant overlap in postbaccalaureate and baccalaureate education constituent organizations and associated relationships. There are, however, nuanced constituents and associated services in the postbaccalaureate enrollment organizational field. Furthermore, the field is comprised of numerous players—too many to address in this chapter. As an alternative to offering an exhaustive account of the field, there is utility in focusing on a few prominent field constituents that serve significant roles in informing postbaccalaureate education. The chosen constituent bodies of interest and relevance to advancing skills and expertise, particularly toward appropriating SEM in alternative contexts, are professional associations—which are virtually absent from enrollment management literature and research.

Advancing SEM in alternative contexts necessitates cultivating broader and deeper awareness of the field among colleagues and professionals who promote, support, deliver, and shape postbaccalaureate education. To this end, professional associations serve an essential function in any organizational field; they operate as interest groups that strive to achieve and sustain collective mobility (Macdonald, 1995). An important role of professional associations is to support "the construction and maintenance of intraprofessional agreement over boundaries, membership, and behavior" (Greenwood, Suddaby, & Hining, 2002, 62). Collectively and reciprocally, association members "represent themselves to themselves" (61) by upholding normative field work and related best practices. Furthermore, professional associations facilitate the legitimization and regulation of knowledge claims and information diffused inside and outside of the profession.

Based on the author's orientation to the field of postbaccalaureate education, a council and four associations have been selected as prominent field organizations: *Council of Graduate Schools, National Association of Graduate Admissions Professionals, University Professional & Continuing Education Association,* and the *American Association for Adult and Continuing Education.* Viewed as communities of practice, these organizations advance knowledge in the field "by hosting a process of discourse through which change is debated and endorsed: first by negotiating and managing a debate within the profession, and, second, by reframing professional identities as they are presented to others outside the profession" (Greenwood, Suddaby and Hinings 2002, 59). Cutting across each organization's mission facilitates a better understanding of how it uniquely applies SEM in a postbaccalaureate context. (See Table 1 for more on each organization.)

In 2010, the Council of Graduate Schools (CGS) marked its 50th anniversary with the landmark report, "The Path Forward: The Future of Graduate Education in the United States." CGS touts advocacy, research, and innovations as its cornerstones and offers a venue for academic administrators to focus on critical issues facing U.S. graduate education.

In 1987, the New England Association of Graduate Admissions Professionals (NEAGAP) forum was founded by a group of admissions professionals for the purpose of "networking with fellow colleagues about their mutual concerns in the growing graduate admissions field." In 1991, NEAGAP was reconstituted as a national organization—National Association of Graduate Admissions Professionals (NAGAP).

The University Professional & Continuing Education Association (UPCEA) was founded in 1915 as the National University Extension Association (NUEA); UPCEA emerged during

Table 1: Postbaccalaureate Education Associations

Organization	Mission	Role/Significance
Council of Graduate Schools (CGS)	To "advance graduate education in order to ensure the vitality of intellectual discovery and to promote an environment that cultivates rigorous scholarship."	The only national organization in the United States that is dedicated solely to the advancement of graduate education and research; "leading authoritative source on information, data analysis, and trends in graduate education."
National Association of Graduate Admissions Professionals (NAGAP)	To support, advance, and engage graduate enrollment professionals by promoting integrity, excellence, and collaboration through education and professional development	"The only professional organization devoted exclusively to the concerns of individuals working in the graduate admissions and recruitment environment."
University Professional & Continuing Education Association (UPCEA)	"Making higher education available to everyone, as well as to ensure that programs and services address societal needs and economic trends."	The original focus was "establishing standards for correspondence schools and distance education." It now offers a space for college and university professionals to shape their institutional understandings of the types of educational programs individuals and organizations seek for professional and personal development.
American Association for Adult and Continuing Education (AAACE)	AAACE "is dedicated to the belief that lifelong learning contributes to human fulfillment and positive social change."	Enacts a strong advocacy role in terms of promoting "relevant public policy, legislation, and social change initiatives which expand the depth and breadth of opportunities for the education of adults;" aims to unify field members by providing leadership, promoting the development and dissemination of theory and research, facilitating the identity negotiation of adult and continuing education as a profession constituted by diverse professionals, and drawing connections between field scholarship and practice.

the era when the Wisconsin Idea and continuing education was taking hold in U.S. higher education.

In 1982, the American Association for Adult and Continuing Education (AAACE) emerged from a series of establishments, dissolutions, and mergers of professional societies and organizations, dating back to the 1920s when the term "adult education" began to emerge in the field.

Altogether the aforementioned council and professional associations represent and facilitate advancing the knowledge and skills of individuals who are vested in understanding and meeting the needs of adult learners. The noted organizations, more or less, facilitate professional spaces where member constituents with strong academic SEM orientations can come together and share knowledge in the sphere of postbaccalaureate education. On one hand, with the exception of NAGAP, the organizations selected are not typical venues attended by most enrollment management professionals. On the other hand, however, professional associations that focus on enrollment and academic services predominantly for undergraduate education—e.g., American Association of Collegiate Registrars and Admissions Officers (AACRAO) and National Association of Collegiate Admissions Counselors (NACAC)—are not customary venues for academic administrators (e.g., deans, associate deans, program directors). Perhaps the greatest potential for developing—and therefore further institutionalizing and professionalizing—SEM for postbaccalaureate education is discovering a nexus, or binding thread, that is core to each organization. A plausible starting point is contemplating the adult student from a learner-centered SEM orientation, which effectively brings together student-focused and academic orientations.

A LEARNER-CENTERED SEM ORIENTATION

> *Education is a social process. Education is growth. Education is not a preparation for life; education is life itself.*[3]

From its inception, Maguire (1976) emphasized that enrollment management should be aligned with "maintaining a humanistic vision of what fundamentally constitutes a good education" and traditions "that contribute to 'making a life not merely a living'" (18). Brown (1995) points out, however, that "education credentials have become the prerequisites for holding the vast majority of high rewarding jobs in America" (2). Moreover, job "churning" which destabilizes enduring careers in any one organization, compels individuals "to continually update their knowledge

---

3. John Dewey, "My Pedagogic Creed," *School Journal* 54 (1897): 77-80.

and skills," and thus places the onus on individuals "for developing their own learning plans" to ensure employment stability (Kohl 2000, 13). Kohl emphasizes that "people need continuous learning to stay occupationally relevant and the population interested in self-enrichment learning activities has mushroomed" (19).

Case in point, as suggested in a recent *New York Times* article, it is plausible that the master's degree may soon become the new bachelor's degree (Papano 2011). Furthermore, the development of postbaccalaureate certificate programs, oftentimes viewed as degree program feeders and suitable dropout options for educational "attainers," have become perhaps the most viable option for individuals seeking shorter and more cost-effective ways to differentiate themselves in an increasingly competitive job market. Attaining a postbaccalaureate degree, however, remains highly desirable among credential-seekers; thus, new master's and doctoral program development is mounting.

In most cases, a postsecondary educational institution aiming to expand or modify their degree offerings must vet the addition or "substantive" change through their chosen accrediting body. In addition to institutional accreditation, many colleges and universities also rely heavily on programmatic accreditation, granted by an entity that sets standards for acceptable levels of educational quality within a specific discipline—e.g., Association to Advance Collegiate Schools of Business (AACSB), Accreditation Board for Engineering and Technology (ABET) and American Psychological Association (APA) Committee on Accreditation (CoA). The advent of academic entrepreneurship and rapid program innovation has situated accreditation as a critical SEM issue. Moreover, a wave of new "credentialism" is partly fueled by postsecondary education executive, administrative, and academic leaders who view the development of new programs and degrees as a panacea to their enrollment problems.

Sundry postbaccalaureate degree choices include: 1) non-terminal master's degrees (e.g., MA, MBA, MS); 2) terminal master's (e.g., MFA, MSW, MPA); 3) terminal, non-professional doctorate (i.e., PhD), and 4) terminal, professional doctorate degrees (e.g., JD, MD, DBA). Beyond completing coursework, individuals seeking postbaccalaureate credentials may be required to fulfill one or more of the following "competency" or "experiential" curricular components: 1) theses, 2) capstone projects, 3) dissertations, 4) practicums, and/or 5) internships. These additional programmatic requirements can complicate issues of student persistence and institutional retention that are often associated with the conferment of a postbaccalaureate degree versus attainment of a graduate education or professional development certificate.

Arguably, individual pursuits for an enlarged portfolio of postbaccalaureate credentials can relegate postsecondary education as a commodity—degrees, certificates, connections—to be bought, consumed and leveraged solely for professional advancement. Conversely, adult learners may experience postbaccalaureate education as a transformative learning process. Merriam,

Caffarella, and Baumgartner (2007) explicate three key concepts of transformative learning that come into play for those "learning in adulthood": 1) life experience, 2) the nature of critical reflection and 3) transformative learning and development (144). Boucouvalas and Lawrence (2010) stress that "whereas experiential learning results in an expansion of knowledge, transformative learning is both epistemological and ontological, often involving a change in world view" (41). In his explication of "investing in learning," Bowen (1977) avows:

> *Our lives cannot be divided meaningfully between production and consumption—between means and ends. The activities we call means are as much a part of our lives and as much influence on our well-being as the activities we call consumption. (379)*

Thacker (2004) poses these provocative questions: "Is education a product? Is the student a consumer?" (197). Toward preserving and affirming conservative educational values, Thacker asserts his position: "Education is a process, not a product. Students are learners, not customers." (193). The ever-changing influx of students, demand for flexible programs, and necessity of agile academic planning, forces college and university academic administrators to assess the effects that shifting demographic and geographical compositions of their student body have on program delivery (e.g., in-person didactic, online synchronous, online asynchronous, hybrid, blended), faculty-student engagement, student development, and student learning.

Dolence (1993) posits that there is an inexorable relationship between SEM and an institution's academic programs. Dixon (1995) emphasizes the significance of understanding the students' learning needs of vis-à-vis faculty's academic expectations. On one side, academic programs depend on student enrollments (directly, or indirectly, through subsidies from more financially viable programs) for their existence; on the other side, students enroll at institutions largely because of the strength of particular academic programs, embodied and facilitated by the faculty. Notions of mutual fit of student and faculty interests, needs, and expectations have both relational and practical implications. Conceptualizing SEM in a context that attends to more diverse populations who seek out postbaccalaureate education necessitates a nuanced understanding of the juxtaposition of adulthood and studenthood; the nexus of the two is learning.

Student development as theory, research, and practice emerged from the scientific study of human development (Evans et al. 2009). Adulthood notwithstanding, learners are cautioned to "be skeptical of all educational pitches that ignore [their] studenthood" (Thacker 2004, 197). Thacker also emphasizes that learners should be just as leery of strategic uses of studenthood in higher education marketing dogma. From a student development lens, SEM is a holistic approach to planning for and addressing the learning needs of students. From a SEM lens, student development underscores "the ways that a student grows, progresses, or increases his or her developmental capabilities as a result of enrollment in an institution of higher education" (Rodgers 1990, 27). Harris (2010) argues that enrollment management professionals are responsible for more than supporting the enrollment and retention of students; they are also responsible for "caring about [students] as individuals" (90).

More broadly defined, student development is "the application of human development concepts in postsecondary settings so that everyone involved can master increasingly complex developmental tasks, achieve self-direction, and become independent" (Miller and Prince 1976, 3). Affective and behavioral transformation notwithstanding, student development theories focus on intellectual growth that can result from faculty engagement with students in a learning context. Plausible positive outcomes of student learning, however, are fundamentally tied to the particular instructional model in use. In other words, the method of learning from which students' intellectual growth is cultivated can, and most often will, yield distinct learning outcomes.

Kohl and LaPidus (2000) point out that "higher education institutions which are prepared to incorporate postbaccalaureate learners into their institution-wide mission rather than treating such education as a tangential activity are likely to have the greatest appeal to learners" (xiv). Hershey and Blanchard (1988) identify four stages of learners that foreground a learner-centered SEM orientation: 1) dependent learners, 2) interested learners, 3) involved learners, and 4) self-directed learners. Dependent learners look for and expect a teacher to direct their learning. Interested learners are motivated and confident; however, they come to subject matters with little or no knowledge, which renders them moderately self-directed. Involved learners possess skills and knowledge relevant to a subject, and therefore are well-positioned to explore specific content with the assistance of a subject matter expert who can guide them through their learning. Self-directed learners "are both willing and able to plan, execute, and evaluate their own learning with or without the help of a subject matter expert" (117).

Until now, there have been no efforts to develop a learner-centered SEM orientation. It is salient to note that SEM orientations are not mutually exclusive. In fact, Bontrager (2008) promotes bringing together different SEM orientations and directly addressing the "necessary juxtaposition of concept and process, as well as institutional and student interests" (17). He argues that administrative, academic, and market-centered orientations each imply the implementation of activities that although not student-centered should ultimately attend to student needs. Bontrager emphasizes that misappropriations of typified SEM orientations can result in attention being steered away from students and toward the interests of institutions and governing bodies. Thus, student success should be a focal point of any SEM agenda.

To that end, a learner-centered SEM orientation promotes student-centeredness, explicated by way of a student-focused orientation that accentuates "student as learner," as suggested by Thacker (2004). By interlacing and augmenting (with brackets, "[ ]") a student-focused SEM orientation with an academic SEM orientation, I construct a learner-centered SEM orientation that humbly embraces and exemplifies "adult learning theory" (see explication of "andragogy"[4] in Knowles, Holton and Swanson 2011) and "learning in adulthood" (Merriam, Caffarella and Baumgartner 2007).

A *student-focused orientation* to SEM:

focuses first and foremost on responding to the needs of the individual student at the in-stitution and on improving the one-on-one, interpersonal climate of the organization.... parallels the particular humanist mode of inquiry, with its focus on abstract learning and inquiry that enhances goals that serve broad humanitarian purposes....driven to understand the individual student and his or her experiences; it bases decisions upon such understandings....individual case study and detailed assessments and anecdotes of particular students or student groups are the most meaningful and influential sources of information (Kalsbeek 2007, 7).

An *academic orientation* to SEM:

focuses on broad purposes, emphasizing the general human benefits of the enhancement of learning and advancement of knowledge....is marked by a preference for structural decentralization, creativity, flexibility, and nonhierarchical lines of authority....parallels conceptual humanist mode of inquiry, with its focus on abstract learning and inquiry that enhances goals that serve broad humanitarian purposes ...emphasizes student learning outcomes, assessing the educational needs of communities, professions, and society, and focuses on how academic programs can be enhanced to promote broad human welfare (Kalsbeek 2007, 7).

A novel *learner-centered* orientation to SEM:

---

4. The Wikipedia entry for "andragogy" includes the following: "Especially in the USA 'andragogy' in the tradition of Malcolm Knowles, labels a specific theoretical and practical approach, based on a humanistic conception of self-directed and autonomous learners and teachers as facilitators of learning."

focuses first and foremost on responding to the [developmental] needs of the individual [learner] at the institution and on [promoting and supporting] the [andragogical] [learning culture] of the [academic spheres] of the organization....[also] focuses on broad purposes, emphasizing the general human benefits of the enhancement of learning and advancement of knowledge.... emphasizes student learning outcomes, assessing the educational needs of communities, professions, and society, and focuses on how academic programs can be enhanced to promote broad human welfare.... parallels the particular humanist mode of inquiry, with its focus on [adult] learning and [cultures of] inquiry [and growth], that enhances [social actions] that serve broad humanitarian purposes.... driven to understand the individual [learner] and his or her [common and distinct] experiences; it bases [learning goals] upon such understandings....[learning dimensions] and detailed assessments and [reflections] of particular [students] or [learner] groups are the most meaningful and influential [learning outcomes] (Kalsbeek 2007, 7).

I believe that learning is the new SEM frontier that has yet to be fully discovered in its conceptualization, and therefore remains scarcely explored or appropriated. A learner-centered SEM orientation recognizes that learners' self-concept, readiness, experience, orientation and motivation (Knowles, Holton and Swanson 2011) to learn are paramount to their student success and the viability of their respective college or university. This alternative take on SEM, and expansion of the orientations explicated by Kalsbeek (2007), are intended to incite new ways of conceptualizing SEM in a postbaccalaureate context. Moreover, a SEM focus on learners and learning is an explicit reminder that people seek education with some learning outcomes in mind. This is merely the beginning of contemplating how enrollment management professionals might shift from primarily addressing recruitment and retention administrative matters, and alternatively ascertaining understandings that enable them to paradoxically honor and confront learning—in relation to student success—at their institutions.

CONCLUSION: SEM SUCCESS FOR POSTBACCALAUREATE EDUCATION THROUGH A LEARNING, TRANSDISCIPLINARY FOCUS

Hossler and Kalsbeek (2008) emphasize that SEM "structure should follow strategy and so should reflect the particular, idiosyncratic institutional culture, climate, and character" (7). A learner-centered SEM orientation places learning at the heart of SEM organizing; it challenges critical viewpoints that SEM appropriation is achieved by way of structural positioning, political leveraging and organizational value shifting. Noteworthy, SEM recently garnered the attention of management theorists who maligned "enrollment management" as a "mundane innovation" of "precarious values" (Kraatz, Ventresca and Deng 2010). Interestingly, Kraatz et. al argue that "enrollment management poses a predictable (if incipient and often unrecognized) threat to established organizational values." They write:

> *Specifically, we emphasize that the EM structure undermines the autonomy of key internal elites and thereby lessens their ability and inclination to "defend the values entrusted to them" (Selznick, 1957: 94). We also argue that EM allows market values to unobtrusively penetrate a college and provides these values and their advocates with a structural and political foothold inside the organization. We buttress these theoretical arguments about EM's prima facie significance for organizational values with evidence from previous higher education research documenting its longer-term consequences for organizational value attainment* (Kraatz, Ventresca and Deng 2010, 1523).

Henderson (1998) reminds us, however, that "enrollment management was a practical necessity before it became a theoretical basis for organizing" (12). At the inception of enrollment management, Maguire (1976) and his colleagues at Boston College firmly believed and demonstrated that career-oriented "market prediction and institutional response," in the form of enrollment management, should not come at the cost of "value-oriented education" (18). Nonetheless, the constitutive and transformative potential of SEM is not always perceived as desirable and beneficial to American higher education. Hossler (2004) recalls that while attending an advisory board meeting for a national higher education organization, "a leading scholar who focuses on issues of access and equity leaned across the table and said quietly: 'Enrollment managers are ruining American higher education.'"

Quirk (2005) admonishes that chief enrollment managers have imposed business strategy techniques and "market-driven competition at the heart of the university" (128). He comes to rest, in the same article, where the introduction to this chapter began: mission and market. Taking a more balanced position, Quirk challenges the claim that chief enrollment managers are ruining American higher education. Contrary to merely "the cutthroat quest for competitive advantage," he steps back and considers the "work in the profession":

> *Although competition increasingly threatens a university's principles, the most innovative work in the profession comes from enrollment managers who attempt to align market with mission....Indeed, the sophisticated methods of enrollment management may be the only way for schools to hang on to their principles while surviving in a cutthroat marketplace* (Quirk 2005, 129).

I firmly believe that appropriations of SEM in the postbaccalaureate context have significant potential to destabilize market-laden criticism of enrollment management, and push colleges and universities beyond normative boundaries and isomorphic organizing that separates administrative and academic SEM orientations. Moreover, I posit that liminal learning borders may hold the greatest promise for value-centered organizational arrangements and actions. I argue that some of the most successful chief enrollment managers are those who consistently and actively advocate and create space for voices of the absent and contingent to be heard, felt and experienced. The stark reality is that underrepresented, underserved, and disenfranchised students often lack the requisite knowledge to navigate the milieu of higher education. It is, therefore, imperative for enrollment management professionals to understand that student success is a complex, messy, and slippery construct that often eludes facile imperatives to define and circumscribe normative frames of reference and predictive behaviors that co-opt orderly conceptions of SEM, marginalizing innovative approaches and foundations that promote and support transformational learning.

Consigning SEM to a single orientation as a "value-threatening administrative innovation" (Kraatz, Ventresca and Deng 2010, 1523) disregards, and may reject SEM's relevance as structure, process, practice and profession. I contend that SEM can break free of constrained disciplinary boundaries and subsequently rise above and beyond interdisciplinary thought.[5] At its most innovative state, the transdisciplinarity of SEM appropriation renders it as both research and practice that interlaces disparate disciplinary knowledge and action. Whereas an interdisciplinary approach creates its own theoretical, conceptual and methodological identity, a transdisciplinary approach goes one step further; it is "based upon a common theoretical understanding, and must be accompanied by a mutual interpenetration of disciplinary epistemologies" (Van den Besselaar and Heimeriks 2001, 2). Transdisciplinary actions are 'borderwork' that links scholarship and practice across disciplinary boundaries, thereby developing cross-disciplinary understandings that transcend the generalizing, decontextualizing, and reductionist tendencies of discipline-based approaches (Horlick-Jones 2004).

Arguably, transdisciplinary imperatives, such as SEM, promise the greatest hope to realize a much needed transformation of American higher education. In *The Heart of Higher Education*, the authors suggest "putting wheels" on much needed transformation through conversations (Palmer and Zajonc 2010, 126). Palmer and Zajonc insightfully point out that higher education structures, particularly disciplinarity, encourages fragmentation and isolation that inherently leads to the privatization of work and actions. That is, purely disciplinary approaches

---

5. This paragraph contains text and ideas from Snowden (2010)

are effectively accomplished behind "closed doors" out of view of others (128). In a related, but slightly different turn, Johnson (1995) argues that the "hinged door allows a selection of what gets in and what gets out" (259). Hence, unyielding disciplinary discourses and standpoints can constrain the influence of novel ideas of a particular discipline. Moreover, disciplinary dissonance oftentimes enables individuals to "effectively 'black box' the work of others...while at the same time being able to depend on and make use of the products of their labors" (Suchman, 1995, 58). In short, "remaking the American university" (Zemsky, Wegner and Massy 2005) into a "liberating and capacity-building environment" depends on transformative conversation, integration, actualization and participation that aims to recover and renew a commitment to holistic education (Palmer and Zajonc 2010, vii).

I believe that discovering and unleashing the transformative power of SEM's transdisciplinarity is an intriguing and constructive alternative to cursorily typifying the construct and practice as "congenial though often mundane" (Kraatz, Ventresca and Deng 2010, 1521). Moreover, I challenge enrollment management professionals to look beyond commonplace conceptions and appropriations to answer a revived and befitting clarion call: "We need to match our talents with the identified gaps and contribute to this evolving profession" (Black 2004b, 19). Toward that end, this chapter is border-work; it fills a gap in enrollment management literature by introducing a novel standpoint that calls attention to the dearth of scholarship on SEM in the postbaccalaureate context, and in respect to postsecondary education learning.

If indeed the rise and enactment of SEM has played a significant role in imposing "competition at the heart of the university" (Quirk 2005), then it is imperative for enrollment management professionals to recalibrate our actions around the higher calling of education—learning. The development, enactment, and promotion of a learner-centered SEM orientation can yield appropriations that are extraordinarily innovative and value-laden, particularly in respect to discovering critical intersections and creating stronger connections between enrollment management and accreditation processes that place foci on learning outcomes. Moreover, employing a learner-centered SEM orientation in the postbaccalaureate context aims to counter the claim that enrollment management is an "ostensibly innocuous" innovation with "value undermining effects" (Kraatz, Ventresca and Deng 2010, 1521).

In conclusion, I put forth that SEM in the postbaccalaureate context should have:

- A distinctive history, including key individuals that influence its development, penetration and entrenchment in higher education.
- Institutional organizing principles that structure valued-laden actions and convey meaning, rationality, and purpose—in terms of its emergence, evolution and maturity; professions that it embodies.
- Interconnected organizations comprised of professionals with an astute awareness of interorganizational dependencies within the graduate, professional and continuing education domains.
- Organizations, professions, and professionals that attend to valued interests and noble efforts to promote the diffusion, adoption and persistence of SEM as an essential and still-developing bastion in American higher education.

10

INTERNATIONAL INITIATIVES WITHIN ENROLLMENT MANAGEMENT

Chris J. Foley
Director of Undergraduate Admissions
Indiana University-Purdue University Indianapolis

Christine Kerlin
Vice President, University Center and Strategic Planning (retired)
Everett Community College, WA

CHAPTER 10

"In the twenty-first century, more than ever before, an education that focuses exclusively on a student's home country is inadequate. Understanding the world today is analogous to being able to read the street signs in a major city."

—Dumont and Pastor, 2010

INTRODUCTION

With over 690,000 international students enrolled in U.S. post-secondary institutions and over 260,000 U.S. students studying abroad, the subject of international education on college and university campuses is not new (Open Doors 2010). However, the *integration* of international education into strategic plans and enrollment management for many colleges and universities is new, and its importance is increasing. For professionals in institutions where consideration of the role of international student enrollment and international programs is emerging, this chapter will help them focus on the rationale, value and implications of international education initiatives in strategic enrollment management. Those in institutions already engaged in the international aspects of enrollment management may find this chapter helpful in broadening their perspective.

The challenge for international educators is to speak about their office's activities in the terms of enrollment management. This can be difficult for international educators who are used to thinking in terms of international education as a "social good" that has positive consequences for the campus and society as a whole. However, in an enrollment management environment, simply saying something is worthwhile is not sufficient. There are many "worthwhile" things in which an institution can engage, and in a world of diminishing resources, a college or university must choose among many worthwhile activities. The challenge for international educators is to make the case that international activities are not only worthwhile, but a valuable investment of institutional resources. And, just as important, international educators need to be a voice at the table during institutional strategic planning to ensure that the institution's view of its horizons includes consideration of international initiatives.

Enrollment management relies on many key elements, such as alignment with the institution's overall mission and strategic plan, the student life cycle from prospective student to graduate and donor, comprehensive planning across an organization, data collection and analysis, an emphasis on the academic program, and other issues outlined in this book. International educators, and a broad cross-section of an institution's leaders, must understand that the integration of international education in enrollment management is built on a number of these key elements, several of which are discussed in this chapter.

SECTION I: THE "ENROLLMENT PORTFOLIO" AS AN INTERNATIONAL ENROLLMENT MANAGEMENT METAPHOR

In an interview with *The Greentree Gazette*, President Art Kirk of St. Leo University compared running a university to running a mutual fund (Kirk 2009). In his comparison, creating the right student "enrollment portfolio" is similar to developing an investment portfolio. Each year, institutions engage in enrollment management to recruit, enroll and retain not just the right number of students, but also the right "mix" of students (for example, geographic origin, ethnicity, academic preparation and interest, socio-economic status, etc.). This strategy may not only meet the desire for a stimulating educational and social environment or for a deliberate type of tuition revenue, but it also reduces reliance on populations in a limited demographic set. As with investment portfolios, it is important to diversify an institution's enrollment portfolio to minimize the impact of any single influence. Adding international students to the "enrollment portfolio" is another way to diversify enrollment and reduce vulnerability that results from too narrow a set of incoming students.

For example, if Big Campus State University depends on a significant portion of its revenue from non-resident tuition of students predominantly from New York, New Jersey, and Chicago, and an economic crisis hits these particular areas, like the one which began in the latter half of 2008, Big Campus State University may look to ramping up its international recruitment as a way to replace these non-resident tuition dollars. As another example, a community college with an aviation maintenance program may have historically established a strong flow of students from local high schools so that a drop in the 18-year old demographic could manifest as a problem for the campus or workforce; however, establishing relationships with civil aviation organizations in selected countries could regain enrollment losses by expanding international student enrollment.

The portfolio metaphor can be carried further. The international portion of an enrollment portfolio is not a single segment, but a collection of smaller ones. Diversification within the international enrollment is also important. Reliance on only one or two countries, or on one country's government scholarship program, can be risky if any one of those segments takes an economic fall or changes policy. This scenario is all too real for those who remember the financial distress of the late 1990s caused by the sudden reduction of students from Japan, Korea, Malaysia, and Indonesia when those economies faltered.

But just as with investment portfolios, over-diversification can also impede success. Diluting recruitment resources across too many international markets may limit results. It is important to know an institution's goals and resources in order to build a focused enrollment plan. For a large public institution, it may be feasible to target ten to twenty countries in two to four geographic regions of the world, in concert with an analysis of the match between institutional strengths and student interests. For small institutions and/or for those institutions with a narrower set of program offerings, perhaps five to ten countries in two to three regions of the world may be appropriate. Within these markets, it may be efficient to designate primary, secondary, and tertiary markets. For example, Mumbai, Bangalore, and Chennai may be primary markets and the rest of India may be a tertiary market. This allows for prioritization in recruitment opportunities in each area. It also facilitates the development of communities of students with common cultures on the campus.

The effort to develop an enrollment portfolio with an international component requires solid data collection and analysis, both internally and externally. Determining goals and identifying strategies and tactics should be driven by a thorough understanding of the type of institution, the types of international students who would be a good match, the ability to support international students, the resources available to successfully recruit, retain and graduate international students, and the perceived opportunities in other countries. Further discussion of the importance and use of data is found in Section III: The International Professional as Data Miner, on page 207.

After identifying the segments of the enrollment portfolio, it's time to build pipelines. Pipelines can't be built overnight, and it's important to invest at the right time in a particular market to take advantage of a boom in interest from a particular country. Here, again, the investment portfolio metaphor is apt. Like investment positions, timing is critical. It takes investment over time to build the right contacts, prospect pool, alumni, etc. to have a good return. These investments can take several years to develop. Moreover, opportunities can develop suddenly, and those institutions that are already there will see the greatest benefit. This requires some foresight, usually strengthened by a close reading of international trends and staying tuned to what other institutions are doing.

Determining the right mix of student and institutional interests is important, and this must be done on an institution by institution basis. Colleges and universities need to determine the depth and elasticity of their resources, tolerance of risk, enrollment goals, and institutional mission. All of these requirements are similar to those of developing an investment portfolio, and like investment portfolios, creating the right enrollment portfolio and establishing an international position in it, can be essential to weathering the changing winds of enrollment patterns.

Meeting enrollment and retention goals and achieving the optimum mix of students underlies many enrollment management efforts. And, as described above, there are many considerations that contribute toward success. The following sections outline other aspects of integrating international efforts into enrollment management.

SECTION II: MAKING THE CASE FOR THE INTERNATIONAL INVESTMENT

To be successful, international services and recruitment offices must understand the basics of enrollment management. Depending on the institution, enrollment management may focus on the recruitment and enrollment of students as well as extend to retention programs and the array of academic programs; it may even cross into capital expansion, alumni, and development. From an international perspective, enrollment management could include the programming and advising for international students, study abroad programs, institutional marketing, advancement, internship and co-op opportunities, and alumni relations in addition to the recruitment and initial enrollment of international students.

Though it is critical that international enrollment match an institution's sense of mission and desire to foster a "social good," such as the achievement of an international perspective in campus life, it is not uncommon for enrollment managers to calculate return on investment (ROI) perspectives. International recruitment is an expensive investment. International travel is expensive, the costs to evaluate international credentials are substantial, and specialists who work with international students are also generally more costly than the typical "road warrior" approach of a domestic admissions office. An institution may find it worthwhile to analyze its recruitment expenses versus tuition revenue as one way to understand ROI, using a method such as in Table 1, on the following page.

Table 1: Return-on-Investment Comparison of International Recruitment at a Public Baccalaureate Institution

Student Type	Cost to Recruit One Student*	Revenue from Tuition over 4 years	Return on Investment for One Student
In-State Student	$594	$23,798 ($5,949 per year)	$40 for each dollar spent
Out-of-State Student	$4,381	$82,560 ($20,640 per year)	$18 for each dollar spent
International Student	$4,903	$82,560 ($20,640 per year)	$16 for each dollar spent

*Note: In this sample, recruitment costs include staff salaries and benefits, materials and supplies, travel, and other related expenses. In reality, each institution may have its own method of calculating ROI for recruitment depending on whether personnel, scholarship, or other expenses are included in the costs.

In the example in Table 1, the return for each dollar spent to recruit an international student is 11% less than that for an out-of-state student. In this scenario, the number of out-of-state students is relatively low—some 4% of the incoming class. If the institution had a much larger out-of state population (say 20-40% of the incoming class), the cost to recruit these students would drop and the return on investment would increase dramatically. However, unless the institution expands its international population at a comparable rate, the cost to recruit an international student would remain expensive. If the discussion simply revolved around tuition generation and there were limited resources, the enrollment manager (or enrollment committee) would most likely place the institution's resources in recruiting domestic students because he or she would have to spend more money to recruit fewer international students. On the other hand, there is still a substantial return on investment that can compel an institution to see value in international recruitment.

Another example of making the case for the inclusion of international enrollment in the institution's student mix is to develop a more detailed business plan on a larger, long-term scale. Compared to the ROI analysis as seen in Table 1, Table 2 provides a simplified illustration of how a small college might plan to expand its international student enrollment by looking at expense and income for a whole initiative, rather than on a per-student basis.

Table 2: Sample International Initiative Business Plan

International Education Initiative Expense and Income Model - Annual Projection	
EXPENSES	
A) International Education Office:	
Director, International Student Services, salary and benefits	100,000
International Student Advisor, salary and benefits	65,000
Program Assistant, salary and benefits	42,000
Travel	45,000
Goods and services, printing, postage, etc	10,000
Memberships and professional development and conferences	8,000
Advertising, marketing	40,000
Office Set-up	3,500
B) Instruction, Intensive English Language Program faculty	50,000
C) Instruction, for Faculty Development, Curriculum Development, Faculty Exchange, etc	40,000
D) Administrative Services Overhead	30,000
Total initial investment, 2011-12:	433,500

Note: This analysis assumes that the college reformulates the resources currently used to enroll 30 international students, and creates an International Education Initiative with additional staffing and instructional resources with enrollment growth goals. For the purposes of this model, all students, expenditures and income are considered "new".

Figures in the "Loss/Gain" column represent investment for the first two years, then income that can be allocated back to the international initiatives and/or to campus-wide needs.

ENROLLMENT PROJECTIONS AND INCOME 5-Year Plan	Cost of staffing and resources	Addition of 5% annual increase in salaries and expenses overall plus additional staffing	Student enrollment goals (headcount)	Annual income from tuition/ fees, est $8,000 each	Loss/Gain
2011-12: Current Year, with staffing, expenses and investment using items above as a basis	433,500	N/A	30	240,000	(193,500)
2012-13: Continue with staffing and resources as outlined in the base above	433,500	455,175	50	400,000	(55,175)
2013-14: Continue with staffing and budget as outlined in the base above	455,175	477,934	80	640,000	162,066
2014-15: Due to increased enrollment, add an International Student Specialist at $70,000	525,175	551,434	120	960,000	408,566
2015-16: Expand housing options with a one-time $700,000 capital investment and part-time housing and campus life coordinator ($40,000). Tuition increases to $9,000 per year.	1,265,175	1,328,434	170	1,530,000	201,566
2016-17: Expand Intensive English Language Program by $50,000. Add a dedicated credential evaluation specialist ($70,000)	748,434	785,855	220	1,980,000	1,194,145

For such plans to succeed, international educators must understand how enrollment management planning is done at their institution. Students and programs that add value to the educational experience are important factors for enrollment management, which, at its best, is more than a strict assessment of dollars and cents. But expenses, income, and return on investment are nonetheless central to the health of an institution and the inclusion of international enrollment and programs must withstand financial scrutiny. Tables 1 and 2 may spark ideas for a method to analyze ROI at an institution by integrating international initiatives into enrollment management.

SECTION III: THE INTERNATIONAL PROFESSIONAL AS DATA MINER

Proposing and assessing international enrollment initiatives requires good data not only to conduct an ROI assessment, but to plan, manage and assess ongoing efforts. Anecdotes and information "from the field" can be helpful to understand the nuances of quantitative data, but an enrollment management plan should have quantitative data as a foundation for its strategies. Enrollment managers must gather as much data beforehand as possible, establish regular reports or "dashboards" to monitor key indicators, and integrate new data as needed to determine what is happening in the enrollment landscape and take any necessary action to maximize the effect of programs to recruit, retain and graduate students (Duniway and Wiegand 2009; Yale 2010).

In general, international enrollment managers have had a harder time collecting data on these students. It is important to observe what types of data points are of value to campus discussions and to then collect similar data points for the international populations. It is imperative to become a part of these discussions at the early stages, if possible, and if not, to then align any program assessments with those metrics that are of value to the campus. Once collected and presented, gaining entrance to leadership discussions will become easier. Identifying these metrics of value is essential even if the data is not currently collected because they can help inform resource allocations and show an interest and understanding of campus values and goals that can then be expanded to include these new international elements. As a result, the first step for international enrollment managers is not to just get access to data, but to identify what data should be collected. The second step, then, is to start collecting it for future use.

Two types of data are helpful: institutional data and market data. Institutional data helps to understand internal enrollment trends while market data puts the institutional data into context as well as identifies potential markets.

Institutional Data

Planning must begin with an accurate review of the current situation. International educators need to know not only how many international students are on campus, but more granular data points such as:

- Where do applicants come from?
- Where do the enrolled students come from?
- What is the yield on prospects to applicants? Admit rate? Admits to enrollees?
- What are their retention rates (first to second semester, first to second year)?
- What are the graduation rates of international students?
- What are the most popular majors?
- What type of financial assistance is requested, and what is given, if any?
- What portion of graduate research assistants or graduate instructors are international students?
- Do graduates return to their home country?
- Do graduates transfer to other institutions, and where?
- Do graduates get jobs?
- Do graduates donate to the institution?

Most importantly, how does this data compare to the similar data points for the general population of the institution? If they compare positively, these can be good reasons to expand these elements of the institution's portfolio. If they are negative, they may require new strategies and, in some cases, resources to improve.

Unfortunately, many institutions neglect to build information systems that are sufficient to collect robust data sets for international students. Things as simple as sufficient space for international addresses and for visa status, or the ability to manage international naming conventions (for example, space limitations or students with single names) are often overlooked. Assuring that student information systems collect necessary and correct information is important for international student enrollment analysis. It also benefits those schools that enroll large numbers of domestic students with international backgrounds.

Market Data

From a recruitment perspective, knowing where to recruit is just as important as knowing how to recruit international students. Though institutional data is most helpful, it is data about the students who are not currently enrolled that will help place this data into context and determine the following:

- How mature are the markets in which the institution is currently strong?
- Is there potential to grow these markets?
- Where are similar markets with good potential?
- Who are the competitors and collaborators in both established and new markets?

An important reminder: Do not ignore those international students already in the U.S. For some colleges and universities, the U.S. is the largest feeder country of international students. These students are exchange students, dependents of staff working in businesses in the U.S., dependents of government staff, recent immigrants, students enrolled at 2-year colleges, or students at boarding schools. Many times, these students are overlooked by U.S. college and university recruitment programs because they are not "domestic" from a citizenship perspective yet they are not "international" from an education background. But they are, in an international recruitment perspective, "in your own back yard."

For students in other countries, the amount of market data available is not as robust as that for domestic recruitment. Still, there are resources about international enrollments that can inform your assessment of market potential. Here are a few sources:

- *Open Doors* is an annual survey of international student enrollments and study abroad published by the Institute of International Education (IIE).[1] Though this report does not allow for granular analysis, it does provide a general idea of market position. For example, if there are 216 students from Kazakhstan studying in the U.S., and an institution has 22 of them, this is a market share of 10% of the students from Kazakhstan in the U.S. An institution should weigh its chances of increasing that market share in light of the potential growth opportunities in that market. The *Atlas of Student Mobility*, also published by IIE, is a more thorough analysis of student flows to and from countries.[2] Though not all countries are profiled in this resource, it does have a good representation. The data not only include numbers of students studying abroad, but where their top destinations are as well as demographic data (like college-aged population and average income) that help enrollment managers understand the viability of expanding a market in a particular country.
- Testing services (like SAT or TOEFL) publish annual digests of their results. These digests include information on international students who took the examinations, and in some cases, the testing service will provide greater access to this information for research, like the Enrolment Planning Service through the College Board.[3] These tools

---

1. See: http://www.iie.org/en/Research-and-Publications/Open-Doors
2. See: http://atlas.iienetwork.org/
3. See: http://professionals.collegeboard.com/higher-ed/recruitment/eps

indicate how many students took their tests and what their grades were, as well as family data. For a test like the SAT, one can determine how many good students are in a particular country, and how many of them intend to study in the U.S., since the SAT is an exam typically taken only by students hoping to study in the U.S.

- As recently described in *The Chronicle of Higher Education*, the U.S. Department of Commerce provides information about and connections with country and regional educational services (Fischer, 2011a). Education U.S.A. also provides country and regional information and advisor assistance for both international students and U.S. institutions.[4]
- Developing a data-sharing or other type of consortium with peer institutions can also be beneficial (Fischer 2001b). Though perhaps more cumbersome than the other data sources (which are a quick web-search or book away), understanding what happens at similar institutions can be even more helpful because student flows will differ from institution to institution. Urban institutions, for example, will attract a different type of student than rural institutions. Community colleges may attract different students than large universities or residential private colleges.

SECTION IV: CONSIDERATIONS FOR EFFECTIVE INTERNATIONAL ENROLLMENT MANAGEMENT

Each institution differs in its approach to international enrollment, programs and services. This section provides some food for thought on the strategies and tactics that may affect the way an institution approaches the successful integration of international enrollment and international programs with its overall enrollment management planning.

Recruitment, Admissions and Enrollment Services

International applications are usually handled by either a sub-unit of the admissions office or the international advising office. Though neither model is superior to the other, each does have particular strengths and weaknesses.

If it is housed with domestic admissions, it is easier for the international admissions unit to stay on the same page with domestic admissions standards and recruitment. In addition, the unit can gain efficiencies in recruitment by piggy-backing with domestic initiatives, realize savings by bundling publications, website references and portals, and tap into data entry pools and contracting with fulfillment houses that handle mass mailing tasks. However, because it

---

4. See: http://educationusa.state.gov/

becomes part of a larger admissions office, it is possible for the international admissions office to get side-lined or pushed aside. Since the bulk of most enrollments at U.S. colleges and universities are made up of domestic students, international admissions professionals may have to fight to make sure international education goals are met in this environment, and they can be seen as an irritant in recruitment initiatives (for example, always needing that extra address line in the database or determining for certain that SAT may not be taken in some countries). For some schools, inclusion in the mainstream admissions operation may mean that international inquiries and applications are handled by a generalist rather than an international specialist.

In the international services setting, the situation is almost the opposite. Here, the international admissions unit is valued because it is the source of the students they serve, and there is an understanding of "things international." However, here the international admissions group may not have the resources necessary to recruit and process applications from abroad (e.g., travel budgets, adequate technology, etc.) or an office that maximizes efficient processing of applications, and staff may be pulled away to advise current students in busy times. Moreover, international admissions practices and policies may get out of sync with domestic admissions policies which can lead to equity issues.

Either model can be successful as long as there is sufficient support of the international admissions unit. The key, like many things in enrollment management systems, is communication and coordination. In some cases a hybrid model can be developed where parts of the admissions and recruitment responsibility can be shared across departmental boundaries. In other settings, just as is the case with other elements of enrollment management, a coordinating committee might be a successful model. Instead of depending upon a strict organizational structure to manage the international aspects of enrollment, some campuses manage them through a committee structure that relies on cooperation and communication.

In most cases, practices in the recruitment and admission of international students are very similar to those of domestic students. In an increasingly globalized world, the expectations of prospective undergraduates are similar whether they are in New York or Seoul. The growing involvement of U.S. "helicopter" parents in the recruitment process is not new to international recruiters who have long been used to recruiting parents as much as students. A focus on outcomes, rankings, and speedy personal responses are important to both international and domestic applicants. However, despite their similarities, international applications typically differ in four major ways that are important for enrollment managers to acknowledge.

Applications Coordinated by Overseas Agents and Partners

A growing number of institutions are creating relationships with overseas organizations and institutions through which the development of a prospective student and his/her admission application is forwarded to the U.S. institution. These relationships are often formed for the sake of improving international student flow to the institution and perhaps bringing a desired sector of the "enrollment portfolio" to the institution. Inherent in these partnerships may be unique processes for handling and responding to these applications. Special admission criteria may apply or follow-up information may be different than for other applicants. Attention needs to be paid to this differential handling, often requiring additional resources.

The use of "overseas agents" may be seen as controversial. Abuses can occur that result in lack of standards, inappropriate placement or falsified records, for example. Institutions engaged with overseas agents should exercise care in their selection, create detailed agreements, and monitor the process and outcomes carefully. As of this writing, guidelines are being considered by professional organizations (Fischer 2009; Ivory 2011; McMurtrie 2008).

Credentials Evaluation

International students, of course, typically come from another educational system. This means that somewhere in the admission process, someone will need to interpret the international academic records so that they can be assessed using admission standards developed for students from U.S. high schools and colleges. This usually involves specialized skills, either of in-house staff or an outside credentials evaluation agency. [5]

An institution's decision about handling international credentials can reflect its commitment to including international enrollment in its overall enrollment planning. For example, institutions that actively recruit international students toward target enrollment goals will realize that one of the competitive factors in enrolling and retaining international students is an astute and timely evaluation of their secondary and perhaps post-secondary transcripts from their home country. Whether a credential evaluation service or their own staff does the evaluation, it is important that the process be clear to the applicants and backed up by knowledgeable staff. This requires an institution to invest in the continuous professional development of its staff so that the right admission, placement and transfer credit decisions are made. Delays in admission

---

5. The website of the National Association of Credential Evaluation Services (NACES) is found at www.naces.org and provides a resource for locating credential evaluation services. Though a credential evaluation service can provide an institution with a careful analysis of a foreign transcript, it still remains the responsibility of the institution to interpret that analysis and apply admission and transfer credit standards appropriate to that institution.

decisions and confusing information about the possible transfer credit indicated by credentials can undermine the resources spent on recruitment. Skilled personnel and clear processes also support the identification of fraudulent transcripts from prospective students and save the institution from difficult situations.

At the community college, this actually has a wider effect, since many community colleges enroll students who live in the U.S. now, but have educational records from another country. In such cases, expert staff and a clear process are a benefit to the whole institution, not only the international program.

Visa Documentation

Besides international credentials, international students also require visa documentation to gain entrance into the U.S. It is essential that institutions maintain their ability to issue this documentation. This adds a very important factor in the international aspects of enrollment management because it involves an element of necessary "compliance" with federal policy. Like being a provider of financial assistance, institutions assume a certain level of legal obligation to comply with federal immigration policies. This can come with necessary investments in the training and staff necessary to remain in compliance with federal regulations, but it can also be a helpful trump card in debates over resources because remaining in compliance is not optional. It is a necessity.

Part of this process is, of course, the demonstration by students that they have adequate funding to support their studies in the U.S. Collecting and reviewing this information can be cumbersome for the student as well as the office, and it is another element that colleges and universities must account for in their enrollment management plans. However, there is a benefit to receiving this information because it can give institutions yet another indicator of a student's intention to enroll. If a student submits this required information, chances are higher that they will enroll, and if they do not, odds are they will not enroll because they cannot enter the U.S.

As with other elements in the processing of admissions, it is essential that the issuance of visa documentation for new admits be issued very quickly. Commonly, it is believed by admissions professionals that "the first I-20 wins," and a fast response can improve the yield from this population. Also, having the staff available to help work with new admits to prepare them for their visa interview can be very beneficial in building a strong relationship with future students.

Language Barriers

Though not applicable to all international students, language barriers are real issues in working with international students and their families. Those students whose native language is not English are often unfamiliar with the vocabularies used in U.S. colleges and universities. Familiar terms like "transcript," "high school," "college," "grade," or "credit" can be foreign to non-U.S. educated students, regardless of their native language. Furthermore, the concept of having to apply for college is commonly unfamiliar to non-U.S. students. Therefore, it is crucial for the international offices to continuously work within the enrollment management setting to ensure that student service units are linguistically "international friendly."

Scholarships and Financial Assistance

International students are typically not eligible for federal or state financial assistance, and they generally must privately fund much of their education. Because of this, scholarships can be important in recruiting and retaining international students. In addition to being able to assist students in funding their education, scholarships are an important source of prestige for international students. U.S. parents generally appreciate being able to say that their student is going to college "on scholarship"—regardless of the size of the scholarship. This is often the case in international societies as well. A scholarship can "leverage" a student's decision to enroll at the institution.

In many enrollment management systems, the method of awarding scholarships is highly sophisticated (Kalsbeek and Hossler 2008). Because many scholarships are essentially "discounts" on tuition, the need to properly plan for them is essential to ensure that the institution achieves its revenue goals while attracting the right types of students to the institution. Moreover, the institution needs to make sure the scholarship offer hits the right "price point" for a student in a way that will persuade the student to enroll. If the college or university offers too little scholarship, the student may not enroll. However, if the institution offers too much scholarship, then the institution is losing money that could be used for other things, including scholarships for other students. In the domestic context, these packaging strategies can be quite sophisticated. It is important, then, for international educators to be at the table during scholarship discussions.

The inclusion of international students in general scholarship schemes can differ by type of institution. It is more common for private institutions to package international students along with their domestic students. Public institutions, on the other hand, are less likely to do so because they may have fewer scholarships for non-resident students. Since international students are often lumped into the non-resident pool, they may not be eligible for scholarships at public institutions. Some institutions may provide some limited tuition discounts for new international students and then provide more access to scholarships for continuing students. Community colleges, whose low tuition may be attracting some international students in the first place, often don't see themselves as positioned to offer locally raised funds to international students. However, there are many examples of community colleges that provide focused scholarships as well as tuition discounting for international students.

Criteria can be another common difficulty for scholarship awards to international students. For instance, if a scholarship requires a certain SAT or ACT score, but the institution does not require an SAT or ACT score for international students, then many will not be eligible. The same may be true if a scholarship requires documented federal financial aid eligibility based on the FAFSA. It is important, for this reason, that international educators participate in scholarship or tuition waiver discussions to make sure that criteria do not inadvertently exclude international students or to learn about available alternative awarding criteria.

Cost is a significant factor in the decisions of international students, and incorporating some institutional strategies to address this concern is an important aspect of an international enrollment management plan.

SECTION V: RETENTION

Enrollment management is more than enrollment targets, recruitment tactics and entry processes. Those efforts certainly do provide a strong foundation for student and institutional success if done well, but an equally critical component of enrollment management is the continuous emphasis on the student's journey through the institution.

This is as true for international students as it is for domestic students. International student success and retention efforts will vary in different institutions, and may differ somewhat from the efforts directed at domestic students.

Orientation and Advising

Typically, an institution should assure that international students are engaged in a specialized orientation process that enables them to learn about the norms and behaviors of the institution and the American society. Orientations also provide practical advice ranging from transportation to banking, medical care, campus vocabulary and more. An orientation can also provide a warm welcome and a way to assure new international students that there are supportive staff and future friends to help them (Fischer 2011c; Sewall 2010).

Advising for international students includes academic guidance as well as procedures and services that help students stay in compliance with their student visa status. It is important that academic advisors and the students themselves understand that what may be possible for a domestic student (such as taking a part-time credit load) may not be within the rules for an international student's visa status. It is also possible that transfer options, internship opportunities, and career tracks will be different for international students.

Student Life

Housing options can make or break an international student's enrollment decision and experience. For those institutions without residence halls, care must be taken to support student access to local housing or family home-stay options. Institutions with residence halls must consider deadlines, how roommates are assigned, and how theme-based housing may or may not be appropriate. Residence hall staff needs education and training regarding international cultures and student needs.

International student clubs or other organized activities may be appropriate on a given campus. For many community colleges, where "residence life" is not a component, finding ways for international students to socialize broadly is a challenge that must be met.

SECTION VI: BEYOND ENROLLMENT TARGETS

This section focuses on making a case for the inclusion of international enrollment in overall enrollment management planning, as well as describing a number of the factors in international enrollment management that align with institutional enrollment planning. The admissions, financial aid and retention aspects described above are good examples of the wide range of operational considerations that would have to underlie a serious and successful commitment to assuring that international enrollment is not simply an additional number in the overall enrollment portfolio metrics. As with managing the enrollment of domestic students, sound operational resources, strategies and activities are the ingredients for successfully achieving goals.

International initiatives in institutional enrollment management are not limited to a focus on international student enrollment. Integrating other international aspects can also play an important role in institutional enrollment success, such as study abroad programs, alumni development, internationalizing the curriculum, faculty exchange, and more. Two examples of how these topics can stimulate successful enrollment and student success are described below.

Study Abroad

Study abroad is increasingly critical to enrollment management. As an internationalized education becomes ever more important, U.S. students are looking for colleges and universities that can offer a wide range of study abroad opportunities. Institutions can assert that they offer extra value to students through these opportunities, thus building an additional attraction for new and continuing students, including new types of students they wish to attract (Connell 2010; Hulstrand 2011).

As with international enrollment, specialized resources are needed to support an effective study abroad program. Advisors need to be familiar with study abroad options, and resources need to be devoted to developing and overseeing these programs. Destinations need to be continuously reviewed to make sure that students are safe, and procedures need to be developed to handle emergencies and crises. Partnerships with overseas institutions for exchange purposes need to be viable and mutually supported.

There is also a fiscal element to study abroad. Because U.S. colleges charge tuition to their students, they must make sure that they plan for students to study at another institution, and that fiscal arrangements are made that will not inappropriately compromise the institution's budget. For example, in the traditional exchange program model, students typically simply

---

IUPUI Promotes Study Abroad

In 2008, Indiana University-Purdue University Indianapolis launched its "RISE to the IUPUI Challenge." RISE stands for Research, International, Services and Experiential learning opportunities. The initiative seeks to engage students more deeply in their learning. Each undergraduate student is challenged to include at least two of the four RISE experiences into their degree programs. The international portion targets students from within the U.S. to engage in the global environment.

Students can fulfill the international requirement through specific coursework (e.g., area studies classes or seminars taught via teleconference in collaboration with classrooms in another college) or study abroad opportunities. To support this effort, special scholarships were created to encourage students to study abroad, and offered to students as freshmen. In addition, the university established one of its top scholarships (the Plater International Scholarship Program) to attract high ability students who were interested in international studies.

---

exchange seats. The U.S. student continues to pay tuition to the U.S. institution, and the international student does the same at his or her institution. As long as these exchanges are 1:1, the U.S. institution is generally fine. However, when not enough U.S. students participate in the exchange, U.S. institutions can find themselves giving away seats to the in-coming exchange students. It is therefore important for institutions to carefully integrate exchange programs into their enrollment planning.

Not all study abroad programs use a 1:1 exchange model. Some are created and led by a faculty member at a distant site. Others take advantage of another institution's program(s) by referring their students to such a program and then utilizing a transfer credit agreement to re-capture the credit (and the student).

Alumni

The relationship between an institution and student does not end with graduation. Because of this, enrollment management should be closely linked with alumni associations and college/university foundations. The missions of each of these units co-mingle with those of enrollment managers, and it is vital that they do the same for international alumni as well. Alumni can prove to be great contributors to recruitment (e.g., by hosting overseas receptions or contacting prospective students), retention (e.g. by helping prospective students see the value of a degree), and fundraising (e.g. for scholarships). Not only that, enrollment management activities such as marketing can also help support the missions of the alumni association and foundation by generating "buzz" about their alma mater. Education is an investment in oneself, but the value of this investment can change over time, depending upon the reputation of the college or university. This reputation is not just built by the activities of faculty and athletics, but just as much by the students who apply and enroll to the institution. Just as growing interest from a prospective student is a good thing for an institution, it is also good for alumni because the value of the degree they already have grows as well. Therefore it is important for enrollment management offices to work closely with their alumni offices as well as their foundations for their mutual benefit.

SUMMARY

In creating an international enrollment strategy, international educators should consider the following steps:

1. Assess the enrollment management mechanisms currently employed on the campus.
2. Assess the type of data needed regarding international education (internal and external) that can inform institutional enrollment management strategies; start collecting the data if not currently available, such as:
   a. Current international enrollment trends on campus; describe these trends in terms of the larger enrollment management plan.
   b. Areas of potential growth as well as potential threats to international enrollment.
3. Re-align current resources to best capitalize on growth areas while minimizing the dangers of threats.
4. Create an enrollment plan to outline how to use these resources that includes:
   a. Goals for international recruitment.
   b. Goals for service to international students to promote access and retention.
   c. Goals for involving current students from the U.S. in international initiatives (such as study abroad).
5. Reach out to alumni living abroad to assist with this enrollment plan.
6. Assess the effectiveness of these initiatives.
7. Assess changes in the enrollment environment.
8. Return to step #1.

Enrollment management is increasingly crucial to the enrollment success of universities and colleges. With an emphasis on resource management, data-driven decisions, and long term planning, enrollment management has become more than a simple office or division on college campuses and more of a philosophy of developing synergies across units. To be successful, international educators must adopt the language and methodologies of enrollment management to maximize their effectiveness in garnering support for the internationalization of their campuses. By being effective stewards of their resources, but also using elements of enrollment management to plug into conversations around the institution, international educators can not only be a participant but a leader in enrollment management conversations within U.S. colleges and universities.

11

SEM AND EXECUTIVE LEADERSHIP

Kevin Pollock
President
St. Clair County Community College

CHAPTER 11

Expectations for higher education leaders are high, varied, and numerous. Leaders are expected to be visionary, decisive and articulate, but also to share information, purposes, commitments, and struggles (Rouche 2011). Effective leaders must know and understand their faculty and staff; insist on realism, set clear goals and priorities, follow through, reward the doers, expand people's capabilities, as well as know themselves and their limits. An institution takes on the culture of its leader (Bossidy 2002).

Strategic enrollment management (SEM) can provide leaders of educational institutions with the tools to connect community, regional, and national initiatives with campus goals. It can create a data-driven culture that is focused on student success and provides avenues for breaking down campus silos. If connected with the right leadership SEM will take a leading role on a campus in future planning, decision making, and the direction of a college.

Strategic enrollment management can be defined as "a concept and process that enables the fulfillment of institutional mission and students' educational goals" (Bontrager 2008; Bontrager and Pollock 2009). Why is SEM important on a campus? Simple: to increase the number of successful students. It is a hard concept to argue against, although it isn't unusual to find resistance and pushback to SEM initiatives. The pushback may come from faculty concerned that a focus on enrollment and a call for increasing the success of students really means the lowering of academic standards, grade inflation, and a push to pass academically unprepared students. In this case faculty should be shown that SEM can mesh with an academic master plan (Clemetsen 2009). It may come from enrollment services staff concerned that they will be held solely responsible if specific enrollment goals are not met. It may come from any part of the campus concerned about changing practices, job descriptions and responsibilities, and the campus culture as a whole.

Therefore, it is logical that any implementation of a SEM model be inclusive and done in a collegial manner. This will go a long way toward staff and faculty understanding SEM and assist in creating a student success model that effectively takes a leading role on a campus. How it is organized, what "players" are involved, and to what extent the executive leadership and the faculty embrace the model will determine its success. One thing is certain: there is no single model that works on every campus. The question then becomes: How do we work with campus leadership to create and enhance a strategic enrollment management model that is the best fit?

LEADING THE TRANSITION TO SEM

Why is SEM leadership important? Strategic enrollment management is more than an attempt at simple manipulation of enrollment. It can easily be misunderstood by upper level administration as just an enhanced approach to admissions, marketing and financial aid and thus becomes solely the responsibility of these few units. Because it is more encompassing, it is easy for campus leaders to underestimate the scope and breadth of what is needed on a campus to implement a successful SEM model. Successful implementation of a SEM model can change the entire culture on a campus as well as be a linchpin toward addressing larger issues.

While SEM ultimately cannot be limited to these departments, the creation of a SEM model often starts in the student services area since admissions or financial aid officers are the first ones exposed to SEM through conferences, seminars, and interactions with other student services colleagues. A major task at the outset is not only providing the campus with information as to how SEM works, but also showing the potential benefits to both students and the institution. Campus colleagues can be enlightened to the fact that SEM can:

- Be a catalyst for establishing comprehensive enrollment goals.
- Promote academic success.
- Promote institutional success.
- Address specialized student challenges.
- Help create a data-rich environment.
- Strengthen internal and external communications.
- Increase campus collaboration (Bontrager 2008; Bontrager and Pollock 2009).

Perhaps most importantly, under SEM everything can be examined through the eyes of the student. Class schedules, tutoring, testing, course placement, developmental education, advising, financial aid, and more can all be reviewed and adjusted to help maximize student success.

The focus of the campus becomes the student. The success of the student becomes the paramount goal and decisions are made with an eye toward what is best for the student. This does not mean that there should be a total trade-off of administrative efficiency and that a campus should be run by catering to every student wish and demand. It means that the decisions should be weighed with an eye toward how they impact students and if they actually assist or hinder student progress. If this is done, the very manner in which staff and faculty interact with students can change.

Indeed, change is the foundation for implementing a new or improved SEM model. To realign an institution according to SEM principles, barriers must be broken down between departments, divisions, programs, staff and faculty. Mature SEM models influence departmental structures, staffing, and the efficient use of staff resources. Ask the question again: Why is SEM leadership important? Tied hand in hand with strong campus leadership, it can become the driving force for a cultural change that will focus on the success of students (Pollock 2004).

The magnitude of change involved with transitioning to a SEM model points to active leadership from the chief campus officer—president or chancellor— and the executive leadership team. However, while top-level leadership is ultimately required for full, successful implementation of SEM, effective SEM transitions do not always start at the executive level. In fact, it has become an oft-repeated fallacy that without initial support of the chief campus officer, it is not possible to adopt a SEM approach. A common corollary of that perspective is the lament, "I wanted to implement SEM but I could not get buy-in from campus leadership." Top-level support from the outset is an advantage, to be sure. However, it is not always required.

Among institutions that now employ robust SEM models, many began their transitions with more of a grass roots approach. As noted in the prior section, SEM awareness often begins with directors of enrollment service departments. When institutions take their initial, fledgling steps toward a SEM model, they sometimes appoint a chief enrollment management officer, often promoting the director of an enrollment service department. This often occurs well in advance of a true commitment to the change of campus culture required by SEM. Often it is these mid- to upper-level managers who first lead the SEM charge. They compile data, involve a wider group of campus stakeholders in enrollment planning, create new, well-informed enrollment initiatives, and, finally, achieve stronger enrollment outcomes that garner attention and create buy-in from executive leaders. This form of leadership—modeling effective SEM process and demonstrating its effectiveness—has been the catalyst for many successful SEM transitions.

EXECUTIVE LEADERSHIP

The prior comments about the importance of "grass roots" SEM leadership notwithstanding, to achieve a sustainable transition to a SEM model requires buy-in from the chief campus executive. Presidents and chancellors must have a clear vision of what their institutions can and should be and carefully articulate that vision to inspire those on a campus. One of a leader's main roles is seeing to the creation of a vision and strategic plan for a campus. A SEM model will provide an opportunity to create a vision that is inclusive and is focused on the student.

The role of the president in the implementation of a successful SEM model hinges on the executive's level of involvement, understanding, and support. Inherent in the executive's ability to deploy a SEM model is gathering together the diverse forces on a campus into a working, coherent group dedicated to student success. The chief executive's role is the big picture, setting the scene for all that comes afterward. To do so, the executive will need to determine the roles of other executive leaders on the campus such as cabinet-level administrators, and potentially, a chief enrollment management officer. As such, the executive at an institution should be able to explain why, in his or her opinion, the implementation of a SEM model is important and why it will be strongly supported.

Executives, their leadership teams, and eventually faculty leaders, must be able to define the reasons for pursuing SEM. They should identify the issues leading to a decision to implement SEM. In addition, all leaders should be prepared to explain what issues the campus is facing and why they are facing them. The desirable outcomes for SEM should be identified, whether they are increasing enrollment, improving student retention, or altering the mix of students. Mature SEM organizations utilize more refined enrollment targets to inform other aspects of campus planning, such as forecasting staffing levels, merging departments for efficiency, and projecting facility needs. The determining factors will be different on each campus, as will specific goals and sub-goals. Leadership should build SEM into the vision and strategic plan for the institution. It certainly will have a major impact as it will be heavily goal-oriented and data-driven.

Throughout the planning process, executive leaders should make the success of students the top priority on campus. Leaders who are truly "student-oriented" will create a campus culture which constantly searches for solutions that look out for the best interest of the students. It is one thing to state that a campus has a "student-first" outlook, but quite another to put it in writing, tie it to a vision and strategic plan, and prove it with data. Once pieces of a SEM model are in place all leadership must support it, financially and through discussions with the campus community and the community at large. The chief executive should be the student's biggest advocate.

Understand that this will be a departure from some traditional educational models and will change the culture on a campus. When viewed through the student "lens," every traditional process can be challenged. Is the student schedule created in the best interest of the students or the faculty? Are bills and payments scheduled around what is best for the student or "what has always been done"? How are students advised? Which student support mechanisms are effective? Are the cafeteria and bookstore hours best suited for students? Campus leaders may be surprised to find how many campus processes actually benefit staff and faculty and are barriers for the students. Along the way, it is important to make sure goals are measurable and fit into the strategic plan. Utilize data to present facts to faculty, staff and the public and to allow discussions on how to improve the program based on specific information rather than just "talk." SEM can easily be dismissed by some on campus as just another educational "flavor of the month" that should be ignored until it goes away. This can be countered by presenting data and allowing true discussions to take place.

The president should follow up with both the process and the results. It would be self-defeating to put the program in place and then not monitor it and be an advocate for it. Through this the president will have a better understanding of who is involved in the student success model, as well as their concerns, issues, ideas and roles.

If a president does not have a firm grasp of the enrollment management concept there are numerous ways to gain that knowledge. Seminars and conferences provide opportunities to learn about multiple facets of enrollment management. One example is the annual SEM Conference sponsored by the American Association of Collegiate Registrars and Admissions Officers (AACRAO). SEM also provides the opportunity for consultants and advisors to come directly to campuses and assist in the building of enrollment management systems. Another learning opportunity for a president is to value the experts on his or her own campus that are in the student services area. Many could have years of experience and background in SEM and student success models. Bringing these individuals into campus planning discussions—if that is not already the case—can be an effective initial step.

IDENTIFY THE DRIVERS AND "PLAYERS"

Any successful student success model encompasses all areas on the campus; therefore it is important to recognize the potential players in the model, as well as those external entities that monitor the success of an institution. Recognizing both internal and external drivers and their roles will help shape a SEM model. Some of these drivers will benefit directly from having a SEM model. Others may never have direct involvement in the system but will still benefit from a model that encourages student enrollment and retention. All of these are parts of a bigger picture and leadership at any institution should look at all models through lenses representing each driver.

Numerous questions will need to be answered by campus leadership. Who should be involved? What sort of structure will be utilized: committee, coordinator, division? How will issues regarding reporting lines, accountability, and campus culture shifts be addressed?

A successful strategic enrollment management model is incorporated into the fabric of everyday work on a campus. Staff and faculty should understand its importance, what their roles might be, and how a combined effort will help lead to the goal of having more successful students. Training for faculty and staff will be critical, from the standpoint of learning about SEM and also how each area impacts students and can be modified to help increase student success.

Internal Drivers

- **Students**—Students are the whole reason to create a SEM model on a campus. Each piece of the model should be reviewed through the eyes of students and modified to provide the maximum amount of support needed for students to be successful. One suggestion is to review all of the processes through which students must navigate in order to do such things as apply, register, complete financial aid, pay bills and enroll for classes. Students will have higher expectations for their college experience; they will be interested in streamlined courses focused on what they need and offered at more convenient times and places. They will want proof that they are getting "their money's worth" (Rouche 2000).

- **Faculty**—Faculty have more direct contact with students than does any other group on a campus. It is critical for faculty to be involved from the beginning in the creation of a SEM model. Areas of faculty concern may include the perception of the lowering of academic rigor and standards to assist in enrollment goals; therefore, faculty must be involved in the creation of a student success model at the earliest of planning stages. Faculty will be charged with creating and reviewing learning outcomes and developing measurable assessment components. Learning outcomes should be created that best represent what students should know when they leave one course and go into another or go directly into the workplace (Rouche 2006). Another area of faculty concern might be finding the balance between academic freedom and the call for more academic accountability. One must keep in mind that faculty members are also under more public scrutiny than ever. "Public interest in faculty's duties, responsibilities, and time on task; legislators' questions about what students are getting for their tuition dollars; and like concerns have become serious intrusions into the business of higher education. Today, more than ever, the methods and criteria by which faculty performance is evaluated will be aligned more closely with documented outcomes than with intent or effort" (Rouche 2000). Assessment of outcomes might call for the overhauling of curriculum and the development of measurable student outcomes. These types of outcomes can be tied directly to strategic enrollment management efforts and student success models. One benefit for faculty involved in SEM is that data from measurable goals will help them respond to public calls for "proof" that learning is occurring in classrooms.

- **The Chief Campus Officer**—Regardless of where the creation of a SEM model is initiated on a campus, there must be wholehearted buy-in from the president or chancellor. Without that buy-in, complete support, and participation by the president, no SEM model can live up to its potential.
- **The Board of Trustees**—Board members should understand the importance of a student success model and its accompanying data in a bigger picture context. SEM can be one of the major guiding principles on a campus. Informational presentations to the board about goals and data will provide updates to trustees as they help shape the future for a college.
- **Upper Administration**—This group can include executive cabinet members as well as directors and others who need to lead a cohesive day-to-day operation that helps students move through an educational system. Administrators must understand and support SEM, be able to lead change on the campus and work through potential cultural changes.
- **Enrollment Services staff**—Outside of faculty participation, this group will carry a large load of the SEM model implementation, and be responsible for nearly everything outside of the classroom, including many critical support mechanisms for students, such as advising and tutoring, student recruitment, admissions and orientation. It is easy for others on the campus to point to this area and assume that the success of students falls under its realm, but it needs to be noted that this group cannot be solely responsible for the success of students. As stated previously, often it is the enrollment service departments that initiate SEM practices on campus, and ultimately lead the change and the creation of a campus-wide SEM plan.

External Drivers

It is easy to identify and focus on the internal drivers on a campus. However, external drivers must be considered when creating a strategic enrollment management system.

- **Local**—Especially for community colleges, the response to local needs and expectations is important. Program offerings matching these needs, flexible class offerings, and the ability to show strong financial stewardship of local tax money are just a few critical areas that can be related to SEM objectives.
- **State**—State funding and educational initiatives, required data submissions, and the need to show increases in student success are just a few areas that are tied to a SEM model. State lawmakers have withdrawn billions of dollars in funding for public education (Wildavsky 2011). Expectations for change are abundant and the need to provide data related to measurable goals may become the norm rather than the exception.
- **Federal**—On perhaps a grander scale than the state level, the federal government is involved in many aspects related to SEM, such as financial aid and grant opportunities. Various data reports must be submitted to the government each year, many of them related to the success of students and completion rates. Expectations for success are climbing. Federal calls for an increase in graduation rates would lead America to have the highest proportion of college graduates in the world. To assist in accomplishing this goal, colleges can create SEM models that will establish better collaboration with K-12s, increase student retention by eliminating roadblocks, grow enrollment, move toward more data-driven decision making, increase financial aid, and redesign remedial education (Cook 2011).
- **National Educational Initiatives**—There are numerous national initiatives that can be tied to a SEM model. Achieving the Dream (ATD) is just one example. With a focus on a data-driven approach that helps find gaps where students fail, ATD provides a pathway to help increase student success. Policymakers and private foundations have also set ambitious goals for improving the rate at which Americans earn college credentials (Bailey 2011). Other initiatives include the American Graduation Initiative, the Voluntary Framework for Accountability, and the National Community College Benchmarking Project. These initiatives can all be directly related to strategic enrollment management, data collection, and a call for more accountability.
- **Accreditation**—National accreditation is moving toward a more result-based data collection that may include areas such as student enrollment and success.

POSITIONING SEM TO TAKE A LEADING ROLE

By recognizing the internal and external drivers and how SEM is related to each, it can be noted how SEM can take a leading role on a campus. As such, it is also easy to see the pivotal role campus leaders must take for a SEM plan to become operational and successful. What sort of steps can be taken by leaders to move an institution into a SEM plan and have it take a leading role in campus decision making?

Vision and Strategic Plan

An expectation on a campus is that one of the president's main roles is to create the vision for where an institution is headed and then to create the plan that is the roadmap to that vision (Rowley, 1997). If the vision for the future is not focused on the success of students, it needs to be adjusted. The vision statement itself should include specific language about the focus on student success.

SEM provides the opportunity to make the success of students the driving force on a campus. It can help spur discussions that can lead to crafting a vision and a strategic plan focused on students. While SEM takes a leading role in planning the future of an institution, it is not the sole force driving the creation of a strategic plan. Rather, it can help focus a campus on its highest priorities for planning, the success of students.

Creating a strategic plan is an opportunity for an institution to think long-term when planning for the future. The involvement of all campus leadership is critical in the integration of SEM. By aligning SEM plans with the budget process, recognizing student success as a campus-wide responsibility, and creating an open communication model that provides updates to the entire campus, SEM takes a leading role in future planning (Sharp 2009).

Once a plan is created, goals can be formed, that once completed, will move the campus forward with an eye on the needs of students. Goals for enrollment are only a portion of an overall plan. Goals from all other areas can flow from the main student focus. From this, areas that hinder student success can be identified and modified.

Statement of Importance

From the beginning, the president and leadership team must emphasize that student success is the paramount objective of the institution. There must be no doubt about the importance of SEM and the long term commitment to a strong, ever evolving student success model. A strong executive leader will make a bold statement about the campus direction and will make it clear that the emphasis on students is the main focal point of the institution. If a leader states that all decisions will be weighed with an eye toward what is best for students and their success, SEM automatically takes a leading role in campus decision making.

The president should set the stage for all that follows by clarifying the value and importance of a healthy enrollment for the whole college. This includes reviews of appropriate programs and course offerings, relevant delivery modes and schedules, as well as quality entry and retention services (Kerlin and Serrata 2009).

As noted before, SEM can be successful without such involvement of an executive leader, however, it should be easy to see that the stronger the commitment of an executive leader to a SEM model, the higher the potential of that model's success.

Collegiality and Inclusion

SEM encompasses the entire campus. In order for a student success model to be effective it must include the input of those parties involved. When a model is completed there should be specific goals and measurements for success; therefore, the building of a student success model should include representatives from all areas of the campus. This can be done through various methods: student focus groups, surveys, staff meetings, all campus meetings, blogs, and other methods that allow input.

While the president may set the overall direction and tone for future SEM discussions the main thrust of the work must come from a group, or groups, creating goals, targets, and measurements. SEM takes a leading role on the campus as departments, programs, and divisions set goals related to the success of students and begin to work together to ensure those goals become reality.

Each area on campus impacts student success; therefore, input from all areas is critical. Faculty and academics, student services and retention, auxiliary services and human resources each have their own role to play in the success of students on a campus; however, they must also see how everything is interconnected. To better understand and then craft a SEM plan they each need to provide input, comments, suggestions, and ideas, relative not only to their own areas, but across the campus.

As a campus focus shifts toward an enhanced student success model, one outcome is an increased interaction among various campus constituencies. This can provide opportunities for faculty and staff to learn more about their colleagues, move out of their silos, and see the campus from a bigger picture view, one that is presented through the common goal of increasing the success of students. From this, a better understanding and appreciation of co-workers may be an additional outcome.

Defining Student Success

If an institution does not have its own definition of student success, how can it measure anything and determine whether goals, policies, programs and initiatives are helping to improve a student's opportunities for success? The definition should be short and to the point. One good example is the following definition of student success: Students completing their educational goals in the most efficient manner.

This simple definition recognizes that students may have different or shifting goals, especially at community colleges where many students never intend to complete a degree at the associate level. This definition, with an emphasis on efficiency, recognizes the multitude of processes that impede student progress. Many of these processes may have been created for the efficiency or benefit of staff or faculty without understanding the impact on students. Is the class schedule well thought out? Does it create an easy path for students? Are tutors and advisors working hand-in-hand with faculty? Is there a required orientation?

Institutions can create their own definition, or rely on one that is used by another institution. Either way, the definition must fit the needs of the institution as well as the student and be recognized on the campus as a foundational piece of the student success model.

Defining Goals

As the campus moves through the process of creating a vision and strategic plan that is focused on student success, the creation of goals becomes the next challenge. While setting an overall enrollment goal may be desirable, leadership must remember that many types of students attend college. Specific target goals can be set for specific markets of students; however, since a true student success model encompasses the entire campus, goal setting for an institution can be more than just determining enrollment objectives. SEM takes a leadership role on the campus through the development of goals. Many goals that are set are not simply short-term, but should influence those on campus to become more forward thinking as SEM goals begin to impact multiple departments and programs.

Note that sometimes goals can be at cross purposes and offset each other. For example, a goal of increased enrollment may offset a goal of increasing net revenue if increased tuition discounting occurs. Another example might be a goal to increase enrollment on a campus without the supporting capacity or infrastructure (Black 2004).

Identify vital issues and rate them in importance. Ask what it will take to make a difference. Goals that are set will impact numerous areas: enrollment, marketing, program mix, policies and procedures. Whatever the method, it is important to remember that goal development must be done in a collegial manner in order to obtain buy-in from the parties involved. Finally, goals that are set must be measurable.

Creating a Data Agenda

With numerous local and federal pressures for student performance tests and effectiveness measures documenting institutional performance, it becomes critical for colleges to develop measurable outcomes, mostly related to student success and data collection (McClenney 2004). Learning outcomes must be identified for courses and programs. Additional measurements might include everything from year-to-year retention success, number of admission applications and financial aid awards, number of visits to support services and the percentage of students who receive a D, F, or W in specific programs and classes. Measurements might also include enrollment headcount, student quality, student diversity, retention rates, graduation rates, student satisfaction, staff satisfaction, and/or institutional image (Black 2004). Once data is collected it should be presented to the campus so that faculty and staff can see progress and note areas that need improvement.

Executive leaders should know where their institution stands in regard to institutional research. Is there a need for an institutional research department? Are staffing levels adequate? With the shift toward measurable goals, and an increase in accountability, institutions may find themselves unprepared to provide needed data collection and research if there is no dedicated role for institutional research.

Accounting for State and Federal Initiatives, Grants, and National Educational Initiatives

As noted by Rouche, "with numerous federal and local pressures for student performance testing and effectiveness measures documenting institutional performance, colleges have much to gain by a serious focus on meeting these growing and increasingly invasive demands" (Rouche 2006). There are a number of national groups and initiatives examining student progression and completion measures. Many of these initiatives now include success indicators as well as final outcome measures.

Some common completion metrics include graduation rates, transfer rates, number and percentage of degrees and certificates awarded, time to degree and credits to degree. Intermediate metrics include enrollment and completion in developmental education, success in "Gatekeeper" English and mathematics courses, credit accumulation in the first year and Fall-to-Fall and Fall-Spring retention (MCCA 2011).

Campus leaders must address local, state, and national initiatives, mandates, and accountability metrics as they create strategic plans, budgets, and staffing. Nearly everything noted in these metrics falls into the strategic enrollment management sphere and its impact on student success. SEM will help lead to the future success of many institutions where strong leaders utilize the initiatives and benefits provided by SEM planning and accountability metrics.

Tying together local, state, and federal mandates and initiatives with campus planning provides a greater sense of legitimacy to the plan while emphasizing the lead role SEM is playing on the campus.

Professional Development

While many professional development initiatives at any institution may increase individual or departmental expertise, it is imperative that a concerted effort be made to provide professional development that will expand knowledge in the area of student success. Faculty and staff that attend professional development sessions should be asked to proceed with a student success lens as they view new materials, ideas and concepts. SEM, therefore, takes a leading role in professional development and the direction of the college.

The area of professional development is wide open when SEM is considered; anything that can help staff and faculty better understand student needs, as well as methods for better campus collaboration, will move a campus forward. For example, faculty can look at student outcomes, measurable goals, online offerings, class schedules, and methods for the transferability of classes. All staff can be trained in customer service, working with difficult people, and best practices in advising, counseling, financial aid, and other service methods. Executive staff can also attend conferences and programs that will provide them with better skills and knowledge in working in such areas as legislative issues, educational law, and the latest national initiatives for higher education. It would be in the best interest of the institution to "prepare all employees through a strategic staff development program for their role in creating and sustaining student pathways to completion" (O'Banion 2011).

Accountability and Responsibility

As noted earlier there is a call for greater accountability for higher education institutions. As data is gathered and used to help support campus decision making, it would behoove campus leaders to release data to the campus community. Open communication is the key. While data should not be used as a weapon against those on the campus, it should be utilized to hold individuals, programs, and departments accountable for their actions and decisions. This will almost certainly cause a change in the campus culture.

SUMMARY

While strategic enrollment management models may be initiated by others on the campus, or by the president, the executive leader's role in the creation of a SEM model is pivotal. Therefore, it is imperative that the leader:

- Define the reasons, issues, and rational for pursuing SEM and be prepared to articulate its importance.
- Recognize the diverse internal and external drivers and their roles.
- Determine who should be involved and in what manner.
- Tie SEM to the vision and strategic plan.
- Help determine the main components of the SEM plan.
- Set goals and establish accountability.
- Include measurements.
- Understand budget implications.
- Provide related professional development.
- Communicate with the campus.

If the campus leadership can take these critical steps in the creation of a SEM plan, SEM itself can become a leading force on the campus, making the success of students a focused, campus-wide goal.

12

INCREASING VALUE THROUGH PERSONNEL TRAINING AND LEARNING

Ronald J. Ingersoll
Sr. Consultant Advisor
EMAS Pro.

Doris M. Ingersoll
Sr. Consultant Advisor
EMAS Pro.

CHAPTER 12

CHANGE IS COMING: GREET IT WITH INNOVATION AND CREATIVITY

Harvard will always be Harvard. But what about the rest of us?

Welcome to the creative era. To fuel the 21st–century economic engine and sustain democratic values, we must unleash and nurture the creative impulse that exists within every one of us, or so say experts like Richard Florida, Ken Robinson, Daniel Pink, Keith Sawyer, and Tom Friedman. Indeed, just as the advantages the United States enjoyed in the past were based in large part on scientific and engineering advances, today it is cognitive flexibility, inventiveness, design thinking, and non-routine approaches to messy problems that are essential to adapt to rapidly changing and unpredictable global forces; to create new markets; to take risks and start new enterprises; and to produce compelling forms of media, entertainment, and design.

There is no shortage of best-seller hyperbole in such claims. But there is also no doubt that today's economic, social, political, and ecological challenges require something other than traditional, routine responses. . . . .

Simply put, America cannot maintain a competitive position in the world order unless we better understand how to nurture creative talent and put in place policies and practices to do so. Nor can we just leave it to chance that we are adequately training rising generations to assume their roles as creative workers and responsible citizens (Tepper and Kuh, 2011).

In 1997, Peter Drucker predicted that within thirty years big university campuses would be "relics" because of the untenable tension between rising costs and stagnant quality of education. Drucker's prediction, as that of a writer and consultant with a great track record of predicting the future, should certainly make us cautious (Lenzner and Johnson 1997).

CREATING INSTITUTIONAL VALUE THROUGH PERSONNEL EXCELLENCE

Value is a key variable in whether a college meets its enrollment goals. If the student believes a school offers distinct value, he or she is more likely to enroll and persist. Over the last decade colleges and universities have increased value by creating outstanding residence facilities, elegant fitness centers, shopping malls in student services, and other physical changes. Some colleges also compete for top scholars to create value in the academic area. All of these ventures are very costly and increase the cost of postsecondary education (Taylor 2010). Given the current economic climate for higher education, institutions will have a difficult time continuing to invest in the physical attributes of their campuses.

The good news is that there are other viable options to create value.

The biggest value that a school can offer is motivated personnel with the best possible skills, knowledge, and attitude as they work with the public, people around them, and students. As colleges and universities move into the next five to ten years, the need to improve and grow will increasingly depend on their capacity to provide the best experience possible and have the potential to change, and frequently. This will depend on the creativity and innovative capacity of a college's staff, faculty, and administration.

Staff, administration, and faculty must develop skills and undertake innovative practices on a continuing and purposeful basis. While most schools have human resource departments that conduct training and coordinate training resources, there are few colleges that devote part of their strategic directions to having an exceptional formal, targeted personnel development program designed to create value and foster innovation.

ENROLLMENT MANAGEMENT: INITIATING A CULTURE OF PERSONAL DEVELOPMENT

Value can be gained from every interaction between the college and a student. The development of skills, knowledge, and attitudes is critical for each individual at the University.

Training and development programs should begin with the enrollment program and everyone associated with it. This includes staff and administrators at all levels who work with admissions, financial aid, the registrar's office and other enrollment service departments. Additionally, it includes student workers, faculty volunteers, and faculty or departments that seek support in efforts to work directly with students. Everyone who has contact with students should undergo some training or development. This process includes students from before inquiry to becoming alumni. Yes, from "before inquiry" because students often initiate the enrollment process on their own using the school's Website, Facebook, Twitter, and other platforms before they inquire.

Enrollment managers must imagine how a well-prepared staff or faculty member can engage students as they consider attending their college or university. It is not just one office or one program but the whole school that is involved. It is not only what the students must do but what the college and the student must do to best prepare a student for the future. A student must perceive and believe that an institution's skills, knowledge, and attitudes are consistent with their own vision of the future and how to get there.

KEY AREAS FOR CHANGE MANAGEMENT

Through this approach to training and development of campus staff, faculty, and administration, changes in the how, why, where, and when we work with students are needed now. We are entering a period where change may be constant and where complexity is the norm. These changes are most likely to occur for colleges and universities in the following areas.

Programs and Services: To accommodate the changes they face now and in the future, colleges and universities must commit to constantly improve the performance of all personnel. Change will require new behaviors and outcomes that may be unfamiliar, and even uncomfortable. For example, campus administrators must now understand how to use increased amounts of data for advising and other work with students at all levels, from inquiry to graduation.

Retain Valuable Human Resources: Some of the best enrollment and student success programs include staff and administration that have been together a long time, are effective, and work hard. During times of hiring or retrenchment, it is essential to keep or hire the most effective people possible to work with students. The aim should be to maintain the quality of effort at the highest level possible, and to develop personnel to a higher and higher level each year.

Technology: Changes in this area clearly impact recruiting and learning. Schools may be recruiting students who have been taught with programs like those of the Khan Academy, where technology is heavily used to support student and faculty collaboration and interaction.[1]

---

1. http://www.khanacademy.org/

Programs like those at Purdue University which developed Signals in partnership with SunGard (2009) tightly bind students to their programs, allowing early identification of problems and intervention opportunities. Programs like these will lead to changes in the methods and focus of SEM work.

STAFF DEVELOPMENT AND SUCCESSFUL OUTCOMES

Staff development efforts will positively impact multiple areas, including:
- *Increased engagement for potential students:* This helps the student to understand the school and increases enrollment and retention.
- *General increase in yields from inquiries to enrolled students:* An increase in engagement occurs at all levels.
- *Improved retention:* Students who enter highly engaged tend to stay.
- *Improved use of data:* People at all levels of the institution need to understand and discuss data implications, convert data into information and develop the knowledge to take action based upon findings. This increases dramatically the ability to do the right things at the right time.
- *Better first impressions of the campus:* The way people feel after contact with the school represents the "brand" for the school.
- *Student success strategies are revealed.* This empowers more people in their work with students and others.
- *Better and more effective enrollment planning:* Discussions and use of creativity increase options available in planning.
- *Better connections between academic and enrollment areas.*
- *Better implementation of new services or technology.*
- *Enhanced retention of good staff.*

GETTING STARTED: A SUCCESSFUL STAFF DEVELOPMENT PROGRAM

The key goals to start or improve a successful staff development program are:
- Understanding what you want, why you want it, and the value it will have to your campus and its students.
- Getting the buy-in of the people involved from the beginning.
- Developing a capacity for "future-ing," or working with the connection between current and future campus practices and developing new directions.
- Working with the people at your institution who are currently responsible for the programs associated with education and training.

These goals are elemental to success in this area. Enrollment managers must be prepared to focus and refocus the program to help it stay on track; much of the capacity to do this depends on how it is established.

Before you meet with staff you need to have a good idea of what you need and why. You must resolve, through discussions and interaction with stakeholders, to move in a new direction with training and education. You need to be able to provide specific reasons for this new direction when you have your meeting with Human Resources (HR). You need to be solidly convinced that the program you want to develop is going to contribute to the value of your school and will enhance the effectiveness of your programs. You must be certain that, without this program, there will be negative consequences for your school and its students. Negative consequences of not pursuing a staff development program might be cited as students being less successful, your enrollments falling short of goals, and people generally being less satisfied with the college and its programs.

Engage a team of people to explore the options with you to develop the program. The process should develop enthusiasm and energy. If it does not, the program is probably not going to work even if you manage to start it. Once you are convinced that your campus needs some kind of personnel development, you are ready to proceed and let the development of the ideas and direction begin.

FORMING THE TEAM

The first step, if you are convinced that a new program is needed, is to form a team. This is a sub-team of the school's strategic enrollment management team. It is often most appropriate that the chair of the group be the senior enrollment person. The team should include people from all levels of the enrollment group, and faculty who generally are familiar with and work well with enrollment. This is not a permanent team but a task force that is prepared to address the single topic of training and education. If the right composition cannot be found within the school's enrollment team, new members should be invited to join the subgroup.

The personnel development team explores and develops new approaches to creating value for the school and ensures that innovation and creativity are the basis for much of the thinking from a day to day basis. It must receive its charge from the senior enrollment person who should seek the endorsement of the president for the work of the team, not just with words but with sincere energy and with the expected outcome of a formal recommendation or report sooner than later.

Another useful tack to take is to include a representative of the office or group (usually HR) that normally does the training or education for the school as a member of the team. The qualification is that he or she would not try to direct the discussions but rather serve as a resource or advisor to the group.

IDENTIFY THE GOAL OR VISION

The team should develop a statement that addresses the kind of attention that is needed in personnel training and education. How is this different from what is happening now? Answering this question may be a good assignment for the representative from human resources. What should be done? What will this provide for the school and for potential and current students? What might happen if this is *not* done? It is important to periodically remind people that the team is not saying something is wrong but that the programs and approaches may need to be different in order to provide stellar service and foster student success.

CONDUCT A PRELIMINARY NEEDS ANALYSIS

A good way to consider the need for training and education of your campus human resources is to look at the function or activity set, and to imagine the ideal state while assessing where the college is now. Then ask yourself the question, how critical is this activity or step, how much is the gap, and how much value will it add to the students' perception or engagement with the school? A sample list of areas for consideration is presented in Table 1.

The information in Table 1 was created from conversations with staff at a midsized community college about the skills, knowledge, and attitudes needed for an effective enrollment service office. In every area there are sets of skills, knowledge, and attitudes that are important for the immediate success of the college. But the personnel development team must also consider how these sets might be different in the future.

On this particular campus, the staff felt uncomfortable with things relating to data. The team might ask, "Is this a serious problem on which to focus given the future which is likely to use data more instrumentally?" If so, could training and education play a significant role in helping the staff feel more comfortable with data? At what levels should it be addressed? What are staff responsibilities involving data, and how much is done with the senior people? How much data training and education is needed outside the enrollment area and how much is needed within it?

A chart resembling Table 1 can be used in most offices. Items in italics represent what staff felt they are very good at. Items in bold represent areas in which the staff felt they needed help.

Table 1: Identification of Staff Development Needs for a Community College

Skills	*Listening*	Planning	Collaborating
	Questioning	Using information well	Getting involved
	Relating	Organizing	Deciding
	Time Management	Setting priorities	Preparing
	Stress management	Writing	Selling
	Quantitative	Expressing	Interviewing
	Analysis	Investigating	Collecting
	Technical	*Speaking*	Gathering
	Self-Management	*Remembering*	Problem solving
	Networking	*Relating*	"People Making"
	Researching	Entertaining	Contact
	Communicating	**Reporting**	
	Creating	Summarizing	
	Thinking	Problem Solving	
		Recording	
Knowledge	*School*	Relationship	
	Market	Management	
	Diverse	Communication	
	Self	Motivation	
	Marketing		
	Knowledge Management		
Attitudes/ Behavior	*Positive*	*Friendly*	
	Works hard	Open	
	Impassioned	Acts positively	
	Cheerful	*Smiling*	
	Pleasant	Outgoing	
	Joyful	Energetic	
	Gentle	**Trusting**	
	Happy	Driven	
	Sociable	Enthusiastic	
	Playful	Goal oriented	
	Excited	Courageous	
	Reflective	Pushes boundaries	
	Opportunistic	Sharing	
		People oriented	

The results of this exercise should take the view of the enrollment manager into account. Does he or she agree with the assessment? That is, does the staff have the self-proclaimed skills in certain areas such as listening or planning? If the staff feels they are not very sharing, trusting, and energetic, leadership needs to explore this. Staff may not react well to program changes in areas they feel very positively about.

A TYPE OF PROGRAM FOR EVERY LEVEL

Getting started, it is important to distinguish between training and education and tactical or strategic initiatives.

Training is concerned with gaining a new skill or technique. Learning to run the new software would be training. Learning how the system works and to be able to change the system would likely be called education. Training and education is whatever is done to produce more value for the people using the services and the people delivering it. One might associate training only with people who have clerical or support functions. This is not true; training at every level may be needed. We have often found that senior people do not know how to use the telephones, fax machines, or have the basic computer skills for the particular system they are using. They rely on others to cover for them. Many provosts or vice presidents are unable to make a Skype call without support from coworkers.

The idea of differentiating between tactical people and strategic people is vital. We should be looking at development for all levels of people from the Chief Enrollment officer to the office staff mailing a letter. Everyone can improve skills and contribute to new approaches that add value to the public perception of the school. Education may be needed at any or all levels in the organization. The more people are trained in the principles of communication, the more they can hone skills on a daily basis to contribute possible innovations in that area.

Table 2 lays out possible training program initiatives for a year.

DEVELOPING INNOVATION AND CREATIVITY

The capacity for innovation and creativity can be developed through more than workshops – although workshops can build energy around new approaches.

The following is a list of core abilities and skills found in creative people laid out by Tepper and Kuh (2011):

- The ability to approach problems in non-routine ways using analogy and metaphor;
- Conditional or abductive reasoning (posing "what if" propositions and reframing problems);

- Keen observation and the ability to see new and unexpected patterns;
- The ability to risk failure by taking initiative in the face of ambiguity and uncertainty;
- The ability to heed critical feedback to revise and improve an idea;
- A capacity to bring people, power, and resources together to implement novel ideas; and
- The expressive agility required to draw on multiple means (visual, oral, written, media-related) to communicate novel ideas to others.

These characteristics are not required of just one or two individuals, but of the entire campus personnel population. A "Creativity Climate" is needed (Florida 2002). This can begin with work in the enrollment area and diffuse throughout the college or university.

Table 2: Areas of Potential Staff Development (Staff/Initiative)

Recruiters/ Admissions Representatives	Developing better presentations for potential students that enable prospects to remember the presentation and the college.
Recruiters/ Admissions Representatives	Establishing and monitoring social communities online.
All	Gaining effectiveness through collaboration.
All	Improving understanding and use of software.
Staff	Answering phones with proper protocols and etiquette.
All	Learning how to follow up effectively.
All	Increasing creativity and innovation now.
Senior staff	Using analytics for real-time decisions.
Senior staff	Improving strategic planning.
Faculty	Gaining relationship management skills with prospective students.
Faculty Advisors	Helping students to achieve their goals.

METHODS

You should have some ideas about the possibilities for delivering the program. These options will give you the language to use in your conversations to initiate the program. Again, this is where the task force or team can be helpful. Are there additional methods and how do people feel about each in terms of your school's program?

Table 3: Summary of Methods Used for Staff Development

Delivery method	
Classroom	People are accustomed to these traditional methods since they involve face to face contact. They are relatively inexpensive and allow for an exchange of ideas.
Workshop	
Seminars	
Mentor	These can be effective but are sometimes expensive and may take a long time.
Coaching	
Conferences	Conference attendees should be expected to bring knowledge back and present the key "take-aways" from the conference. Attendance should depend in part on how the conference meets the learning needs of the office.
Video Conference	
Online conference	
Video Tutorial	These are short videos that usually pertain to a specific topic.
Partly online	Hybrid activities are delivered partly online and partly in class. This provides some face-to-face contact but requires less frequent travel or time on site.
All online	
Reading	Some of us get a lot out of reading, and key findings should systematically be shared with others in the organization. This might be done through seminars, newsletters or mailings.
Visits	Often, visits between offices can be used to learn the roles and daily responsibilities of various offices on campus.

A key factor in methods is to share activities with colleagues. This is obvious for conferences, reading, and visits. These activities can be expensive and a lot can be gained through providing the information to a broad audience and discussing it. For example, if someone is attending an AACRAO meeting, they would attend sessions and report on the outcome and key points. The office might attend special workshops such as those conducted by IBM around analytics. Upon return to the school, attendees would present and possibly apply the material to their work.

ASSESSMENT

One very important part of developing a successful program is the assessment. An assessment needs to be part of any training or educational program, and it needs to be done in such a way that it is informative not punitive. The assessment should tell you if the objectives of the effort have been met. If there are a few people that did not connect with the program, work with them. If nobody got it, change the program and redo it. It is important to do formative assessments during the activity to determine how things are going. The summative assessment identifies its overall success. These should not be tests but forms of feedback that tell us two things: the college is serious about its ongoing venture being a success, and the program will be evaluated and improved each year.

NEXT STEPS: IMPLEMENTATION

You now have an understanding of what you need for the development of a personnel training and education program and its systematic evolution. You are prepared to go to the next step and formulate your program in cooperation with the people at your school who offer the services.

Three approaches are available to you. The first is to see if the program can be developed and conducted by the campus offices responsible for training and development. More than likely, they will be ready to respond.

The second approach is to develop the program yourself. It is likely you will need to do this to meet some of your needs. Attendance at conferences and reading may likely be conducted immediately in your program. If you move in this direction you need to make a decision about who will be the person to move it along. You may select one of your staff who wants to develop his or her skills for the future. You might also engage someone who is experienced with training and development programs. This could be expensive and may include additional costs for hardware and software involved with the program.

The third possibility is to develop a hybrid program of shared responsibilities between the enrollment management and training staff at the school. This may be the preferred outcome at many colleges and universities.

SO WHERE DO YOU GO? DRIVING AND RESTRAINING FORCES

The use of a restraining forces/driving forces model as shown by Table 4 may be helpful in developing an action plan. In identifying forces, the objective is to decide which restraining forces can be lessened and which driving forces can be made more powerful. As you are doing this, you may find new restraining and driving forces. Hashing this kind of model out with staff from several areas on campus is a good way to get involvement from people who will be part of the program. It is also a good way to ensure that you have included and addressed most of the issues at stake.

Table 4: Forces to Identify (Sample)

Restraining Forces	Driving Forces
Time	Need to compete
Cost	Need to cope with change
Perception of loss of territory by Human Resources	Need for creativity
Organizational silos of duplicate activities	Use of a cross functional team
Clouded vision	Cite benefits to the school
Lack of awareness	Cite benefits to the student
Lack of interest	Create enthusiasm
Lack of resources	Involve people in the decision
Lack of vision	Educate
Lack of belief	Believe

This type of table points out the importance of the team in the overall process.

Clearly in most schools, the cost and time will be the hardest factors to address. Using a team should help address all of the rest of the factors.

IN SUMMARY

Viable recruitment and student success efforts depend on increasing the value of education to potential students. The development of skills, knowledge, and attitudes of the institution's personnel is a way to increase value that costs less than new buildings, additional personnel, or the use of financial aid as incentives to enroll. To succeed in training and education efforts, there must be agreement as to the need for the effort, the areas where the effort will be focused, the methods to deliver the program, and a means for assessment. The program should include all staff levels in the enrollment service areas, including senior members. Ideally, this will become a model for increasing service levels and value to students throughout the institution.

13

SEM AND CHANGE MANAGEMENT

Ronald J. Ingersoll
Sr. Consultant Advisor
EMAS Pro.

Doris M. Ingersoll
Sr. Consultant Advisor
EMAS Pro.

CHAPTER 13

The future of Strategic Enrollment Management (SEM), with its emerging emphasis on student success, is tied to the ability of colleges and universities to address and adapt successfully to the myriad of external and internal forces that create significant change agendas for higher education. Their ability to adapt successfully is critical. The change agendas are linked directly to budget and themes that are related to enrollments of all kinds. In this chapter the forces impacting higher education are discussed, change agendas and types of adaptations are explained, a change process is developed, and change management tools are identified.

THE DRIVING FORCES FOR CHANGE

In physics a force is defined as any influence that causes an object to undergo a change in speed, direction, or shape (Knight, Jones and Field 2010). In the environment of colleges and universities, these forces for change come from both the external and internal environments. Because institutions react to these forces, it is critical to have a firm grasp on the nature of the forces in order to make the appropriate adaptations.

Forces in the external environment have always driven the way schools view enrollment and how it is managed. In the early to mid-seventies, enrollment staff focused on one force: demographics. The internal forces for change were not strong. The answer to the demographic problem was solved by hard work and better communication with students. Ingersoll (1988) discovered that dramatic changes in enrollment could be produced with almost no change on the part of the school. If changes in the school were made, they were often cosmetic, such as landscaping or cleaning up or adding some services. Today, things are different!

External Forces of Change

In the external environment, forces are coming from the federal and state governments, individuals, groups, media, and authors who are writing books for the general public that are generally critical of higher education (Kamenetz 2011; Hacker and Dreifus 2011). Such forces place the onus on colleges and universities for lowering the costs of education, providing more financial aid, becoming more accountable, operating with more transparency, increasing completion rates, increasing the percentage of the population of the country with degrees, providing more students in the sciences, technology, engineering and mathematics (STEM programs), offering more courses and programs for non-traditional students, controlling salaries, and generally doing a better job in meeting the needs of the public the institution serves (Hacker and Dreifus 2011; Taylor 2012; DeMillo 2011; Kamenetz 2011).

Another external force is the rise of alternatives (competitors) to traditional campuses such as for-profit schools and open course programs. Today, for example, students can take a course online from Massachusetts Institute of Technology and get a certificate of completion. The student doesn't receive credit, but does get the certificate. In time, this will lead to credit for these options by some outside agency (Eaton 2008).

Internal Forces of Change

Today, forces inside schools must be included in the agenda for the future. These include the mission statement; teaching/research; the teaching/learning process; the influence of technology on courses and programs; funding for departments; customer relationship programs; a reallocation of resources in response to STEM goals; and many more. Colleges and universities should help the public understand these forces and how they influence the decisions and actions of the school.

Are changes in the higher education system inevitable? Calls for change have been gaining greater voice in recent years, but obstacles have been identified by researchers. Bontrager (2008) reviewed extensively the need for fundamental change in American higher education, particularly to improve student access and equity. Kezar (2009) produced a thorough article about change in higher education, stressing the difficulty and the slow rate of change at the postsecondary level. He suggested that change in higher education was complex and much harder to achieve than change in businesses. In 2010, Jones and Wellman laid out the issues that face higher education with a focus on finances. The authors indicated:

In fact, there is never a good time to talk about fundamental changes in higher education. In the worst of times, nobody has the time for conversation about long-term solutions: all of the energy is devoted to keeping the enterprise afloat. In the best of times, the pressure for change is relieved and the participants necessary to the conversation don't want to contemplate the (inevitable) recurrence of bad times.

Processes must be put into place to encourage timely, positive, productive, and sustainable responses to the many forces that bear upon schools at this time, especially because these forces are likely to continue to gain momentum.

STRATEGIC ENROLLMENT MANAGEMENT IN TIMES OF CHANGE

In any response to the change forces, maintaining the number, type, quality, and other variables that characterize new and continuing enrollment for a school, as well as the funding required to achieve enrollment goals, must continue to be a high priority. To do this year after year requires close attention to internal and external threats and opportunities, a capacity to make decisions about how to address these forces, and the ability to implement tactics necessary for both institutional and student success. These capacities lead to systems that become more complex as well as more competitive each year. In this context, the SEM agenda depends on the forces schools are in a position to address, which varies for each institution. In all cases, the enrollment manager should set the stage for effective conversations that determine what forces should be considered; coordinate the analysis; and establish a process for achieving the enrollment "state" the school desires. The options considered must be closely linked to budget and funding. In undertaking these activities, enrollment managers become change agents for their schools.

Senior enrollment staff must be ready to lead a successful change in their area. They must also be ready to participate effectively in change efforts throughout the school. Changes in other parts of the institution are often needed to meet both school enrollment goals and goals of the individual students attending. For example, adapting to increases in nontraditional, older students may be a challenge, but may be essential for enrollment success. Colleges and universities must have strong processes and the right skills and knowledge to produce positive outcomes for the school and students. Those practicing SEM must embrace change and work with people and ideas to facilitate positive results in and outside the enrollment area.

A two-year community college in a small town in the Northeast with several branch campuses. The faculty met throughout spring to create a new approach to serving the needs of non-traditional students. The president was convinced this market was viable, based on some data provided by institutional research and two board members, yet the results every year were poor. New student enrollment was down, retention was struggling, and the environment was unpleasant to work in. In general, the faculty was resistant but the president insisted that courses for this cohort be offered each term. She requested that faculty come up with a plan to make the nontraditional student experience more pleasant and to offer a streamlined program through which students could progress quickly without lower standards. The faculty came up with a cohort program in which a student could take three classes each term. However, it meant a lot of work for students. The faculty also decided to offer two programs online and develop a third program as a hybrid, partly online. However, this approach did not take into consideration the preparedness of the students to the technology and workload needed to succeed with these instructional approaches.

ॐ

During this process, the enrollment office was not consulted, not involved in the marketing process nor in handling the students. The result was that only one cohort was formed, and it did not persist through the year. Most campus staff and faculty took this as evidence that the school should not pursue offering distance learning or catering to the non-traditional market.

In this scenario it is clear that the involvement of senior enrollment personnel is critical in the designing of a viable program.

This examination of forces that influence the direction of higher education clarifies that:

- Colleges and universities will need to grapple with change more often in the future (Selingo 2011).
- The changes will be increasingly complex and occur over shorter time periods (Tapscott and Williams 2010; Christensen and Eyring 2011).
- The time to send an idea through several committees and then get buy-in from everyone involved will get shorter and shorter (Christensen and Eyring 2011).
- The financial and human resources to address change become more limited each year as budgets adapt to current and future realities.
- Success in this effort will require skills, knowledge, and attitudes that support the change effort.

IMPORTANT CHANGE VARIABLES AND PROCESSES

As the approach to change and adaptation unfolds, there are key variables that contribute to an enhanced opportunity for success. Attention to these variables is essential.

Institutional Culture

Our lack of understanding about the role of organizational culture in improving management and institutional performance inhibits our ability to address the challenges that face higher education. As these challenges mount, our need to understand organizational culture only intensifies (Tierney 2008).

The base for successful change efforts rests in the culture of the school (Wurston 2008; Kezar and Eckel 2002). This theme is covered in more detail in Chapter 5. Campus culture may be defined as the patterns of organizational behavior and shared values, assumptions, beliefs, or ideologies that the faculty and administration have about the organization and its work. To anticipate how the culture may manage change, consider the following questions:

Area	Observations
What is the power structure? Is it top down or distributed?	Identifying the power structure will clarify who must be consulted before initiating a change effort. If top-down, the top person has to be convinced before the effort is undertaken. Sit-down conversations with the leader are particularly helpful.
Is the school open or closed to new ideas?	Consider the ideas or concepts that have been a focus of the school. If people go to meetings and discuss the content of the meeting when they return to their daily responsibilities, the culture is open to new ideas.
How is information shared and used?	If the enrollment office has ready access to data with reliable people to provide it, then campus culture is open to using the data for new directions. Consider whether any data is kept under the table.
How do people communicate?	Consider whether staff uses email, phone, memo, meeting, coffee breaks, video, etc. to determine how best to communicate change initiatives.

Area	Observations
Who has influence?	The actors in the organization with influence may be the president, deans, faculty and/or students; understanding the extent of their influence is important because they are the people you need to work with.
What are the levels of trust, caring, and concern about students and people in general?	To gain insight, ask an outsider for their reactions after they have visited the school.
How much change has occurred in the last five years?	Look at the changes that have occurred, how the culture or the system influenced the change and how long the process took for each. Specific examples and the process used for each are valuable resources.
What kinds of changes were attempted and did not occur?	Look at examples and changes sought that did not occur, and how the culture or the system influenced the outcome.

Answering these questions can help an enrollment team or others develop a pathway for a change effort. It also must be clear that there may be no "right" culture. Whether the change process is functional or dysfunctional depends on specific school circumstance and its culture. If the school is achieving its goals, making good decisions, and experiencing a general positive thrust, the culture might be made stronger and better able to support change. On the other hand, if the school is struggling with enrollment and student success, the culture should be studied for ways to best initiate change so that the campus experience is improved for students, faculty and staff.

Innovation, Creativity and Collaboration: Everyone Is Involved

While there is room for much variety in campus culture, three characteristics must be present in any culture of success today: creativity, innovation, and collaboration. The words creativity and innovation have been used for years to describe important characteristics of any successful effort in enrollment (Selingo 2011; Tapscott and Williams 2010; Rogers 2010), but limited innovations show up over a year's time despite the frequent use of the term on campuses.

Today creative efforts and innovation are needed from all the individuals and groups that make up a college or university. The small changes that accumulate to create a better value to students and the external world are the important ones. Examples may be:

- How a phone is answered.
- How the campus tour is done.
- How visitors experience the campus.
- How distance education is supported.
- How programs are delivered to non-traditional students.
- How remediation is addressed.
- How improvements are made to the development of new academic and service programs, considering how people learn, the role of faculty, and how to advise various types of students effectively.

The culture must always be looking for better ways to serve the needs of students and others with whom the school has contact.

A Systems View

At all colleges and universities, there are interconnections between offices that are getting more and more complex every year. Even in small schools the web of connections can be complicated. What happens in the academic programs, for example, has an impact on all offices and staff. Poor technology can scuttle even the best efforts to make positive changes in enrollment. Because of this, viewing the school from a systems point of view is essential. In fact, schools are an example of complex systems that learn as they work (Nicolis and Nicolis, 2007; Wheatley 2006).

There are very few programs, activities, or services that can be viewed in isolation. Figure 1 shows a systems view of the work done at the University of South Florida (USF) in the development of their student success program.

Figure 1: Systems View for Change Management on Campus

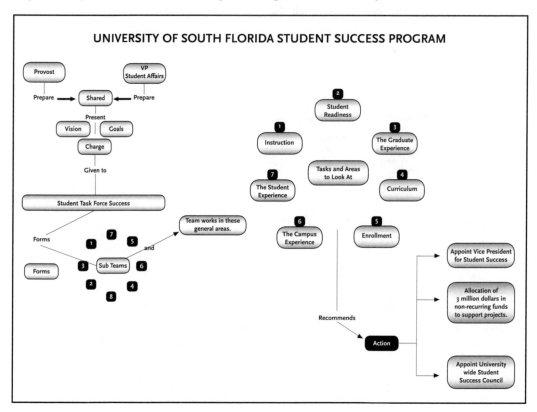

UNIVERSITY OF SOUTH FLORIDA STUDENT SUCCESS PROGRAM

In this system one can see the relationship matrix that needs to be formed throughout the campus in order to improve student success.

At USF, the vision and the charge of senior people was essential for the project. The president wanted to move the university to a new level of success. From the beginning of the project it was clear that this was a university-wide project. The initial presentation to the Student Success Task Force was given by the Provost and the Vice President for Student Affairs.

The changes that were required to improve student success needed to reach everyone at the school, so eight sub-teams went to every part of the university. The material from the visits emerged as very important to the final result.

Recommendations indicate changes to be implemented across the University. This requires that systems be mapped and that the metrics and coordination of the work be effectively done.

Encourage Dialogue

It is important to encourage the use of a dialogue process when considering change (Bohm, 1994; Senge, 1994). The physicist David Bohm originated a form of dialogue where a group of people talk together in order to explore their assumptions of thinking, meaning, communication, and social effects (Wikimedia Foundation, Inc., 2012). This approach brings to light assumptions and thinking about many issues, especially the development of successful new ventures. This process requires no discouragement of contributions or viewpoints and results in an agreement of what has to be done and how. With the use of dialogue, many problems of implementation can be addressed as the change plan is developed.

Collaboration

Along with dialogue is the need for collaboration. Colleges and universities are very complex, with a limited ability for an individual or a small group of people to identify needs and the means to meet them. For the best results, working together should be encouraged. Taylor believes that "…there can be no meaningful reform of higher education without redesigning departments in ways that will support more extensive collaboration among faculty members and students working in different fields" (Taylor 2012). For true collaboration, tools have to be used, including discussion boards, wikis, white boards, chat resources and a place on- and off-line for a place to hang your hat and meet. Leaders should lead by example, by using collaboration tools in their work on a day to day basis.

HELPFUL PROCESSES AND TOOLS

How many higher education institutions have a process in place for managing change? Often the process is invented after the need for the change is identified, and the process is then carried out on an ad-hoc basis. Having both a team and a process in place provides the school with a head start in creating innovative and creative responses to opportunities presented each year.

Of course, not every change needs to use the team and process. If you are thinking of changing a high school visit schedule or an off campus site or program, there would be little need for a "change," though there would be a need for communication. Generally changes that happen in a specific department or program would not need the team or process that involved the whole university. A team could be identified within the department or program. Changes that involve many parts of the institution would fall into the institutional change model.

Change Models

While there are many ways to organize the change process, we have found that two models serve well as a change process. These are Kotter's 8 Step Model and the Focus, Analyze, Develop, Execute (FADE) model (Kotter 1996). We have used both models in work with two- and four-year schools. Some schools use parts of the models or adapt the concepts to produce their own approaches. In addition to these two models, we introduce the "present state/desired state" model as a way of starting any process. Sometimes the change process can come from the top and be implemented quickly, as in the case below:

> *Paul LaBlanc, President of Southern New Hampshire University was a change agent by introducing online learning as a focus of the university. He sought faculty input but removed the ability of the faculty to veto nwew programs. President LaBlanc "negotiated a governance structure that gave the online outfit more elbow room" because he knew that this program needed to get underway before the market was saturated with competitors offering courses* (Mare 2011).

Figure 2. A Way of Coordinating Thinking about Complex Systems

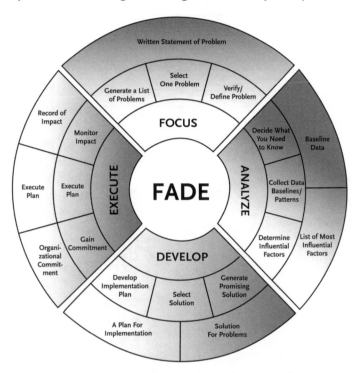

There are yet other methods that may work to bring the institution together for planning change.

FADE

FADE can be used with the present/desired state model to pursue the change process (Evans and Lindsay 2005; Organizational Dynamics, Inc. 2011). A campus department identifying a University-wide change project illustrates the use of the process. The first step of the change team would be to **focus** the effort. The focusing determines if there is a real need to change and develop the present state. The **analysis** would identify the various elements of the system and how to work with them. The **develop** portion of the model is a period of time in which the change effort is constructed. Finally, it is time to **execute** the change effort.

If the project is undertaken, the development of the project might then use the Kotter model, as described in the following section. If the change process was short or relatively simple, the

Figure 3. Kotter: Eight Point Process

1. Establish a sense
   of urgency
   2. Create a guiding
      coalition
      3. Develop a vision
         and strategy
         4. Empower broad
            based action
            5. Generate
               short-term wins
               6. Consolidate gains
                  produce more wins
                  7. Communicate the
                     change vision
                     8. Anchor new
                        approaches in the culture

FADE model might be all that is needed. The FADE model allows for the documentation and the thinking about change to take place and be recorded in a consistent pattern. This diagram representing the whole FADE process, solutions for problems are a part of the **develop** category.

Kotter

The Kotter model includes some of the steps in the movement from present to desired state. The Kotter model is valuable in structuring or developing the work of enrollment teams and is particularly suited to colleges and universities. The model addresses the culture and vision of the school and how these factors shape change efforts. The model also stresses communication and the importance of the guiding coalition in the process. It speaks to the importance of highlighting short term wins and the constant communication of the change vision among all staff.

Kurt Lewin

This is a classic model for change (Bumes 2004).

Figure 4. Overview of a Communication Process

Unfreeze ——→ Change ——→ Refreeze

In any situation, individuals and groups enter into the process with their own unique be-liefs, values, opinions, and experiences. Before any exchange they may already have a position that should be identified, whether they are aware of it or not. The first task in a change process, then, is to understand the vantage points of the people who need to be involved in the change. For example, faculty may have a very different view of student success than the student services staff. Their view may focus on learning and academics, while the student services staff may view the issue as a student development challenge. Those with such opposing views need to come together to address the issues. The faculty may need to understand the student services view as being learning focused and as a key factor in student development. This illustrates how each has to "unfreeze" their views and feelings to develop a unified approach.

In this process several strategies or activities may be used, such as discussions, readings, videos, trips to other schools, and just time spent together in dialogue trying to reach an un-derstanding and agreement on a change. If the group gets to the point where people agree that there may be another way to do business, then the "change" process can be developed and implemented. The people involved should have a mutual set of opinions and beliefs that are consistent with the new process or rule. With the implementation in process, it must be so well accepted that "refreezing" makes the new way of doing things an integrated part of the student success process.

Process Management

One of the best tools to work with is the concept of process management (Rummler and Brach 1995; Rummler, Brach, and Rummler 2009). This is a way of visualizing a process and under-standing its purpose, flow, and product. The approach also fits well with the present/desired state analysis. By creating "is" process maps and "should" process maps, great progress can be made in understanding the way a system works. These types of maps can be created for the organization, offices, and individual job performance. These maps also represent the institution well in terms of a complex system.

Individuals or groups can carry out this process. The more people that are involved in the mapping the better, with the results assessed in terms of achieving a desired state. Meetings can be held with the intent of mapping and discussing the present and desired pathways to success. All the people involved should have a chance to contribute to augment successful change.

Present State/Desired State

This technique is often conducted along with any other change management process, and can also stand alone as a way to move to a desired state or situation, and is particularly suited to the work of groups.

In brief, the model is used when a group wishes to move from some undesired present state to a positive desired state (see Figure 5). The assumption is that a group seeks to resolve a problem or opportunity by changing the present way things are done. The outcome is the desired state. The present state/desired state model can be pursued by any office or program, and may serve as the starting point of the school's change process. Those who identified the opportunity generally should be part of the campus-wide change team if it becomes a broader change initiative.

Figure 5: Moving into a Future Desired State from a Less Desirable Present State

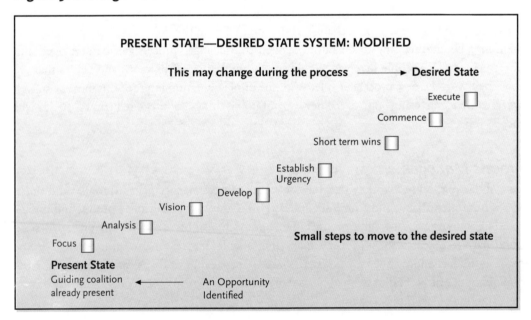

The next step in the model is to lay out the plan to reach the desired state. The initial steps may involve questions about resources, and driving and restraining forces that may need to be addressed (See Figure 6). Usually the steps are small and achievable so that everyone can see that progress is being made and so that issues can be addressed if the progress slows down (Jones 2009).

In applying this model, it is important to remember that emergent issues may cause revisions in the steps, the time frame, and the desired state. This type of model helps keep the change process on track.

There are some features of the approach that need to be considered. There could be branches in the process. At one or more of the steps through the process actions could be taken that are parallel to the main flow and going in the same direction. At some point, the pathways need to reconverge. It is also likely that the desired state may change during the project. The system is very easy to use to keep track of the changes that occur and the realignment of the process in terms of new directions or the development of new pathways.

Figure 6: Force Field Analysis as a Way of Addressing Complex Issues

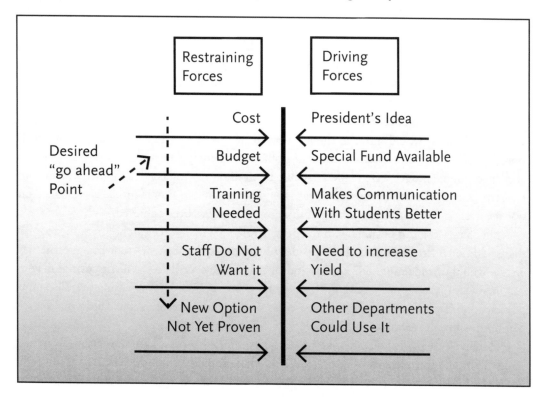

Force Field Analysis

Force Field Analysis is a powerful model that is used with the present state/desired state model or other approaches. This is another concept developed by Kurt Lewin to find and examine all of the variables included in a complex situation (Bar-Gal and Schmid 1993).

In any situation, there are restraining forces that keep people from reaching a desired state just as there are driving forces that push them toward it. The Force Field process starts with a clear understanding of the desired state and the identification of variables that influence the movement towards it. Collect as many variables as possible and divide them into restraining and driving forces. The vertical line represents the position of the project at present, with the goal being to move that line to the left until it is clear that the desired state can be obtained. If the line moves to the right as the process unfolds, it means that the restraining forces are such that the goals cannot likely be achieved.

The next step is to rate the variables on their degree of power, from top to bottom. The training needed may be a weaker restraint than the budget. In this model the fact that the staff does not want it may be the strongest restraint. This process is repeated on the right, with the facts that the President had the idea and that there is money available being the most positive driving forces and thus located at the top. Once this process is completed the line may be located further to the right or the left with the variables now rated. Now one needs to know any additional restraints or driving forces. If there are, the process should be repeated with the new ideas and the final chart created.

The next question becomes: which of the restraining forces could be weakened? If they are weakened, the bar would move to the left toward the decision point. Perhaps there might be staff discussion that could weaken the staff's objection. Perhaps the budget concerns would be alleviated if more money were made available. If a restraint is weakened, are other restraints increased? Does the weakened restraint create any new ones? Note also, if a force is weakened but was relatively minor in the beginning, nothing significant has been achieved.

The same work can be done with the driving forces. Which force can be strengthened? Are there additional driving forces? Perhaps identifying other departments that can use the new system would provide more proponents and/or reduce the overall cost. The discussion may result in lowering the significance of the president seeking the goal and increasing overall campus participation. Be warned not to pressure people so they hesitantly agree but fail to make a real commitment to the process.

The Force Field Analysis often identifies new resources and activities, as well as restraints, which were not considered in the original idea; these should be considered. In any case, the Force Field Analysis is an effective model that can be very useful in complex situations.

Beckhard's Formula

Richard Beckhard developed a model for the change process and some advice about making change (Beckhard 1992). His formula states that dissatisfaction, vision, and first steps must be greater than the degree of resistance in the environment.

Beckhard's formula is as follows:

Dissatisfaction x Vision x First Steps (use of desired state model) > Resistance

He believes that you need to have a huge amount of dissatisfaction, or a great vision, to initiate change. People who are for or against the idea already have the first steps in mind, so clarifying the goal can allay people's feelings about what may happen.

Beckhard also indicates that it is important to *manage the transition* to a new way of doing business. Frequently the new process will start while an older process is in place. The change must have its own management process to ensure success. This is illustrated by the University of South Florida effort to build a student success program. There was a strong vision by the President and the vice presidents about what the future should bring. While the level of satisfaction with current student success efforts was not high, the leadership identified that more needed to happen for the university to realize its goals.

PUTTING IT ALL TOGETHER

The success of colleges and universities depends on their ability to manage the change process. Change is going to be a part of the life of any college or university. Small changes will occur frequently, sometimes daily, while significant changes may occur yearly. In any case, a college's ability to manage the change process is essential to the success of the school and its students. The following is an overview of themes around which change efforts might be built.

- *Create the right structure and process.* Because enrollment is a critical part of the institution's financial success, the responsibility for the data and the change process should be in the enrollment division. This covers all of the functions below. Enrollment management becomes responsible for monitoring the forces, keeping people informed, and initiating and facilitating the process. Many change management models have been presented in this chapter. Your institution may already have a process in place works well. If so, just be certain that whatever process is chosen can be followed with ease and is expected to result in specific outcomes.

- *Get the right change manager.* Assign the task of leading the change management process to an individual with the interest, commitment and energy to direct the effort. The function itself should be in the enrollment office. If there is no one that meets these requirements within the enrollment office, transfer someone to it or look to other departments.
- *Get the right people.* Identify those individuals on campus who seem most positive about and interested in change. Form a team to develop the change process for the school. The team must have the support and the encouragement of senior administration and the faculty.
- *Build the infrastructure.* Build the databases needed to assess the need for change. This includes internal and external data, and qualitative and quantitative data. Access to readers, magazines, articles, listening sessions, surveys, and demographic data is important, as is the capacity to use analytical tools for assessment.

14

A STRUCTURE FOR SEM PLANNING

Bob Bontrager
Senior Director, AACRAO Consulting and SEM Initiatives

Tom Green
Senior Consultant, AACRAO Consulting

CHAPTER 14

As the many topics addressed in the preceding chapters amply illustrate, strategic enrollment management is a multifaceted enterprise. Indeed, its comprehensive nature is both the strength and the challenge of SEM. Transformative enrollment work necessarily touches virtually every aspect of institutional operations. Effectively managing a larger number of those aspects will generally determine whether a school does or does not meet its enrollment goals in a sustainable way, over the long term. However, doing so is far easier said than done given the complexities inherent to postsecondary institutions.

With those realities, individuals reading this book, or who otherwise are practitioners of SEM, may find themselves at a loss as to how to either introduce SEM concepts at their institution, or refresh the implementation of SEM where prior efforts have stalled. Either of those tasks is made more daunting by the fast-moving nature of SEM, as addressed in previous chapters. SEM practitioners today—arguably more than ever—are attempting to hit a rapidly moving target. The purpose of this chapter is to help improve the aim of those charged with providing leadership to SEM planning.

The content of this chapter is based on defining SEM as *a concept and process that enables the fulfillment of institutional mission and students' educational goals* (Bontrager 2004, 2008, 2009). In practice, the purposes of SEM are achieved by:

- Establishing comprehensive goals for the number and types of students needed to achieve the desired future of the institution.
- Improving students' academic success by improving access, transition, persistence, and graduation rates.
- Enhancing institutional success by enabling more effective enrollment and financial planning.

- Creating a data-rich environment to inform decisions and evaluate strategies.
- Strengthening communications with internal and external stakeholders.
- Increasing collaboration among departments across the campus to support enrollment goals.

Some will read this chapter and have difficulty reconciling the comprehensive, long-term planning model it describes with the urgency they face in achieving near-term changes to their enrollment outcomes. There is no question that recruitment and retention efforts must persist as a campus begins to engage a longer-term planning model. Opportunities and good ideas should continue to be taken advantage of as they arise. Thus, it is only natural that planning continues on parallel tracks, one attending to day-to-day operations and planning for the next semester or academic year, and the other positioning the institution for long-term enrollment success.

At the same time, the reality is that many institutions find themselves locked into a short-term planning cycle, attempting daily to respond to a steady stream of anecdotes of recruitment or retention shortcomings, along with a virtually endless list of strategies and tactics for correcting them. The result is often a conglomeration of initiatives, each of which has some merit, but that lacks cohesion and alignment. The result is staff overload, limited return on resource investments, and failure to meet enrollment goals. The SEM planning model described in this chapter addresses those issues.

SEM PLANNING FRAMEWORKS

To effectively manage the complexities of SEM requires that planning be organized into manageable components. Attempts to do so within a single model or diagram tend to be unwieldy. To achieve a higher level of "manageability," the authors have developed three "frameworks" around which to align an institution's SEM processes, its organizational structure for decision-making and continuous improvement, and its development of strategic enrollment plans with cross-campus input, integration, and buy-in. Taken together, these frameworks constitute a planning model and roadmap for transforming an institution into a SEM organization.

The SEM Process Framework (Figure 1) emanates from continuous improvement concepts. The feedback loop of gathering data, inclusion and shared governance, monitoring of results and adjusting course is one that will be familiar to those who have worked with similar processes in the past, such as accreditation self-studies and strategic plan development.

The framework outlines recommended process steps and who is responsible for completing them, with the "who" further illustrated and described in Figure 2. Within the

Figure 1. The SEM Process Framework

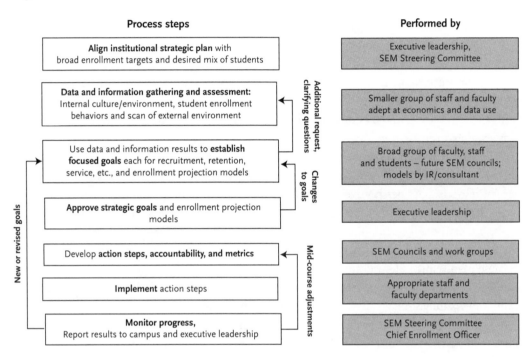

process steps as illustrated in Figure 1, several crucial concepts are embedded. First, the framework places the setting of enrollment goals within the broader strategic planning framework of the institution. While it is not uncommon to find some reference to enrollment in an institution's overall strategic plan, it is less common to find such goals defined sufficiently to allow for sound enrollment planning. The linkage between the institution's strategic plan and the SEM plan must then rest at the Executive Leadership level, where the broad vision of the institution is formed and/or translated into operational plans. The addition of the SEM Steering Committee broadens the discussion beyond the executive team and adds the enrollment focus to it.

Second, the broad enrollment goals and mix of students are researched and supported by data and information that inform the broad goals against internal and external constraints and opportunities. This assures the institution that its decisions are based on sound and thorough research, avoiding planning by anecdote or decisions that are insulated from demographic and market trends. Because this is largely a research function, the team is smaller and comprised of individuals with the skills and resources to perform this work. Including faculty with interests in this type of research can be an asset to inclusion and provide some expertise (such as economics theories and resources) that may be hard to find in staff teams.

Enrollment projection models can be used to test the assumptions or goals developed in the planning process. The models allow the institution to understand how the inputs (new enrollments) and improvements to student success (increased retention and persistence) interact to produce enrollment outcomes. This can be a profound element of the process framework, as it adds a "reality check" to the assumptions being brought into the planning work, especially when it is a widely inclusive one.

Third, the process framework assumes broad involvement of persons across campus, from different administrative levels, departments, and roles, including faculty. This is important in several respects. The perspectives of faculty and staff outside the enrollment management offices expand the understanding of recruitment and student success with the specific culture and context of the institution. It is also important to ensure that the campus broadly embraces the implementation of the plan, participating appropriately and seeking to know its outcomes because involvement allowed their interest to be piqued. The plan is grown from both the top (executive leadership) and the institution's grass roots, its staff and faculty, so that implementation of the plan has the greatest possible chance of being successful.

The academy's culture of deliberation and debate sharpens the plan yet, can derail it into a never-ending loop of more information and more debate without forward motion. Balancing the time for deliberation with the need to move forward to a plan with specific and measurable goals can be achieved through careful selection of participants and seasoned leadership. In respect to the process framework, the issue here is the effort required to achieve a plan with *clear timelines* for each step listed in the process framework that are established at the outset. The roles of individuals in enrollment planning are further differentiated between committee/staff work, goal setting and recommendations, and approval. Establishing *clear expectations for participation* is crucial to a smooth planning process. Councils must know that their role is to develop detailed recommendations and that the decisions to accept them rest with executive leadership, where connection to the broader institutional issues of budget, vision and governance exists. The assignment of individuals to various roles is further described in the following section.

SEM ORGANIZATIONAL FRAMEWORK

Figure 2. The SEM Organizational Framework

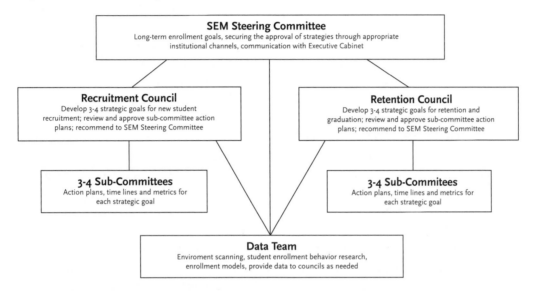

When engaging in any significant planning process on a campus, process leaders typically seek broad, cross-functional input and buy-in. But what does that actually mean for SEM planning? Who should be involved at which stage of the process? Partial answers to those questions are identified by the previously-described process framework. Additional guidance is provided by the SEM Organizational Framework. Like the Process Framework, the Organizational Framework is built on several assumptions.

First, effective SEM planning requires senior-level leadership, reflecting the cross-functional nature of enrollment initiatives and the importance of enrollment outcomes to fulfilling broader institutional goals. Placing senior officers from academic affairs, student affairs, and enrollment management as co-chairs of the SEM Steering Committee can establish an important precedent and model for achieving campus-wide engagement, and the value of doing so. While governance of the steering committee may be shared, it is common to see one person emerge as the practical leader of the process. In this instance, it is important for the co-chairs to provide strong and consistent support to ensure that council and team members involved in the process understand the investment of senior leaders in it. Leaders not only define expectations of participants but set the tone for the process. Inevitably, some participants disagree over direction or specific strategies. They may seek cracks in the unity of the steering committee as a mechanism to achieve alternate outcomes or personal agendas. The steering committee must possess the wisdom and insight to see beyond these tactics and present a consistent message based upon student success and institutional vitality.

The same message is further reinforced by the composition of each of the planning groups included in this framework. There may be opinion leaders without whom the process lacks credibility but whose presence extends the time for discussion and debate. To counterbalance those perspectives, other appointments may (and should) include those associate directors and associate deans who are the "doers" of the organization and can be counted on to get the job done. A good team includes both. As goals and strategies emerge, the recruitment and retention councils may need to expand to capture the expertise of those closest to them. Some institutions have successfully utilized the sub-committee structure to gain this inclusion without expanding the size of the council itself, as larger groups can be slower to complete the work due to scheduling conflicts, extended debate, etc.

Second, recruitment and retention efforts deserve equal attention. This runs counter to the lingering perception among many that SEM is focused primarily on bringing students in the door. One of the most important trends of SEM is an increased focus on student success and creating new linkages between recruitment, admission criteria, and retention programming. Third, this organizational framework directly reflects the data-driven nature of effective SEM practice, illustrating the need for all recruitment and retention initiatives to be directly supported by data. This is true both in terms of setting strategic goals initially as well as in generating assessment information to feed back into the planning process.

Finally, the details contained in this organization framework—particularly regarding the composition of the steering committee, councils, sub-committees, and data teams—is subject to adjustment depending on the specific needs and context of a given campus. For example, at a smaller private institution, the provost or vice president for academic affairs might co-chair the SEM Steering Committee, whereas at a larger public university it may be more appropriate for a dean or associate vice president to fill that role. Each institution will determine the mix of participants that validates the process across the institution, fuels its success with personnel who can be relied upon to deliver the plan on time, and stimulates the deliberation of its goals to align it with its broader strategic plan and mission.

Figure 3. SEM Planning Framework

The SEM Planning Framework augments the process and organizational frameworks by identifying the primary topical areas to be addressed in SEM planning. By beginning at the bottom of the pyramid and working up, institutions are provided a roadmap for developing SEM plans that will achieve long term results. The following narrative provides further description of SEM planning phases.

Link to the Institutional Strategic Plan

To be effective, enrollment planning must emanate from the larger mission and strategic plan for the institution. This point is not as obvious as it may first appear. In the authors' institutional and consulting work they have seen many instances when institutional strategic plans were poorly aligned with the goals and programs being carried out by those charged with operational responsibility for recruitment and retention. Often, the main link between institutional and enrollment planning is financial, that is, how many students are required to achieve budget goals for the next year or two. Typically, such planning is primarily focused on the past and what is perceived to be achievable based on enrollment results of the past few years.

By contrast, linking enrollment planning to the institutional strategic plan has a number of advantages. It connects enrollment planning to the full scope of the institutions' mission, vision, and operations—beyond just finances—to include other critical areas such as academics, student life, advancement, and community engagement. Since institutional strategic plans are typically developed for time frames of five years or more, it extends the planning horizon for enrollment planning as well, thereby basing enrollment planning on the institutions' desired future.

Key Enrollment Indicators

By whatever name—key performance indicators or key success factors, among others—identifying the metrics by which you will measure success is critical to any planning process. For strategic enrollment planning, key enrollment indicators—or KEIs—provide the first component of a two-stage bridge between aggregate enrollment goals typically included in institutional strategic plans and the more specific goals required of SEM planning.

Depending on institutional type, KEIs will include enrollment goals across a wide range of student and institutional attributes, as well as performance metrics. Common KEIs include:

Student attributes
    Academic ability
    Academic program interest
    Special skills (fine arts, leadership, athletics)
    Race/ethnicity
    Undergraduate/graduate/certificate
    Financial means
    Geographic origin

Institutional attributes
    Program capacities
    Facility capacities
    Course delivery mode (on-campus, satellite campus, online)

External factors
    Demographics in target student markets
    Economic trends
    External mandates (federal or state governments, governing entities, accreditors)

Performance Metrics
> Recruitment yield rates (prospect-admit, admit-deposit, deposit-enroll)
> Retention rates (first-to-second year, 4-6 year graduation)
> Measurable outcomes for specific enrollment initiatives
> Net revenue resulting from specific enrollment initiatives
> Aggregate tuition revenue

Data Collection and Analysis

The second component of the bridge between aggregate enrollment goals and specific SEM goals is provided through data collection and analysis. Building on points made earlier in this chapter related to the Organizational Framework, this phase of the SEM Planning Framework includes:

Benchmarking: Compiling statistics on the institution's performance on key enrollment indicators over the past three to five years. Compiling numbers farther back is rarely useful given the speed and degree of change in the factors influencing enrollment from year to year.

Compiling new information: Gathering information that has not existed in the past or that may have existed but was not previously included in enrollment planning. Information on KEIs as listed above may not have been collected previously, maintained consistently over time, or directly linked to SEM plans. Filling these data gaps is critical to the SEM planning process. Where historical data simply does not exist, the SEM Steering Committee will recommend protocols and staff assignments to begin collecting it.

Environmental scanning: Collecting data on external factors that directly influence the institutions' enrollment outcomes, with particular attention to future trends. Such data is relatively easy to obtain from a number of governmental and higher education agencies. Usually, various individuals around campus have been monitoring pieces of this data. A primary purpose of the planning model being described here is to bring that information together into a comprehensive data package, in the context of focused enrollment discussions that will enable the data to be utilized for more effective decision-making.

Notes of caution are in order when considering the data collection and analysis phase. There is a fine line between positioning an institution for informed SEM decision-making and getting caught in a counter-productive cycle of attempting to answer every potential question related to enrollment metrics. When the latter occurs, institutions spend copious amounts of time analyzing and reanalyzing increasing amounts of data as readily-apparent enrollment opportunities are passing them by. Neither this stage of the planning process nor the SEM planning model as a whole should be allowed to supersede day-to-day decisions that must continue to be made in order for schools to meet their immediate enrollment goals. Such near-term decision making will gradually and increasingly be informed by the SEM plans that result from the longer-term planning process.

Setting Strategic Enrollment Goals

This phase of SEM planning is a direct outgrowth of an institution's strategic plan, with delineation of key enrollment indicators and data analysis as intervening process steps. Again, to the extent institutional strategic plans identify enrollment targets, they generally do so at a macro level, lacking the specificity required of SEM plans. Such specificity is provided as SEM planners develop KEIs, though simply identifying KEIs is inadequate. KEIs take on meaning as they are benchmarked and examined for future trends in the data collection and analysis phase.

Thus, the next phase of SEM planning is to set enrollment goals for each KEI that are strategic in their linkage to the institutional strategic plan and informed by data. This includes two important components. One is setting "x by y" targets for each KEI, where "x" is the desired change in the KEI and "y" is a designated time frame. The other is prioritizing which KEIs and associated goals will receive primary attention at the beginning, in the middle, and toward the end of the SEM planning schedule. A common pitfall of institutional strategic plans and many SEM plans is to seek to address every enrollment goal at the same time. Such plans often say "we want to enroll more first year students *and* increase their academic credentials *and* increase diversity *and* increase international enrollment *and* improve retention rates *and* reduce the discount rate *and* increase net tuition revenue"—implying that all of these goals will be achieved at the same time.

The reality is that few institutions have the capacity to launch initiatives across a large range of enrollment goals concurrently. Or, perhaps more to the point, rarely can they do so successfully and at an acceptable cost. Like all other types of planning, when institutional resources are spread too thinly across multiple initiatives, outcomes tend to be diminished. It is better to begin with 3-4 initiatives that are deemed to be of highest priority, spend 2 to 3 years refining and establishing them, and then move on to other enrollment goals. This is where the earlier reference to extending the enrollment planning horizon becomes important. Advocates for a particular group of students may not be happy that their group is not among those to receive focused attention in Year One of a ten-year enrollment plan. However, if they can see that such attention will be given in Years Three to Five of the plan, with clear rationale for focusing on other groups ahead of theirs, they generally will be more satisfied than they would be in the absence of a detailed plan for the longer term.

Developing Strategies and Tactics

With the aforementioned planning phases completed, an institution will be well-positioned for implementing enrollment strategies and tactics that have a significantly greater likelihood of being successful. This point warrants emphasis, as it runs counter to the strong temptation to begin enrollment planning at the tactical stage. Where enrollment goals are not being met, campus conversations tend to be dominated by rapid-fire tactical ideas. Common examples include hiring a new admissions counselor, appointing a retention coordinator, acquiring new technology systems, expanding use of social media, improving the institution's website, adding academic support programs, offering more financial aid, increasing advertising, or sending a recruiter to international locations—to name just a few. The list of potential strategies and tactics is virtually endless, leading many institutions to continually add initiatives. The result often is an unwieldy mix of disjointed recruitment and retention efforts that drain staff and financial resources. Such efforts may in fact result in increases in the number of new students or improved retention rates over the short term. However, absent the comprehensive planning process being outlined here, enrollment gains usually will fade after a year or two, or will be much more costly than necessary.

Achieving Sustainable Enrollment Outcomes

The ultimate goal of the SEM planning model is to position an institution for sustained achievement of its enrollment goals over the long term. This approach runs counter to the prevailing perspective on some campuses, where the lure of additional tuition revenue leads to the desire for large enrollment increases as soon as possible. That notion prompts the authors to recall situations when their campuses did achieve significant short term enrollment increases —in one case amounting to a 25 percent increase in new first year students in one year. Tuition revenue did indeed grow significantly that year, as did a range of challenges, including the need to hire adjunct faculty late in the summer to teach added course sections, a strain on residence hall space, and significantly higher demand for academic and co-curricular support services, to name a few.

Institutions are better served by modest growth of two to three percent per year over a sustained period. Those are not the dramatic numbers sometimes sought by those seeking faster growth. But here again, the extended horizon of effective SEM planning comes into play. While annual growth of two to three percent may not be impressive over the first several years, the 20 to 30 percent growth that accrues over the course of a 10 year SEM plan is significant by any measure.

CONCLUSION: PLANNING FOR THE SHORT- AND LONG-TERM

This chapter began by noting the daunting nature of practicing strategic enrollment management in today's environment. The same observation can be made of any complex endeavor. This leads to two concluding points that are closely related. First, SEM is not a quick fix. Given its impact on institutional finances, it is understandable that campus leaders view enrollment outcomes with a high degree of urgency. However, that very urgency can be the bane of the long-term planning process that is required to achieve better results. Second, any complex, long-term process is enacted one step at a time. The point is to get started. By beginning to take the steps described in the SEM planning frameworks, and building on them over time, you soon will achieve stronger, sustainable enrollment outcomes.

REFERENCES

CHAPTER 1

American Association of Collegiate Registrars and Admissions Officers. 1990-91. Board of directors minutes. Washington, DC.

Bontrager, B. 2006. The brave new world of strategic enrollment management. Preconference paper for the 16th Annual Strategic Enrollment Management Conference. Phoenix, AZ. AACRAO.

Britz, J. D. 1998. Maguire reviews the past, forecasts the future, *The Lawlor Review*, VI (3). Minneapolis, MN.

Campanella, F. B. 1974 (November). Papers of J. Maguire. Boston, MA.

Campbell, R. 1980. Future enrollment goals via traditional institutional strengths. AACRAO 70th Annual Meeting. New Orleans, LA.

Caren, W. and Kemerer, F. 1973. The internal dimensions of institutional marketing. *College and University.* Spring: 173-188.

Dolence, M. G. 1993. *Strategic Enrollment Management: A Primer for Campus Administrators.* Washington, DC: AACRAO.

Dolence, M. G. 1999. Phone Interview with S.E. Henderson, Cincinnati, OH.

Fram, E. 1975. Organizing the marketing focus in higher education. Annual Forum of the Association of Institutional Research.

Gleason, B. 2010. World-class greatness at a land grant university near you. *The Chronicle of Higher Education.* September 26.

Haycock, K. 2006. Promise abandoned: How policy choices and institutional practices restrict college opportunities. Washington, DC: The Education Trust.

Henderson, S. E. 1998. A historical view of an admissions dilemma: seeking quantity or quality in the student body. In *Handbook for the College Admissions Profession,* C.C. Swann and S.E. Henderson (Eds.). Westport, CT: Greenwood Press.

Henderson, S. E. 2001. On the brink of a profession. In *The Strategic Enrollment Management Revolution,* edited by J. Black. Washington, DC: AACRAO.

Henderson, S. E. 2005. Refocusing Enrollment Management: Losing Structure and Finding the Academic Context. *College and University.* 80 (3): 3-8.

Henderson, S. E. 2008. Admissions' Evolving Role: From Gatekeeper to Strategic Partner. *The College Admissions Officers Guide,* B. Lauren (Ed.). Washington, DC: AACRAO.

Henderson, S. E., and Yale, A. 2008. Enrollment Management 101. Preconference Workshop, AACRAO's Strategic Enrollment Management Conference (SEM XVIII). Anaheim, CA.

Hossler, D. 1984. *Enrollment Management: An Integrated Approach.* New York: College Entrance Examination Board.

Hossler, D. 1986. *Creating Effective Enrollment Management Systems.* New York: College Entrance Examination Board.

Hossler, D. 1999. Phone Interview with S. E. Henderson. Cincinnati, OH.

Hossler, D., J. P. Bean, & Associates. 1990. *The Strategic Planning of College Enrollments.* San Francisco: Jossey-Bass.

Huddleston, T. 1976. Marketing: The applicant questionnaire. *College and University.* 52:214-219.

Huddleston, T. 1977. Understanding the nature of the student market for a private university. *Journal of College Student Personnel.* 19: 6.

Huddleston, T. 1978. Marketing Financial Aid. *New Directions for Higher Education.* San Francisco: Jossey-Bass.

Huddleston, T. 1980. In consideration of marketing and reorganizations. *The National Association of College Admissions Counselors Journal.* 25 (1): 18-24.

Huddleston, T. 1999. Phone interview with S. E. Henderson. Cincinnati, OH.

Johnson, D. 1991. Notes from enrollment management conference planning meeting. Unpublished; in author's possession.

Kalsbeek, D. H. 2003. Redefining SEM: New perspectives and new priorities. Keynote presentation at AACRAO's SEM XIII. Boston, MA.

Kalsbeek, D. H. 2006. Some reflections on SEM structure and strategies (part one). *College and University.* 81:3.

Kalsbeek D. H. and Hossler, D. 2009. Enrollment Management: A market-centered perspective. *College and University.* 84:3.

Kemerer, F., Baldridge, J. V., and Green, K. 1982. *Strategies for effective enrollment management.* Washington, DC: American Association of State Colleges and Universities.

Kreutner, L. and Godfrey, E. S. 1980-81. Enrollment Management: A new vehicle for institutional renewal. *The College Board Review.* Winter: 118.

Maguire, J. 1976. To the organized go the students. Bridge Magazine. XXXIX (1). Boston: Boston College.

Maguire, J. 1999. Phone Interview with S.E. Henderson. Cincinnati, OH.

Quirk, M. 2005 (November). The best class money can buy. *The Atlantic Monthly.* 294 (4).

Randall, M. E. 1991. Correspondence to Dr. Charles McKinney in his role as president of AACRAO. Copy in author's possession.

Scannell, J. 1999. Phone Interview with S.E. Henderson. Cincinnati, OH.

Sjogren, C. 2005. College admissions: Modify and simplify. AACRAO 91st Annual Meeting, New York.

Smith, C. and W. Kilgore. 2006. Enrollment Planning: A Workshop on the Development of a SEM Plan. Washington, D. C.: AACRAO Consulting Services.

CHAPTER 2

Association of American Colleges and Universities. 2002. *Greater expectations: A new vision for learning as a nation goes to college.* Washington, DC: Association of American Colleges and Universities.

Archibald, R. B. and D.H. Feldman. 2011. *Why Does College Cost So Much?* New York: Oxford University Press.

Arum, R. and J. Roksa. 2011. *Academically Adrift: Limited Learning on College Campuses.* Chicago: University of Chicago Press.

Bean, J. P. 2007, March/April. Saving Higher Education in the Age of Money (review). *The Journal of Higher Education* 78:2, 240-242.

Collini, S. 2011, August 25. From Robbins to McKinsey. *Essay in Higher Education: Students at the Heart of the System.* London Review of Books (33:16). Accessed at www.lrb.co.uk/v33/n16/stefan-collini/from-robbins-to-mckinsey.

Dewey, J. 1916. *Democracy and Education.* New York: The Macmillan Company.

Ewell, P., and J. Wellman. 2007. *Enhancing student success in education.* Washington, DC: National Postsecondary Education Cooperative.

Gose, B. 2005, February 25. Battling college hype and student stress. *The Chronicle of Higher Education.* Section: Admissions & Student Aid (51:25).

Hacker, A. and C. Dreifus. 2010, 2011. *Higher Education?: How Colleges Are Wasting Our Money and Failing Our Kids—And What We Can Do About It.* New York: St. Martin's Press.

Hannan, M. & J. Freeman. 1984. Structural inertia and organizational change. *American Sociological Review*, 49: 149-164.

Hersch, R. 2007. "Going Naked," *Peer Review*, Spring: 4-8.

Keeling, R.P., Ed. 2004. *Learning Reconsidered: A Campus-Wide Focus on the Student Experience* Washington, D.C.: ACPA – College Student Educators International and NASPA: Student Affairs Administrators in Higher Education.

Keeling, R.P. Ed. 2006. Learning Reconsidered 2: *A Practical Guide to Implementing a Campus Wide Focus on the Student Experience.* Washington, D.C.: ACPA – College Student Educators International; Association of College and University Housing Officers–International; Association of College Unions International; National Academic Advising Association; National Association for Campus Activities; National Intramural-Recreational Sports Association.

Kirsch, I., H. Braun, K. Yamamoto and A. Sum. 2007. *America's Perfect Storm: Three Forces Changing our Nation's Future.* Princeton, NJ: Educational Testing Service.

Kuh, G. D. 2008. *High-Impact Educational Practices: What They Are, Who Has Access to Them, and Why They Matter.* Washington, DC: Association of American Colleges and Universities.

Jelinek, M. and C. Schoonhoven. 1990. *The Innovation Marathon: Lessons From High Technology Firms.* Oxford: Basil Blackwell.

Lalami, L. 2009, June 12. California's higher education crisis: Under the barbarian. *The Nation.* Accessed at www.thenation.com/doc/20090629/lalami.

Masterson, K. 2008, September 12. If Kent State beats goals, professor will profit. *Chronicle of Higher Education.*

McNay, I. 2006. *Beyond Mass Higher Education: Building on Experience.* New York: McGraw Hill.

National Survey for Student Engagement's (NSSE). 2007. *Experiences That Matter: Enhancing Student Learning and Student Success.* Bloomington, IN: Indiana University Bloomington.

Nussbaum, M.C. 2010. Not for Profit: *Why Democracy Needs The Humanities* (The Public Square). Princeton, New Jersey: Princeton University Press.

Reiger, T. 2011. Breaking the fear barrier: How fear destroys companies from the inside out and what to do about it. Gallup Press.

Schoem, D. 2002, November-December. Transforming undergraduate education: Moving beyond distinct undergraduate initiatives. *Change.*

Shavelson, R. J. 2007. *A Brief History of Student Learning Assessment: How We Got Where We Are and a Proposal for Where to Go Next.* Washington, D.C.: Association of American Colleges and Universities.

Schneider, C. G. 2010. "The Three-Year Degree Is No Silver Bullet," Association of American Colleges and Universities, http://www.aacu.org/about/statements/2010/threeyears.cfm.

U. S. Department of Education. 2006. *A Test of Leadership: Charting the Future of U.S. Higher Education.* Washington, D.C.: U. S. Department of Education. A Report of the Commission Appointed by Secretary of Education Margaret Spellings, http://hub.mspnet.org/index.cfm/13445.

Zemsky, R.M. 2005. The Dog That Doesn't Bark: Why Markets Neither Limit Prices Nor Promote Educational Quality. In Joseph C. Burke. Ed. (2005). *Achieving Accountability in Higher Education: Balancing Public, Academic and Market Demands.* San Francisco: Jossey-Bass.

CHAPTER 3

DeMillo, R. 2011. Abelard to apple: The fate of American colleges and universities. Cambridge, MA: The MIT Press.

Krezmer, H. and Boublii, A. 2010. *Les Miserables*. DVD.

Senge, P., C. Roberts, R. Ross, B. Smith, and A. Kleiner. 1994. The fifth discipline fieldbook: Strategies and tools for building a learning organization. New York: Currency/Doubleday.

Tapscott, D. and A.D. Williams. 2010. Innovating the 21st-century university: It's time! *EDUCAUSE Review*, vol. 45, no. 1 (January/February): 16-29.

Taylor, M. 2010. Crisis on Campus: A bold plan for reforming our colleges and universities. New York: Knopf.

Tepper, S. & Kuh, G. 2011. Let's get serious about cultivating creativity. *The Chronicle Review* (September 4).

Thomas, D. and Seely Brown, J. 2011. A new culture of learning: Cultivating the imagination for a world of constant change. Charleston, SC: CreateSpace.

University of South Florida. 2009-10. Office of the Provost and Executive Vice President: Student Success, http://www.acad.usf.edu/Office/Student-Success/ and Task Force Report: http://www.acad.usf.edu/Task-Force/Student-Success/docs/Student-Success-Task-Force-Final-Report.pdf

Wilcox, Ralph and Jennifer Meningall. 2009. Letter to Members of the Student Success Task Force (October 23).

CHAPTER 4

Bolman, L. G., & T. E. Deal. 2003. *Reframing Organizations: Artistry, Choice, and Leadership*. San Francisco, CA: Jossey-Bass.

Bontrager, R. 2004. Strategic enrollment management: Core strategies and best practices. *College and University Journal,* 79(4), 9-14.

Bradica, J. R. 2001. Enrollment management: An interdependence model. Unpublished manuscript.

Christensen, C. M., & H. J. Eyring. 2011. *The Innovative University: Changing the DNA of Higher Education from the Inside Out.* San Francisco: Jossey-Bass.

Conrad, C., & M. S. Poole. 2007. *Strategic Organizational Communication (5ᵗʰ Ed.).* Boston: Wadsworth Publishers.

Costantino, C. A., & C. S. Merchant 1996. *Designing Conflict Management Systems.* San Francisco, CA: Jossey-Bass.

Detsky, A. S. 2010. How to be a good academic leader. *Journal of General Internal Medicine,* 26(1), 88-90.

Deutsch, M. 1973. *The Resolution of Conflict.* New Haven: Yale University Press.

Dull, M. 2010. Leadership and organizational culture: Sustaining dialogue between practitioners and scholars. *Public Administration Review.* 107, 857-866.

Frost, P. 2004. Handling toxic emotions: New challenges for leaders and their organization. *Organizational Dynamics,* 33(2), 111-127.

Galtung, J. 1988. *Essays in Peace Research 6: The Next Twenty-five Years of Peace Research.* Copenhagen: Christian Ejlers.

Gibb, J. 1978. *Trust: A New Vision of Human Relationships for Business, Education, Family and Personal Living.* New York: Guild of Tutors Press.

Holton, S. 2008. *Cracks in the Ivory Tower (2ⁿᵈ Ed.).* Thousand Oaks, CA: Sage.

Johnson, D. W., & R. T. Johnson. 1996. Conflict resolution and peer mediation programs in elementary and secondary schools: A review of the research. *Review of Educational Research, 66,* 459-506.

Jones, T. S., M. R. Remland, & R. Sanford. 2008. *Interpersonal Communication through the Lifespan.* Boston: Allyn and Bacon.

Kalsbeek, D. 2007. Reflections on strategic enrollment management structures and strategies (Part Three). *College and University Journal,* 82(3), 3-12.

Kamenetz, A. 2010. *Edupunks, Edupreneurs, and the Coming Transformation of Higher Education.* White River Junction, VT: Chelsea Green Publishing Co.

Katz, R. N., Ed. 2008. *The Tower and the Cloud: Higher Education in the Age of Cloud Computing.* Lexington, KY: Educause.

Keashly, L., & J. H. Neuman. 2009. Building a constructive communication climate: The Workplace Stress and Aggression Project. In P. Lutgen-Sandvik & B. Sypher (Eds.), *Destructive organizational communication: Processes, consequences and constructive ways of organizing* (339–362). London: Routledge.

Keashley, L., & , J. H. Neuman. 2010. Faculty experiences with bullying in higher education: Causes, consequences and management. *Administrative Theory and Praxis,* 32(1), 48-70.

Kemerer, F. R. 1984-1985. The role of deans, department chairs and faculty in enrollment management. *College Board Review,* 134(4-8), 28-29.

Kuh, G. D., & E. J. Whitt. 1988. The invisible tapestry: Culture in American colleges and universities. *ASHE-ERIC Higher Education Reports,* 17, 1-33.

Lewin, D. 1993. Conflict resolution and management in contemporary work organizations: Theoretical perspectives and empirical evidence. *Research in the Sociology of Organizations,* 12: 167-209.

McCorkle, S. 2008. Recognize conflict types, respond accordingly. *Enrollment Management Report,* 12(5), 8.

McKay, R., D. H. Arnold, J. Fratzl, & R. Thomas. 2008. Workplace bullying in academia: A Canadian study. *Employee Responsibilities and Rights Journal,* 20: 77–100.

Penn, G. 1999. Enrollment management for the 21st century: Delivering institutional goals, accountability and fiscal responsibility. *ERIC Digest, ED 432939.*

Pondy, L. 1967. Organizational conflict: Concepts and models. *Administrative Science Quarterly,* 12: 296-320.

Roloff, M. 1981. *Interpersonal Communication: The Social Exchange Approach.* Beverly Hills, CA: Sage.

Slaikeu, K. A., & R. H. Hasson. 1998. *Controlling the Costs of Conflict: How to Design a System for your Orientation.* San Francisco, CA: Jossey Bass.

Thomas, D., & J. S. Brown. 2011. *A New Culture of Learning: Cultivating the Imagination for a World of Constant Change.* Lexington, KY: Thomas and Brown.

Tierney, W. G. 2008. *The Impact of Culture of Organizational Decision Making: Theory and Practice in Higher Education.* Sterling, VA: Stylus.

Twelves, C. F. 2004. *A case study of UNLV students' enrollment and financial services: The trend to blend key student services into a one-stop shop.* Las Vegas, NV: UNLV Theses/Dissertations/Professional Papers/Capstones. Paper 401. http://digitalcommons.library.unlv.edu/thesesdissertations/401

Ury, W. L., J. M. Brett, & S. B. Goldberg. 1988. Getting Disputes Resolved: Designing Systems to Cut the Costs of Conflict. San Francisco, CA: Jossey-Bass.

Wallace-Hulecki, L. 2009. *Reframing Strategic Enrollment Management from the Academic Lens: Theory in Practice (part 2).* Greensboro, NC: SEM Works.

Wilkinson, R. B., J. S. Taylor, A. Peterson, & M. de Lourdes Machado Taylor. 2007. *A Practical Guide to Strategic Enrollment Management Planning.* Virginia Beach, VA: Educational Policy Institute.

CHAPTER 5

Dolence, M. G. 1993. *Strategic Enrollment Management: A Primer for Campus Administrators.* Washington, D.C.: American Association of Collegiate Registrars and Admissions Officers.

Hacker, A. and C. Dreifus. 2010. *Higher Education? How Colleges Are Wasting Our Money and Failing Our Kids—and What We Can Do About It.* New York: Times Books/Henry Holt.

Henderson, S. E. 2005. Refocusing enrollment management: Losing structure and finding the academic context. *College and University.* 80(3): 3-8.

Henderson, S. E. and A. Yale. 2008. Enrollment Management 101. Preconference Workshop, AACRAO's Strategic Enrollment Management Conference (SEM XVIII), Anaheim, CA.

Hossler, Don and D. Kalsbeek. 2009. Enrollment management: A market-centered perspective. *College and University.* 84(3): 2-11.

Kennedy, R. F. 1967. *To Seek a Newer World.* Garden City, NY: Doubleday and Company, Inc.

Smith, C. and W. Kilgore. 2006. Enrollment Planning: A Workshop on the Development of a SEM Plan. Washington, D.C.: AACRAO Consulting Services.

Williams, J. D. 1998. Generations of Service. Unpublished manuscript in author's possession.

CHAPTER 6

Baum, Sandy and Lucie Lapovsky. 2006. *Tuition Discounting: Not Just a Private College Practice.* New York: The College Board.

Baumol, William J. and W. G. Bowen. 1996. *Performing Arts: The Economic Dilemma.* New York: The Twentieth Century Fund.

Bontrager, Bob, Ed. 2008. *SEM and Institutional Success: Integrating Enrollment, Finance and Student Access.* Washington DC: AACRAO.

———. 2004. Enrollment Management: An introduction to concepts and structures. *College and University. 79:3,* 11-16.

Bowen, W.G. 1967. *The economics of the major private research universities.* Berkeley, CA: Carnegie Commission on Higher Education.

Breneman, David W. 1994. *Liberal Arts Colleges: Thriving, Surviving, or Endangered?* Washington DC: Brookings Institution.

Brittan, Gordon G., Jr. 2003, Winter. Public Goods, Private Benefits, and the University. *The Montana Professor,* 13:1, 1-16.

Clotfelter, Charles T. 1996. *Buying the Best: Cost Escalation in Elite Higher Education.* Princeton, NJ: Princeton University Press.

College Board. 1999. *Trends in Student Aid.* Washington, DC: The College Board.

Common Fund Institute. 2010. *2009 HEPI Update: Higher Education Price Index.* Wilton, Connecticut: Common Fund Institute.

Davis, Jerry Sheehan. 2003, May. Unintended Consequences of Tuition Discounting. *Lumina Foundation for Education New Agenda Series, 5:1.* http://www.luminafoundation.org/publications/Tuitiondiscounting.pdf

Delta Project on Postsecondary Education Costs, Productivity and Accountability. 2009. Issue Brief #2: Metrics for Improving Cost Accountability. Washington, DC: American Institutes for Research. http://www.deltacostproject.org/resources/pdf/issuebrief_02.pdf

Dill, David D. 2003. An institutional perspective on higher education policy: The case of academic quality assurance. In J. Smart (ed.), *Higher education: Handbook of theory and research (v. 18,* 669-699). Dordrecht, the Netherlands: Kluwer.

Ehrenberg, R.G. 2006. *Tuition rising: Why college costs so much.* Cambridge MA: Harvard University Press.

Harvey, James, et al. 1998. *Straight talk about college costs and prices: Report of the National Commission on the Cost of Higher Education.* American Institutes of Research, National Commission on the Cost of Higher Education, American Council on Education. Phoenix, AZ: Oryx Press.

Hossler, Donald. 2004. Refinancing public universities: Student enrollments, incentive-based budgeting, and incremental revenue. In E. P. St. John and M. D. Parsons (Eds.), *Public funding of higher education,* Baltimore, MD: Johns Hopkins University Press, 145-163.

Hossler, Donald and J. P. Bean. 1990. *The Strategic Management of College Enrollments.* San Francisco: Jossey-Bass.

Kreutner, Leonard and Eric S. Godfrey. 1980-81, Winter. "Enrollment Management: A New Vehicle for Institutional Renewal." *College Board Review* 188:6-9, 29.

Lingenfelter, Paul E. 2008. The Financing of Public Colleges and Universities in the United States. *Handbook of Research in Education Finance and Policy,* Helen F. Ladd and Edward B. Fiske, editors. Routledge: New York and London.

Mabry, Theo N. 1987. *Enrollment Management.* ERIC Clearinghouse for Junior Colleges. http://www.ericdigests.org/pre-926/management.htm

Middaugh, Michael F. 2005, March-May. Understanding higher education costs. *Planning for Higher Education* 33:3, 5-18.

National Center for Education Statistics. 2010. The Condition of Education 2010. Appendix A Supplemental Tables A-7-2 and A-8-1 (page 2). Washington, D.C.: NCES. http://nces.ed.gov/pubsearch/pubsinfo.asp?pubid=2010028

————. 2007. Education Longitudinal Study of 2002 (ELS: 2002): A First Look at the Initial Postsecondary Experiences of the High School Sophomore Class of 2002. Washington, D.C.: NCES. http://nces.ed.gov/pubs2008/2008308.pdf

National Center for Public Policy and Higher Education (NCPPHE). 2007. Squeeze Play: How Parents and the Public Look at Higher Education Today. Washington, D.C.: National Center for Public Policy and Higher Education. http://www.higher education.org/reports/squeeze_play/squeeze_play.pdf

Office of Management and Budget, The White House. 2000. Circular No. A-21: Cost Principles for Educational Institutions. Washington D.C. http://www.whitehouse.gov/omb/rewrite/circulars/a021/a021.html

Rhoades, G., and S. Slaughter. 1997. Academic capitalism, managed professionals and supply-side higher education. *Social Text* 51(2), 9-38.

————— . 2004. *Academic Capitalism and the New Economy: Markets, State and Higher Education.* Baltimore, MD: Johns Hopkins University Press.

State Higher Education Executive Officers (SHEEO). 2010. *State Higher Education Finance FY 2009.* Boulder, CO: SHEEO. http://www.sheeo.org/finance/shef/SHEF_FY_2009.pdf

————— . 2004. *State Higher Education Finance FY 2003, Technical Paper A (The Higher Education Cost Adjustment: A Proposed Tool for Assessing Inflation in Higher Education Costs).* Boulder, CO: SHEEO. http://www.sheeo.org/finance/techA.pdf

Wellman, Jane. 2006. Costs, Prices and Affordability: A Background Paper for the Secretary's Commission on the Future of Higher Education. Proceedings of the Secretary of Education's Commission on the Future of Higher Education. Washington, DC: U.S. Department of Education. http://www2.ed.gov/about/bdscomm/list/hiedfuture/reports/wellman.pdf

Winston, Gordon C. 2001a. 'Grow' the college? Why bigger may be far from better. *Williams Project on the Economics of Higher Education.* Washington, DC: U.S. Department of Education. http://www.williams.edu/wpehe/DPs/DP-60.pdf.

———— . 2001b. Higher education's costs, prices, and subsidies: Some economic facts and fundamentals. In *Study of College Costs and Prices, 1988–89 to 1997–98*, Volume 2, Commissioned Papers, ed. A. F. Cunningham, J. V. Wellman, M. E. Clinedinst, and J. P. Merisotis, 117–28. NCES 2002-158. Washington, DC: U.S. Department of Education, National Center for Education Statistics.

———— . 1997. College costs: subsidies, intuition, and policy. *Williams Project on the Economics of Higher Education.* Washington, DC: U.S. Department of Education http://www.williams.edu/wpehe/DPs/DP-45.pdf.

Zemsky, Robert. 2003, May. Have We Lost the 'Public' in Higher Education? *Chronicle of Higher Education, 2*, B20.

CHAPTER 7

Bean, J. 1990. Strategic planning and enrollment management. In D. Hossler & J. P. Bean & Associates (Eds.), *The strategic management of college enrollments* (21-43). San Francisco: Jossey-Bass.

Bontrager, B. 2004a. Enrollment management: An introduction to concepts and structures. *College and University,* 79 (3), 11-16.

Bontrager, B. 2004a. Strategic enrollment management: Core strategies and best practices. *College and University,* 79 (4), 9-15.

Brinkman, P. T. and C. McIntyre. 1997. Methods and techniques of enrollment forecasting. *New Directions for Institutional Research,* 93, 67–80.

DesJardins, S. L., D. A. Ahlburg, B. P. McCall. 2006. An Integrated Model of Application, Admission, Enrollment, and Financial Aid. *The Journal of Higher Education,* 77(3), 381-429.

Guo, S. and M. W. Fraser. 2010. *Propensity Score Analysis: Statistical Methods and Applications.* Los Angeles: Sage.

Kalsbeek, D.H. 2008. Defining Enrollment in the 21st Century. Presentation at the inaugural conference for the USC Center for Enrollment, Research, Policy and Practice, Los Angeles, CA, August 4-6, 2008. http://www.usc.edu/programs/cerpp/docs/KalsbeekPaperrevised.pdf

Kalsbeek, D.H. & D. Hossler. 2009. Enrollment management: A market-centered perspective. *College and University,* 84 (3), 3-11.

Wohlgemuth, D. 1997. *Individual and aggregate demand for higher education: The role of strategic scholarships.* Unpublished doctoral dissertation. Iowa State University, Ames, IA.

Wohlgemuth, D., J. Compton, G. Forbes, and A. Gansemer-Topf. 2010, November. *Projections when projections matter most.* Conference presentation at American Association of Collegiate Registrars and Admissions Officers, Strategic Enrollment Management Conference, Nashville TN.

CHAPTER 8

Binder, S. & C. Aldrich-Langen. 1995, Fall. Fiscal and human resources to support enrollment management. *New Directions for Student Services,* (71).

Black, J. 2001. *Strategic Enrollment Management Revolution.* Washington: American Association of Collegiate Registrars and Admission Officers.

Bontrager, B. 2004. Strategic enrollment management: Core strategies and best practices. College and University, 79 (4), 9.

Cornell, C. and S. A. Lingrell. 2011. Managing up: Leading your executive council or board on enrollment issues. General Session Presentation for American Association of Collegiate Registrars and Admissions Officers Ninety-Seventh Annual Meeting, March 15, 2011, Seattle, WA.

Davenport, T. H., J. G. Harris, & R. Morison. 2010. *Analytics at Work: Smarter Decisions Better*

Results. Boston: Harvard Business School Publishing.

Dixon, R. 1995. *Making enrollment management work: New directions for student services.* (Fall 1995 ed., Vol. 71). San Francisco: Jossey-Bass.

Hossler, D. 1984. *Enrollment Management: An Integrated Approach.* New York: The College Board.

Dolence, M. G. 1993. *Strategic Enrollment Management: A Primer for Campus Administrators.* Washington: American Association of Collegiate Registrars and Admission Officers.

Summers, L. H. 2003. Remarks of President Lawrence H. Summers, Harvard School of Public Health Leadership Council, Cambridge, Massachusetts, October 21, 2003, http://www.president.harvard.edu/speeches/summers_2003/hsp-h_deans_council.php.

CHAPTER 9

Black, J. 2004a. Defining enrollment management: The structural frame. *College and University Journal,* 79, 37-39.

———. 2004b. Enrollment management: Defining a profession. In M. Rodgers & H. Zimar (Eds.), *SEM Anthology* (17-19). Washington, DC: American Association of Collegiate Registrars and Admissions Officers.

Bok, D. C. 2003. *Universities in the marketplace: The commercialization of higher education.* Princeton, NJ: Princeton University Press.

Bontrager, B. 2008. *SEM and institutional success: Integrating enrollment, finance and student success.* Washington, DC: American Association of Collegiate Registrars and Admissions Officers.

Boucouvalas, M. & R. L. Lawrence. 2010. Adult learning. In C. Kasworn, A. Rose, & J. Ross-Gordon (Eds.), *Handbook of adult and continuing education* (35-48). Thousand Oaks, CA: Sage.

Brown, D. K. 1995. *Degrees of Control: A Sociology of Educational Expansion and Occupational Credentialism.* New York, NY: Teachers College Press.

Bowen, H.R. 1977. *Investment in Learning.* San Francisco, CA: Jossey-Bass.

Collins, R. 1979. *The credential society: A historical sociology of education and stratification.* New York, NY: Academic Press.

Cohen, Arthur and Carrie Kisker. *The shaping of American higher education: Emergence and growth of the contemporary system.* San Francisco: Jossey-Bass.

Dewey, J. 1897, January. My Pedagogic Creed. *School Journal* 54, 77-80.

DiMaggio, P. J., & W. W. Powell. 1983. The iron cage revisited: Institutional isomorphism and collective rationality in organizational fields. *American Sociological Review,* 48, 147-160.

Dixon, R. R. 1995. Making enrollment management work. *New directions for student services* (71), 19-23. San Francisco, CA: Jossey-Bass.

Dolence, M. G. 1993. *Strategic enrollment management: A primer for campus administrators.* Washington, DC: American Association of Collegiate Registrars and Admissions Officers.

Ellingson L. 2009. *Engaging crystallization in qualitative research: An introduction.* Thousand Oaks, CA: Sage.

Evans, N. J., D. S. Forney, F. M. Guido, L. A. Patton, & K. A. Renn. 2009. Student development in college: Theory, research and practice (2nd ed.). San Francisco, CA: Jossey Bass.

Greenwood, R., R. Suddaby, & C. R. Hining. 2002. Theorizing change: The role of professional associations in the transformation of institutionalized fields. *Academy of Management Journal,* 45, 58-80.

Harris, T. 2009. Enrollment management professionals in community colleges: An exploratory study of their influence on student recruitment and retention. PhD dissertation, Walden University.

Henderson, S. E. 1998. A historical view of an admissions dilemma: Seeking quantity or quality in the student body. In C. C. Swann & S. E. Henderson (Eds.), *Handbook for the college admissions profession*. Westport, CT: Greenwood Press.

Hershey, P., & K. Blanchard. 1988. Management of organizational behavior: Utilizing human resources (5th ed.). Englewood Cliffs, NJ: Prentice Hall.

Horlick-Jones, T .S. 2004. Living on the border: knowledge, risk and transdisciplinarity. *Futures*, 36, 441-456.

Hossler, D. 2004, April 30. How enrollment management has transformed—or ruined— higher education. *The Chronicle of Higher Education*, B3-5.

Hossler, D. 2009. Enrollment management & the enrollment industry: Part 1. *College and University Journal*, 85, 2-9.

Hossler, D., & D. Kalsbeek. 2008. Enrollment management & managing enrollment: Setting the context for dialogue. *College and University Journal*, 83, 2-11.

Johnson, J. (a.k.a. Bruno Latour). 1995. Mixing humans and nonhumans together: The sociology of a door-closer. In S. L. Star (Ed.), *Ecologies of knowledge: work and politics in science and technology* (257-280). Albany, NY: SUNY.

Kallio, R. E. 1995. Factors influencing the college choice of graduate students. *Research in Higher Education*, 36(1), 109 - 124.

Kalsbeek, D. 2007. Some reflections on SEM structure and strategies (Part Three). *College and University*, 82, 3-9.

Kalsbeek, D. 1997. Politics. In R. M. Swanson & F. A. Weese (Eds.), *Becoming a leader in enrollment services*. Washington, DC: American Association of Collegiate Registrars and Admissions Officers.

Karabel, J. 2005. *The Chosen: The hidden history of admission and exclusion at Harvard, Yale, and Princeton*. New York, NY: Houghton Mufflin Company.

Kerr, C. 1988. *Higher education in service to the labor market: Contributions and distortions.* Philadelphia, PA: University of Pennsylvania, Institute for Research in Higher Education.

Kerr, C. 1995. *The uses of the university.* Cambridge, MA: Harvard University Press.

Knowles, M. S., E. F. Holton & R. A. Swanson 2011. *The adult learner: The definitive classic in adult education and human resources development,* 7th ed. London: Elsevier.

Kohl. K. J. 2000. The Postbaccalaureate learning imperative. In K. J. Kohl & J. B. Lapidus (Eds.) *Postbaccalaureate futures: New markets, resources, credentials,* 10-30. Washington, D.C.: Oryx Press.

Kohl, K. J. & J. B. Lapidus. 2000. *Postbaccalaureate futures: New markets, resources, credentials.* Washington, D.C.: Oryx Press.

Kraatz, M. S., M. J. Ventresca and L. Deng. 2010. Precarious values and mundane innovations: Enrollment management in American liberal arts colleges. *Academy of Management Journal* 53:6, 1521–1545.

Kraft, P. D. 2007. *Faculty engagement in campus-wide enrollment management activities: A grounded theory.* EdD dissertation, Montana State University.

Macdonald, K. M. 1995. *Sociology of the profession.* London: Sage.

Maguire, J. 1976, Fall. To the organized go the students. *Bridge Magazine,* XXXIX, 16-20. Boston, MA: Boston College.

Massy, W.F. 2004. Markets in higher education: Do they promote internal efficiency? In P. Teixeira, B. Jungbloed, D. Dill, & A. Amaral (Eds.) *Markets in higher education: Rhetoric or reality?* (13-35). Dordrecht, Netherlands: Kluwer Academic Publishers.

Mastenbroek, W. F. G. 1993. *Conflict management and organization development.* New York, NY: Wiley.

McCarthy, C. 1912. The Wisconsin Idea. New York: McMillan Company. http://www.library.wisc.edu/etext/WIReader/Contents/Idea.html

Merriam, S., Caffarella, R., & Baumgartner, L. 2007. *Learning in Adulthood: A Comprehensive Guide* (3rd ed.). New York: Wiley.

Miller, T., & J. Prince. 1976. *The future of student affairs. A guide to student development for tomorrow's higher education.* San Francisco, CA: Jossey-Bass.

Ollman, B. 1971. *Alienation: Marx's conception of man in capitalist society.* Cambridge: Cambridge University Press.

Palmer, P. J., A. Zajonc, & M. Scribner. 2010. *The heart of higher education: A call to renewal.* San Francisco: Jossey-Bass

Pappano, L. 2011. The Master's as the new Bachelor's. *The New York Times*, July 22. Accessed 12/11: http://www.nytimes.com/2011/07/24/education/edlife/edl-24masters-t.html?_r=1&ref=edlife

Poock, M.C., & P. G. Love. 2001. Factors influencing the program choice of doctoral students in higher education administration. *Journal of Student Affairs Research and Practice*, 38(2), 203 - 223.

Quirk, M. 2005. The rise of the "enrollment manager" and the cutthroat quest for competitive advantage. The secret weapon: financial-aid leveraging: The best class money can buy. *Atlantic Monthly*, 296, 128-135.

Rodgers, R. F. 1990. Recent theories and research underlying student development. In D. Creamer & Associates, *College student development: Theory and practice for the 1990s*, 27-79. Alexandria, VA: American College Personnel Association.

Scott, R. W. 2008a. *Institutions and organizations: Ideas and interests.* Thousand Oaks, CA: Sage.

Scott, R. W. 2008b. Lords of dance: Professionals as institutional agents. *Organization Studies*, 28, 219-238.

Spencer, D.S. 1986, January. The master's degree in transition. *Council of Graduate Schools Communicator*, 1 – 6.

Suchman, L. 1995: Making Work Visible. *Communications of the ACM, 38*, 56–68.

Thacker, L. (Ed.). 2004. *College unranked: Affirming educational values in college admissions.* Portland, OR: The Education Conservancy.

Weisbrod, B. A., Ballou, J. P., & Asch, E. D. 2008. *Mission and money: Understanding the university.* New York, NY: Cambridge University Press.

Winston, G. C. 1993. Robin Hood in the forest of academe. In M.S. McPherson, M.O. Schapiro & G.C. Winston (Eds.), *Paying the piper: Productivity, incentives and financing in higher education,* 229-231. Ann Arbor, MI: University of Michigan Press.

University of Wisconsin-Extension. 2010. History of UW-Extension. Retrieved September, 27, 2011 from http://www.uwex.edu/about/uw-extension-history.html.

U.S. Department of Education. What is the role of the U.S. Department of Education in postsecondary accreditation? Retrieved September, 27, 2011 from http://ope.ed.gov/accreditation.

Van den Besselaar, P., & G. Heimeriks. 2001. Disciplinary, multidisciplinary, interdisciplinary: Concepts and indicators. In M. Davis & C.S. Wilson (Eds.), *Proceedings of the 8th International Conference on Scientometrics and Informetrics - ISSI2001* (705-716). Sydney: University of New South-Wales.

Zemsky, R., G. R. Wegner & W. F. Massy. 2005. *Remaking the American university: Market-smart and mission-centered.* New Brunswick, NJ: Rutgers University Press.

CHAPTER 10

Connell, C. 2010. University of Minnesota Twin Cities pursues an international transformation. *International Educator.* 20 (2): 30-37.

Dumont, S. and R. Pastor. 2010. The internationalization of U.S. universities – Are we making progress? *International Educator.* 19 (4), 52-55.

Duniway, B. and K. Wiegand. 2009. Using dimensional data to address enrollment management questions in higher education. *College and University.* 84 (4): 32-41.

Fischer, K. 2009. Council promotes ethical guidelines for student recruitment agents. *The Chronicle of Higher Education,* May 27, http://chronicle.com/article/Council-Promotes-Ethical/47275.

Fischer, K. 2011a. Commerce Department takes greater role in promoting U.S. higher education overseas. *The Chronicle of Higher Education.* April 8. Available at http://chronicle.com/article/Commerce-Dept-Takes-Greater/126988/.

Fischer, K. 2011b. State by state, colleges team up to recruit students from abroad. *The Chronicle of Higher Education.* April 8. Available at http://chronicle.com/article/State-by-State-Colleges-Team/126982/.

Fischer, K. 2011c. College 101 for non-native speakers. *The Chronicle of Higher Education,* August 7, http://chronicle.com/article/College-101-for-International/128535/.

Hulstrand, J. 2011. One size does not fit all. *International Educator.* 20 (1): 56-59.

Ivory, S. 2011. News Release: NACAC board confirms opposition to commissioned recruiting for international students; Presents alternative action plan. July 28. Retrieved from: www.nacacnet.org/ABOUTNACAC/PRESSROOM/2011/Pages/commissionedagents.aspx

Kalsbeek, D. and D. Hossler. 2008. Enrollment management and financial aid: Seeking a strategic integration. *College and University.* 84 (1): 2-11.

Kirk, A. 2009. A Gazette minute interview. *Greentree Gazette.* March 25. 1-2.

Kisch, M. 2011. Education abroad: Adults only. *International Educator.* 20 (2): 44-49.

Open Doors. 2010. International student enrollments rose modestly in 2009/10, led by strong increase in students from China. http://www.iie.org/Who-We-Are/News-and-Events/Press-Center/Press-Releases/2010/2010-11-15-Open-Doors-International-Students-In-The-US.

Sewell, M. 2001. U.S. colleges focus on making international students feel at home. *The Chronicle of Higher Education,* August 24. http://chronicle.com/article/US-Colleges-Focus-On-Making/124108.

Yale, A. 2010. Expanding the conversation about SEM. *College and University.* 85 (4): 29-38.

CHAPTER 11

Bailey, T., S. Jaggars, D. Jenkins, D. 2011. Introduction to the CCRC Assessment of Evidence Series. New York: Community College Research Center, Teachers College, Columbia University.

Black, J. 2004. Emerging themes and models. *Essentials of Enrollment Management: Cases in the Field.* Washington, DC: American Association of Collegiate Registrars and Admissions Officers.

Black, J. 2004. Enrollment Management Architecture. *Essentials of Enrollment Management: Cases in the Field.* Washington, DC: American Association of Collegiate Registrars and Admissions Officers.

Bontrager, B. 2008. A Definition and Context for Current SEM Practice. *SEM and Institutional Success: Integrating Enrollment, Finance and Student Access.* Washington, DC: American Association of Collegiate Registrars and Admissions Officers.

Bontrager, B. and K. Pollock, K. 2009. Strategic Enrollment Management at Community Colleges. *Applying SEM at the Community College.* Washington, DC: American Association of Collegiate Registrars and Admissions Officers.

Bossidy, L. and R. Charan. 2002. *Execution: The Discipline of Getting Things Done.* New York: Crown Business.

Michigan Community College Association Trustee Conference (MCCAA) Center for Student Success. 2011, July. Issue Paper – Measuring Community College Performance. Traverse City, Michigan.

Clemetsen, B. 2009. Webinar, Strategic Enrollment Management and Instructional Division. *Applying SEM at the Community College.* Washington, DC: American Association of Collegiate Registrars and Admissions Officers.

Cook, B. and T. Hartle. 2011. First in the World by 2020: What Will It Take? The Presidency: Special Supplement. Washington, DC: American Council on Education. www.acenet.edu

Kerlin, C. and W. Serrata. 2009. Data and Decision Making; Strategic Enrollment Management and Campus Leadership. *Applying SEM at the Community College.* Washington, DC: American Association of Collegiate Registrars and Admissions Officers.

McClenney, K. 2004. Keeping America's Promise: Challenges for Community Colleges, in Keeping America's Promise: A Report on the Future of the Community College. Denver, CO: Education Commission of the States.

O'Banion, T. 2011, August/September. Pathways to completion: Guidelines to boosting student success. *Community College Journal.* Washington, DC: American Association of Community Colleges. 82(1), 28-34.

Pollock, K. 2004. Student success: A catalyst for change. *Essentials of Enrollment Management: Cases in the Field.* Washington, DC: American Association of Collegiate Registrars and Admissions Officers.

Rouche, J. and S. Rouche. 2011. The Art of Visionary Leadership: Painting a Face on the Future. Celebrations Publications. Austin, TX: National Institute for Staff and Organizational Development at the University of Texas at Austin.

Rouche, J., C. Kemper and S. Rouche. December 2006/January 2007. Learning Colleges: Looking for Revolution But Embracing Evolution. *Community College Journal.*

Rouche, J. and S. Rouche. 2000, April/May. Facing the New Millennium: Making Friends with the Future. *Community College Journal.*

Rowley, D., D. Lujan & M. Dolence. 1997. *Strategic Change in Colleges and Universities: Planning to Survive and Prosper.* San Francisco: Jossey-Bass.

Sharp, K. 2009. Strategic Enrollment Management's Financial Dynamics. Applying SEM at the Community College. Washington, DC: American Association of Collegiate Registrars and Admissions Officers.

Wildavsky, B., A. Kelly and K. Carey. 2011. Introduction. *Reinventing Higher Education: The Promise of Innovation.* Cambridge, MA: Harvard Education Press.

CHAPTER 12

Angel, D. and T. Connelly. 2011. Riptide: The new normal for higher education. Lexington, KY: The Publishing Place.

Florida, R. 2002. The rise of the creative class: And how it's transforming work, leisure, community, and everyday life. New York: Basic Books.

Hacker, A. and C. Dreifus. 2011. Higher education?: How colleges and universities are wasting our money and failing our children and what we can do about it. New York: Time Books.

Khan Academy. http://www.khanacademy.org/

Kamenetz, A. 2010. DIY U: Edupunks, Edupreneurs, and the coming transformation of higher education. White River Junction, VT: Chelsea Green

Lenzner, Robert and Johnson, Stephan. 1997, March 3. Seeing things as they really are. *Forbes*. http://www.forbes.com/forbes/1997/0310/5905122a_7.html

Purdue and SunGard Higher Education to deliver signals <http:// news.uns.purdue.edu/ x/2009b/091029McCartneySunGard.html>.

Taylor, M. 2010. Crisis on campus: A bold plan for reforming our colleges and universities. New York: Alfred Knopf Doubleday.

Tepper, Steven J. and George D. Kuh. 2001, September 4. Let's get serious about cultivating creativity. *The Chronicle of Higher Education*. http://chronicle.com/article/Lets-Get-Serious-About/128843/

CHAPTER 13

Bar-Gal, D. and H. Schmid. 1993. Organizational change and development in human service organizations. New York: Routledge.

Beckhard, R. 1992. Changing the essence: The art of creating and leading fundamental change in organizations. San Francisco: Jossey-Bass.

Bohm, D. 1994. Thought as a system. New York: Routledge.

Bontrager, B. 2008. SEM and institutional success: Integrating enrollment, finance and student success. Washington, D. C.: American Association of Collegiate Registrars and Admissions Officers.

Bumes, B. 2004. Kurt Lewin and the planned approach to change: A re-appraisal. *Journal of Management Studies*, 31(6).

Christensen, C. & H. Eyring. 2011. The innovative university: Changing the DNA of higher education from the inside out. San Francisco: Jossey-Bass.

Eaton, J. 2008, March 24. The future of accreditation. *Inside Higher Education*, Retrieved April 2012 from http://www.insidehighered.com/views/2008/03/24/eaton

Evans, J., & M. Lindsay. 2005. *The management and control of quality.* (6 ed.). Stamford: Cengage Learning.

Hacker, A., & C. Dreifus. 2010. *Higher education? How colleges are wasting our money and failing our kids and what we can do about it.* New York: St. Martin's Press.

Jones, G. 2009. Organizational theory, design, and change. New York: Prentice Hall.

Jones, D. and J. Wellman. 2010, May-June. Breaking Bad Habits: Navigating the Financial Crisis. *Change: The Magazine of Higher Learning.* Retrieved April 2012: http://www.changemag.org/Archives/Back%20Issues/May-June%202010/breaking-bad-full.html

Kamenetz, A. 2011. *DIY U: Edupunks, edupreneurs, and the coming transformation of higher education.* White River Junction, VT: Chelsea Green Publishing.

Kezar, A., & P. Eckel. 2002, Jul. - Aug. The effect of institutional culture on change strategies in higher education: universal principles or culturally responsive concepts? *Journal of Higher Education,* 73(4), 435-460. Columbus, OH: Ohio State University Press.

Kotter, J. P. 1996. Leading change. Cambridge: Harvard Business Review Press.

Kezar, A. 2009, November-December. Change in higher education: Not enough or too much? *Change: The Magazine of Higher Learning.* Retrieved from http://www.changemag.org/Archives/Back Issues/November-December 2009/full-change-higher-ed.html

Nicolis, G., & C. Rouvas-Nicolis. 2007. Complex systems. *Scholarpedia,* 2(11).

ODI®: Organizational Dynamics Inc. 201). Quality action teams™. Billerica, MA: Organizational Dynamics, Inc. Retrieved from http://www.orgdynamics.com/tqci.html

Rummler, J., & A. Brache. 1995. *Improving performance: How to manage the white space in an organization.* (2nd ed.). San Francisco: Jossey-Bass.

Rummler, G., Ramias, A., & Rummler, R. 2009. *White space revisited: Values through process.* New York: Pfeiffer.

Selingo, J. 2011, July 11. How will colleges innovate as the market is disrupted? *The Chronicle of Higher Education.* Retrieved from http://chronicle.com/blogs/next/2011/07/11/how-will-colleges-innovate-as-the-market-is-disrupted.

Senge, P., Ross, R., Smith, B., Roberts, C., Kleiner, A. 1994. *The fifth discipline fieldbook: Strategies and tools for building a learning organization.* New York: Currency Doubleday.

Tapscott, D., & Williams, A. 2010, January/February. Innovating the 21st-century university: It's time! *Educause Review,* (45:1). April 2012, Retrieved from http://www.educause.edu/EDUCAUSE Review/EDUCAUSEReviewMagazineVolume45/Innovatingthe21stCenturyUniver/195370.

Taylor, M. C. 2012. *Crisis on campus: A bold plan for reforming our colleges and universities.* New York: Knopf.

Tierney, W. G. 2008. *The impact of culture on organizational decision making: Theory and practice in higher education.* Sterling, VT: Stylus.

Wiseman, B. & V. Kaprielian. Methods of Quality Improvement. *Duke University Medical Center.* June 2012. Retrieved from http://patientsafetyed.duhs.duke.edu/module_a/methods/methods.html.

Wheatley, M. 2006. *Leadership and the new science:* Discovering order in a chaotic world. San Francisco: Berrett-Koehler Publishers.

Wursten, H. 2008, December 1. Culture and change management. Item Intercultural Management. Retrieved from http://www.itim.org/articleonchangemanagement.pdf

CHAPTER 14

Bontrager, B. 2004. Enrollment Management: An introduction to concepts and structures. *College and University.* 79(3): 11-16.

————. 2008. *SEM and Institutional Success: Integrating Enrollment, Finance and Student Access.* Washington, DC: American Association of Collegiate Registrars and Admissions Officers.

Bontrager, B., and B. Clemetsen. 2009. *Applying SEM at the Community College.* Washington, DC: American Association of Collegiate Registrars and Admissions Officers.